THE WHOLESALE-BY-MAIL CATALOG™ UPDATE 1986

by
THE PRINT PROJECT

Lowell Miller, *Executive Producer*
Prudence McCullough, *Editor*

ST. MARTIN'S PRESS
New York

The Wholesale-by-Mail Catalog™ Update 1986 is a resource for use by the general public. Companies in this catalog are listed at the sole discretion of the editors, and no advertising fees are solicited or accepted.

THE WHOLESALE-BY-MAIL CATALOG™ UPDATE 1986. Copyright © 1986 by Lowell Miller and Prudence McCullough. All rights reserved. Printed in the United States of America. No part of this book may be used or reproduced in any manner whatsoever without written permission except in the case of brief quotations embodied in critical articles or reviews. For information, address St. Martin's Press, 175 Fifth Avenue, New York, N.Y. 10010.
First Printing/February 1986

ISBN: 312-90379-0
Can ISBN: 312-90380-4

Design by Giorgetta Bell McRee/Early Birds

First Edition
10 9 8 7 6 5 4 3 2 1

CONTENTS

INTRODUCTION

We're pleased to bring you *The Wholesale-by-Mail Catalog Update 1986*. This concise version of the third edition of *WBMC* features revised, condensed listings that include all the vital information you need to shop by mail, and also notes on store locations and hours. It's a shopping guide you can use on the road as well as at home, presented in an easy-to-use format.

Like *The Wholesale-by-Mail Catalog* on which it's based, the *Update* includes firms selling at 30% below list or comparable retail—the traditional definition of "wholesale." You can buy just about anything by mail at discount prices: burglar alarms, Mexican spices, deerskin gloves, Lalique crystal, squash racquets, antique jewelry, original art, magazine subscriptions, French perfumes—the list is almost endless. Using *The Wholesale-by-Mail Catalog Update 1986*, you'll pay what the retailer does *before* the markup, and you won't have to wait for a sale.

Before sending for a catalog or placing an order, be sure to read the explanations of the listing code on page 5—you'll find it easier to understand and use this book.

Happy bargain hunting, and be sure to let us know about your experiences with the firms listed in this book. Turn to "Feedback," page 357, if you'd like to contact us.

THE PRINT PROJECT
Lowell Miller, *Executive Producer*
Prudence McCullough, *Editor*

ORGANIZATION OF LISTINGS

As you can imagine, organizing a book like this requires many decisions. If a company sells fabric, uniforms, and watches, do we list it in the crafts, clothing, or jewelry section? We asked each firm to designate the product category in which it was strongest in terms of selection. To maintain brevity and minimize confusion, we put the firm's listing—the description of all its goods and services—in that category. We then *cross-referenced* the firm in every other applicable category.

See Also: The last page of each chapter of catalogs, headed "See Also," lists firms that carry that category of goods, and gives a brief note on the relevant goods and the location of their main listings. For example, the fictional Handy Dandy Tool Co. sells hand and power tools and some gardening equipment. Its main listing would be in the "Tools" chapter. On the *See Also* page at the end of the "Farm and Garden" chapter, you'd find: "Handy Dandy Tool Co. . . . kneepads, portable rototiller, mini-compactor . . . See TOOLS." So, even though a firm may be listed in "Tools," as in the example above, it may still be an *important source* for a gardening bargain. Bear in mind, then, that *companies are listed in full in only one product category, but they may well warrant your perusal as a source for many kinds of products.* So don't overlook the *See Alsos!*

Patience: Since companies are constantly revising their catalogs and printing new ones, we ask you to be patient while waiting for literature to arrive. Specifically, please allow *six to eight weeks,* unless the firm's listing indicates a longer possible delay.

Whenever we were able to determine a firm's schedule of catalog publication, we included this information in the listing. (The months catalogs are issued are denoted by numbers following the catalog cost.) Use this as a guide when sending for catalogs, and remember that some products, such as flower bulbs, can be ordered only at certain times of the year.

Price Quotes: Some firms do not issue catalogs at all. Most of these operate under a price quote system: you must tell them the exact make and model number of the item you want and they will give you the price and shipping cost, either by mail or phone. Businesses that operate this way are clearly indicated in the listings by "Info: PQ" instead of or in addition to catalog information. Often these price-quote firms have the lowest prices on such goods as appliances, audio and TV components, and furniture; they usually sell well below both the standard manufacturers' suggested list prices and below the less formal minimum prices that some manufacturers try to enforce.

Minimum Orders: In a few cases the very best buys are available from firms that require a minimum order in dollars or goods, though most listings in this book carry no such restriction. Don't be put off by a minimum requirement. If you want something that's a real bargain, chances are you have friends or work associates who'll want it too. Even if you can't find a buying partner, remember that a great bargain can also be a great gift, and you can stock up on a supply of that special product. This will also keep you one small step ahead of inflation.

A Note About Specific Prices: Our criteria for listing companies center on percentage discounts; 30% off today ought to be 30% off tomorrow, or next year, even if *prices* change, unless profit margins become squeezed. Ordinarily, most sellers set their prices in relation to the rest of the market. When you do see specific prices, though, please keep in mind that we live in an unstable economic environment. Prices have probably changed in the time it took this book to reach you and are included only as guidelines.

A Caveat: The Wholesale-by-Mail Catalog Update 1986 is compiled as a resource, pointing you to the bargains available by mail. *Never* order goods directly from this book, even if prices and shipping charges are given in the listing. Always write first and get a catalog or a current price quote, and be sure to follow each company's ordering and payment instructions. All the information in this book is based on our research and fact-checking as of press time and is subject to change.

THE LISTING CODE

To save space and avoid repetition, we've presented some of the information in the listings in a simple coded form at the head of each entry. All the "hard" factual information is listed and abbreviated as follows:

(1) Company name, mailing address, and phone number

(2) Literature form: cat. (catalog), broch. (brochure), flyer, leaflet, PL (price list), etc.; price; "ref." (if the fee is refundable or otherwise redeemable through ordering); "SASE": send self-addressed, stamped, business-sized envelope (#10) with request; "info": price quote or information given by phone and/or letter

(3) "Save": percentage of savings you may expect on the suggested list prices or comparable retail of those goods and/or services. *Do not deduct this percentage from the order total* unless so instructed in the listing text or catalog

(4) Type of goods sold: custom-made, handcrafted, handmade, used, surplus, salvage, etc.

(5) "Pay": methods of payment accepted for orders; assume catalog fees must be paid by check or money order unless listing states otherwise:

    (a) C: personal check

    (b) MO: bank or postal money order

    (c) cert. check: certified check, teller's check, cashier's check, or bank draft

    (d) IMO: bank or postal international money order

    (e) IRC: International Reply Coupon; postal voucher used as payment for catalogs from foreign firms

    (f) AE: American Express credit card

(g) CB: Carte Blanche credit card
(h) CHOICE: CHOICE credit card
(i) DC: Diners Club Credit card
(j) EC: Eurocard credit card
(k) MC: MasterCard credit card
(l) V: VISA credit card

The Dollar Code: The dollar-code symbol ($) represents our opinion of the overall worth of the firm to the average bargain hunter. We take into account the quality of the goods, quantity of the offerings, depth of the discount, and, when information is available, the quality of service. The final judgment is somewhat subjective, but when you've analyzed as many firms as we have, certain ones simply stand out and others fade away.

Four "dollar signs" is a top rating; one is the lowest. *However,* a low rating may reflect a limited number of products and does not indicate that the company is a poor source for those products. There has to be some way of separating the thrilling buys from the merely good. Whenever possible, the ratings reflect our opinion of that firm as it compares to others within the same product category. Exceptions occur when the firm's offerings are so diverse or singular that such comparisons would be misleading.

The omission of a dollar-sign rating should not be considered a "poor" rating of a business. All it means is that we did not feel, for whatever reason, qualified to make a judgment. Companies to which we would have had to give a "poor" rating were simply not listed.

The Envelope Symbol: This shows that the firm accepts mail orders.

The Phone Symbol: This shows that the firm accepts orders over the phone. Many of the firms listed here offer toll-free order lines, and virtually all require use of a credit card to pay for goods ordered by phone. Toll-free order lines (800 numbers) are included in many of these listings, but should not be used to request information or catalogs unless the listing states that this is permitted.

A MINI GUIDE TO MAIL-ORDER SHOPPING

Shopping by mail is one of the easiest ways to get more from two of your most precious resources: time and money. The added convenience of ordering by phone, an option provided by many firms, makes the choice between curling up with your latest batch of catalogs and trudging through as many stores a no-contest decision.

Even though catalog shopping is simplicity itself, the following guidelines and explanations can help ensure hassle-free transactions. If you have questions, your local Better Business Bureau office can provide pamphlets on buying by mail. Additional information is also available from the Direct Marketing Association; 6 E. 43rd St.; New York, NY 10017.

Catalogs: Write for catalogs, including requested payment in the form of a check or MO. Coins, taped securely between pieces of cardboard, are acceptable payment for catalogs costing under $1. Don't use 800 lines to request catalogs and don't charge them to your credit card, unless so instructed.

Price Quotes (PQ): Write for price quotes, include a SASE with your query, and request prices on no more than three items at a time. Ask for the terms of the firm's return policy and shipping costs. Include manufacturers' model and stock numbers; don't use code numbers from other catalogs. Do not use 800 lines to request price quotes unless so instructed.

Phone Orders: Fill out the catalog order blank before calling, and have your credit card at hand. Note the name of the operator or service representative and the date you're placing the order.

Verify the terms of the firm's return policy, if not clearly stated in the catalog. Keep the dated order form as a record of the transaction.

General Tips: Remember to include your return address on all correspondence, and note all enclosures. Keep dated records of all phone calls and letters. Have goods delivered to a street address whenever possible. Don't order products from the information given in this book; write for a catalog or price quote instead. If a problem arises, write to the company and ask for an explanation or request specific action. Contact the Better Business Bureau or the Direct Marketing Association if the problem is not resolved.

ANIMAL

Livestock and pet supplies and equipment, veterinary instruments and biologicals, live-animal referrals, and services.

Some doctors "prescribe" pets for people who have hypertension, since the simple act of stroking the animal seems to lower blood-pressure levels. Most of us adopt pets for less practical reasons, but few are aware of the long-term costs of ownership: keeping the average cat or dog can cost upwards of $10,000 over a typical pet lifetime. The companies listed here can help you realize significant savings on everything from toys and collars to cages, carriers, and even medications.

Those who have yet to choose a pet should see *Getting More for Your Money,* by the Better Business Bureau. It includes a section on selecting cats, dogs, fish, and birds. (See "Resources" for information on obtaining a copy of the book.) If you have a pet, would you like to increase your animal's well-being, longevity, and save yet more money? It's simple: become an informed owner. Attention to routine care pays off in many ways. If you understand the actual nutritional needs of your animal, for example, you'll judge a can or box by its nutrient listing and not the ads. Finding out the essentials of proper grooming can save your pet the unpleasant effects of overwashing and improper clipping, and may save you considerable sums in salon costs. And using simple training techniques developed by professionals should work just as effectively at home as it does at obedience school—and all it costs is a little patience. You can begin your quest for information with your vet, and proceed to the bookstore or library. *The Common Sense Book of Kitten and Cat Care* and *The Common Sense Book of Puppy and Dog Care* (Bantam Books), by Harry Miller, are excellent reference tools. The advice of the incomparable Barbara Woodhouse is especially valuable to owners of recalcitrant or problematic canines, and can be found in *Encyclopedia of Dogs and Puppies* and *Dog Training My Way* (both from Berkley Books), as well as *No Bad Dogs.* Guides to the care of fish, birds, reptiles, and more exotic creatures are also available; consult your local library.

The knowledgeable owner is also less likely to take the pet to the vet at every temporary change in habit or body function, and can evaluate early symptoms of real illnesses more accurately and seek prompt medical attention. Nipping a potentially serious condition in the bud is almost always cheaper than a course of treatment for a fully developed disease. More important to most owners, of course, is the fact that appropriate care is less traumatic for the beloved pet.

Several of the firms listed here retain veterinarians who can answer questions on products and use, but they're not permitted to give specific medical advice. Turn to your own vet for that, and be sure to seek his or her counsel if you plan to administer any vaccines or medications yourself. Know the number of your local 24-hour service that handles medical emergencies (if available), and become familiar with symptoms and first-aid measures you may have to take in order to transport the animal to the clinic. Every pet owner should have such information at hand, and one of the best booklets around is the "Angell Memorial Guide to Animal First Aid," published by the American Humane Education Society and MSPCA. The 22-page guide tells you how to restrain and handle an injured animal, bind a wound, and deal with burns, drowning, heat stroke, problem deliveries, choking, shock, poisoning, and many other problems. Rosters of toxic household substances and plants are included, as well as a list of tips to help prevent accidents and injuries. The booklet is $1; request it by title from the American Humane Education Society; 350 South Huntingdon Ave.; Boston, MA 02130.

One caution when buying animal medical supplies: The FDA requires that you swear to the fact that your purchases of hypodermic syringes, needles, and antibiotics are for animal use only, and that you submit your vet's prescription with your order. Be sure to do this whether the catalog states this regulation or not —it's the law. Check with your local health department before ordering to see whether local ordinances permit receipt of such materials. And don't forget to keep drugs, treatments, and medical instruments out of the reach of both pets and small children.

ANIMAL CITY WHOLESALE; P.O. Box 2076; La Mesa, CA 92041-0318 (619) 469-0188/ Cat.: free/ Save: 10–50%/ Pay: C, MO, MC, V Sells: vet, kennel, and pet supplies/ Shop: 15 other locations nationwide

$$$/ ✉ / ☎

Comment: The twice-yearly catalog from ACW (a division of PETCO) offers solid savings on supplies and equipment for horses, dogs, cats, birds, and fish. A reliable firm, founded in 1965.

Sample Goods: Antibiotics, wormers, instruments, nutritional supplements, skin treatments, insecticides, toys, brushes, grooming aids, horse tack, collars, leashes, feeders, books, and more. Goods range from the department-store variety to specialized items sold to vets, groomers, and kennel operators.

Special Factors: Satisfaction guaranteed; returns accepted on everything except vaccines and instruments for refund or credit; shipping included on orders of $20 or more; min. order $5.

ANIMAL VETERINARY PRODUCTS, Inc.; P.O. Box 1267; Galesburg, IL 61401 (800) 447-8192/ Cat: free/ Save: 10–50%/ Pay: C, MO, MC, V Sells: vet, kennel, and pet supplies/ Shop: Galesburg, IL; also Henderson, NV; Allentown, PA; Roswell, GA; M–F 9–5, all locations

$$$/ ✉ / ☎

Comment: Help your dog or cat "stay healthy, handsome, and contented" with AVP's 84-page catalog. Hundreds of products at up to 50% off list prices; reliable service. Division of Dick

Blick; all outlets accept mail orders (see catalog for locations and phone numbers).

Sample Goods: Biologicals and medications, nutritional supplements, wormers, flea and tick collars and preparations, toys, books, collars and leashes, grooming tools and products, cages, feeders, training devices, and much more. The best prices are on goods bought in quantity, so combine orders with friends to maximize your savings.

Special Factors: Returns accepted; quantity discounts offered on some items; min. order $10.

DAIRY ASSOCIATION CO., INC.; Lyndonville, VT 05851-0145 (802) 626-3610/ Broch.: free/ Save: 40% +/ Pay: C or MO **Sells:** livestock liniment and leather balm/ Mail order only

$$$$/ /

Comment: The Dairy Association, known to generations of herd farmers for its Bag Balm ointment, also sells Hoof Softener and Tackmaster leather conditioner—all at excellent savings. Est. in 1889.

Sample Goods: Bag Balm (formulated to soothe the chapped, sunburned, and scraped udders of cows) is recommended by horse trainers for cracked heels, gauls, cuts, hobble burns, etc., plus use on sheep, goats, dogs, and cats; super for weatherbeaten, chapped hands. A 10-oz. can, over $5 elsewhere, $3 here; 4½-lb. pail, $20.10. Dilators and milking tubes for injured udders also available. Hoof Softener, for cracked and dry horse hooves, is $3.50 per pound. Tackmaster is TLC for leather—a one-step, all-around conditioner, cleaner, and preservative, cheaper than similar products at $1.55 for 4 oz.

Special Factors: Shipping included in prices; phone orders accepted for C.O.D. payment.

ECHO PET SUPPLIES; Box 145; Westland, MI 48185 (313) 425-5293/ Cat.: $1/ Save: to 40%/ Pay: C, MO, MC, V Sells: fish and pet supplies/ Shop: 32841 Park Lane, Garden City, MI; M–F 8–5:30, Sa 9–1

$$$/ / ☎

Comment: Echo Pet Supplies, est. as Aqua Engineers in 1963, offers a plethora of products for tropical and saltwater fish plus goods for gerbils, hamsters, guinea pigs, cats, dogs, and birds.

Sample Goods: Complete aquarium outfits and air pumps, filters, water pumps, heaters, lighting, tank novelties and plants, food, and medicines for fish; cages, shelters, beds, and playthings for birds, rodents, cats, and dogs; leashes, leads, feeding bowls and devices, grooming implements, and nutritional supplements and medications. Also offered: mailing lists of fish clubs by state or for the entire U.S. and Canada, plus lists of product manufacturers, wholesale suppliers, and breeders.

Special Factors: Monthly sales flyers pub. with special savings; information on mailing lists given in catalog.

KANSAS CITY VACCINE CO.; 1611 Genessee St.; Kansas City, MO 64102-5713 (816) 842-5966/ PL: free/ Save: to 35%/ Pay: C or MO Sells: vet supplies and biologicals/ Shop: same address; M–F 8:00–4:30

$$$/

Comment: Livestock farmers, herders, and veterinarians have relied on KCV since 1912 for its comprehensive stock of supplies and equipment. Catalog geared to medical/commercial needs.

Sample Goods: Products for cattle, horses, sheep, hogs, poultry, dogs, and cats—vaccines, antitoxins, flea and tick treatments, grooming tools, wormers, stethoscopes, soaps, tattoo markers, nutritional supplements, and other related items by Franklin, Norden, Tylosin, Trax-M, Havoc, Kopertox, RedKote, Happy Jack, Chaparral, Lindane, Resco, Ritchey, Oster, and Sunbeam.

Special Factors: Vaccines and biologicals sent where ordinances permit; quantity discounts available; min. order $10.

LIBERTY LEATHER MANUFACTURERS; P.O. Box 213; Liberty, TN 37095 (615) 597-7999/ Broch.: 25¢ & SASE/ Save: to 75%/ Pay: C or MO Sells: handmade dog collars/ Mail order only

$$$$/

Comment: Liberty's handmade, bridle-leather dog collars are up to 75% less expensive than similar models, should outlast vinyl, and are more comfortable than chain.

Sample Goods: Liberty offers collars in a range of weights and styles—plain, studded, etc.—and sizes to fit everything from a miniature to a mastiff. A sturdy collar, combined with a stout leash, provides maximum "breakaway" protection for dogs of the leaping, lunging, bolting variety.

Special Factors: Discount prices apply to orders of $20 or more.

OMAHA VACCINE CO., INC.; 3030 L St.; Omaha, NE 68107
(402) 731-9600/ Cat.: free/ Save: 33%/ Pay: C or MO Sells:
vet, kennel, and pet supplies/ Shop: same address; M–F 8–5,
Sa 8–12

$$$/ ✉

Comment: Omaha's 104-page catalog, pub. 6 times yearly,
features thousands of products for livestock, horses, and house
pets. Est. in 1959, OVC does most of its business with livestock
producers and veterinarians.

Sample Goods: Vaccines and biologicals, medications, surgi-
cal implements, grooming tools and preparations, nutritional
supplements, flea and tick products, cages and carriers, leads and
leashes, horse tack, Hush Puppies work gloves, Red Ball boots.

Special Factors: Some pharmaceutical products are available
by prescription only (shipment subject to local ordinances); min.
order $10.

**PBS LIVESTOCK DRUGS; 2800 Leemont Ave. N.W.; P.O.
Box 9101; Canton, OH 44711-9101** (800) 321-0235/ Cat.:
free/ Save: 20–50%/ Pay: C, MO, MC, V Sells: vet and live-
stock supplies/ Shop: Canton, OH; also Wooster, Circleville,
Wilmington, OH; M–F 9–5, Sa 9–12, all locations

$$$/ ✉ / ☎

Comment: The 64-page PBS catalog offers commercial dairy,
beef, swine, and sheep producers a bounty of biologicals and
veterinary products at 20–50% below list.

Sample Goods: Biologicals, nutritional supplements, surgical instruments, ointments, treatments, tags, and much more for all livestock varieties; isopropyl alcohol, Bag Balm, unrefined wheat germ oil, mineral oil, K-Y jelly, disposable plastic boots and gloves, work boots, etc. Remember that the catalog is intended for livestock farmers and not for the squeamish.

Special Factors: Satisfaction is guaranteed; shipping included on some items; min. order $20.

TOMAHAWK LIVE TRAP CO.; P.O. Box 323; Tomahawk, WI 54487 (715) 453-3550/ Broch.: free/ Save: 33–50%/ Pay: C or MO **Sells:** proprietary humane animal traps/ **Shop:** same address; M–F 8–5; also Fingerhut Corp., Minneapolis, MN; Plow & Hearth, Madison, VA

$$$$/ ✉ / ☎

Comment: The U.S. Army Medical Corps, state and federal conservation departments, dog wardens, universities, and others who want to catch a critter without endangering its pelt or life use Tomahawk's box traps. Est. in 1929.

Sample Goods: Traps for everything from mice ($10.11) to large dogs ($136.25), plus fish and turtles, birds, and beavers as well. Models include rigid and collapsible styles, transfer cages, station-wagon and carrying cages, and several with sliding doors made for shipping animals. Special sizes can be made to order. The brochure and price list include dimensions and specifications of each trap and a list of common foods that can be used to lure over 20 animals.

Special Factors: Quantity discounts of 50% available on orders of 6 or more of the same trap; PQ by phone or letter with SASE.

UNITED PHARMACAL COMPANY, INC.; 306 Cherokee St.; St. Joseph, MO 64504 (816) 238-3366/ Cat.: free/ Save: 30–50%/ Pay: C, MO, MC, V Sells: vet, kennel, and pet supplies/ Shop: same address; 3705 Pear St., St. Joseph; M–F 7:30–6, Sa 7:30–5

$$$$/ ✉ / ☎

Comment: UPCO, est. in 1958, publishes a 128-page catalog of thousands of products for dogs, cats, and horses—a must-have for pet owners and professionals.

Sample Goods: Antibiotics, wormers, instruments, nutritional supplements, skin treatments, insecticides, grooming aids, horse tack, leashes and leads, collars, feeders, books, flea collars, toys, feeding dishes and stations, etc. Professional groomers and those who own vain dogs should note the range of ribbons, coat whiteners, nail polish, and similar products.

Special Factors: Quantity discounts available; staff veterinarian; returns accepted within 20 days; min. order $5.

WHOLESALE VETERINARY SUPPLY, INC.; P.O. Box 2256; Rockford, IL 61131 (800) 435-6940/ Cat.: free (5 & 11)/ Save: 20–50%/ Pay: C, MO, MC, V Sells: vet, livestock, and pet supplies/ Mail order only

$$$/ ✉ / ☎

Comment: WVS offers over 8,000 products for cats, dogs, rabbits, cattle, and horses in its 104-page catalog. The firm, est. in 1971, keeps abreast of new developments in research and preventive medicine.

Sample Goods: Vaccines and biologicals, nutritional supplements, surgical instruments, cages and carriers, grooming tools and preparations, leashes and leads, flea and tick treatments, a large selection of books, leather-care products, flashlights, knives, disinfectants and cleaning products, Georgia and Cedar Crest work shoes, Laredo Western boots, and other goods. Many well-known manufacturers—Sergeant's, Lambert Kay, Oster, Roche, Fortex, Farnam, Absorbine, Holiday—are represented, as well as hard-to-find labels and imports.

Special Factors: Authorized returns accepted within 30 days; min. order $20.

SEE ALSO:

Gohn Bros. . . . horse blankets . . . CLOTHING
Puritan's Pride, Inc. . . . pet vitamins, grooming aids . . .
   HEALTH
Star Pharmaceutical, Inc. . . . small selection pet vitamins,
   grooming products . . . HEALTH
Sunburst Biorganics . . . pet vitamins . . . HEALTH
Vitamin Specialties . . . pet vitamins . . . HEALTH
Western Natural Products . . . pet vitamins . . . HEALTH

APPLIANCES, AUDIO, TV, AND VIDEO

Major, small, and personal-care appliances; sewing machines and vacuum cleaners; audio components and personal stereo; TV and video equipment; tapes, discs, and services.

If it plugs in or runs on batteries, it's probably sold by one if not many of the firms listed here. White goods (washers, dryers, refrigerators, and ranges), brown goods (TVs, air conditioners, etc.), small kitchen and personal-care appliances, pocket calculators, phone equipment, sewing machines, vacuum cleaners, and floor machines are featured, and many of the companies also sell blank audio and video tapes, luggage, cameras, typewriters, pens, and video games.

Discounts of 30% to 50% are routine, but smart buyers consider more than price when they're shopping. The Better Business Bureau publishes a number of "Booklets on Wise Buying" that can help you make intelligent purchases. Tracts on appliance service contracts, air conditioning, home computers, microwave ovens, phone purchases, and video equipment are all available. Contact your local BBB to obtain them, or send a SASE for the complete listing of pamphlets and an order form to Council of Better Business Bureaus, Inc.; 1515 Wilson Blvd.; Arlington, VA 22209; Attn: Publications Dept.

Sunbeam publishes a 20-page booklet, "Making Less Electricity Do More," that lists the operating costs of many popular electrical appliances and includes a number of recipes. Request the booklet by title from the Consumer Affairs Dept.; Sunbeam Appliance Company; Sunbeam Corp.; 2001 South York Rd.; Oak Brook, IL 60521.

Consumer Reports reviews name-brand products monthly and publishes summaries of these in its yearly *Buying Guide.* Use the magazine and annual as *adjuncts* to shopping, and note that suggested list and "benchmark" retail selling prices stated with model information may be out of date (this is stated by CU in its guide). *Consumer's Research* also publishes product evaluations and articles of practical interest to consumers.

For additional firms selling appliances and electronics, see "Office and Computing" and "Tools."

AAA-ALL FACTORY, INC.; 241 Cedar; Abilene, TX 79601
(915) 677-1311/ Broch.: $2 (quarterly)/ Save: 35–75%/ Pay:
C, MO, MC, V Sells: vacuums, floor machines, ceiling fans/
Shop: same address

$$$$/ ✉ / ☎

Comment: Clean up, cool off, and save with AAA—top names in vacuum cleaners at 50% below list and the firm's own line of ceiling fans, plus supplies and accessories. Est. in 1975.

Sample Goods: The latest models in canister, upright, convertible, and mini vacuums: Kirby's "Heritage," Compact's canister and upright models, Filter Queen's complete cleaning system, the Rexair Rainbow and attachments, Hoover's home and commercial lines, Eureka's commercial floor buffers/rug shampooers and machines by Mastercraft, Shelton, Panasonic and Royal. Bags and belts stocked. Ceiling fans run from a 36", 3-blade model ($21.95) to a 52" fan with five cane-inset hardwood blades, 3 speeds, reversible rotation, a choice of finishes ($89.95).

Special Factors: No seconds or rebuilt models sold; layaway plan available; all machines warrantied; satisfaction guaranteed; returns accepted within 10 days; C.O.D. orders accepted.

ABC VACUUM CLEANER WAREHOUSE; 6720 Burnet Rd.;
Austin, TX 78757 (512) 459-7643/ PL: free (1, 4, 7, 11)/
Save: 30–50%/ Pay: C, MO, AE, MC, V Sells: vacuums, floor machines/ Shop: same address; M–F 9–6, Sa 9–3

$$$/ ✉ / ☎

Comment: ABC purchases from overstocked distributors, and passes the savings—up to 50% on top names in floor machines—on to you. Selling to informed customers since 1977.

Sample Goods: Rexair's Rainbow and Aquamate carpet-cleaning attachment; Kirby's Heritage upright and Rug Renovator shampoo attachment; the Filter Queen and the compact Compact, a powerful cleaner with "big vac" features that include a motorized power nozzle (under $450 here and as much as $880 when bought from a sales representative). Bags and filters also stocked.

Special Factors: No seconds or rebuilt models sold; layaway plan available; terms of warranties stated in PL; satisfaction guaranteed; returns accepted within 15 days.

AMERICAN VACUUM & SEWING MACHINE CORP.; 2908 Hamilton St.; Hyattsville, MD 20782 (301) 559-6800/ Info: PQ with SASE/ Save: 20%/ Pay: C, MO, MC, V Sells: sewing machines, vacuum cleaners/ Shop: same address; M–F 9–6, Sa 9–5

$$/ ✉

Comment: American, est. in 1965, offers name-brand sewing machines and vacuum cleaners and accessories and supplies for both at 20% off list. Savvy shoppers will *write* for prices and availability info—no PQ calls or catalog.

Sample Goods: The latest models in vacuum cleaners by Eureka, Hoover, Royal, Kirby, and Panasonic; sewing machines by Singer, Necchi, White, Universal, Pfaff, Viking, Elna, Bernina, and New Home. Bags, belts, and attachments are also available.

Special Factors: PQ by letter only with SASE; include mfr. data and model name.

ANNEX OUTLET LTD.; 43 Warren St.; New York, NY 10007 (212) 964-8661/ Cat.: free (1, 5, 9)/ Save: 35–40%/ Pay: C, MO, cert. check **Sells:** audio, video, TV, phones, cameras/ **Shop:** same address; M, T, Th 8–6, W 8–9, F 8–3:30, Su 9–5

$$$/

Comment: Annex Outlet is listed in just about every New York City shopping guide for its consistently good discounts on audio and TV/video equipment, cameras, phones and machines, etc. Est. in 1972.

Sample Goods: Video recorders, portable VCRs, cameras, tapes, and batteries by Panasonic, RCA, Quasar, JVC, Sharp, Fisher, Hitachi, Vidicraft, Recoton, Can Am, Smith-Victor, Bescor, Maxell, TDK, Scotch, Agfa, BASF, Trimax, Sony, Fuji, Memorex, etc. Audio by Technics, Sansui, Sharp, Shure, and ADC; personal stereo by Aiwa, Sony, and Sanyo; auto audio by Blaupunkt, Clarion, and Panasonic; Sony, Sharp, and Hitachi TVs; phones and machines by Panasonic, Sanyo, Uniden, Phone-Mate, Electra, and ITT.

Special Factors: PQ by phone or letter with SASE on items not listed in catalog.

AUDIO VIDEO CENTER, INC.; 4128 S. Florida Ave.; Lakeland, FL 33803 (813) 644-4546/ Info: PQ/ Save: 30–40%/

Pay: MO, cert. check, MC, V **Sells:** video, TVs, audio, satellite dishes/ **Shop:** same address

$$/ ✉ / ☎

Comment: AVC can give you maximum reception at a minimum price—satellite dishes at 5% over dealer cost. Founded in 1981, it also stocks TVs, video, and audio.

Sample Goods: VCRs, video cameras, and TVs by Panasonic, RCA, Quasar, Sony, and Magnavox; a range of video products from Fuji, Kiwi, Smith-Victor, Marathon, Allsop, and Videolink; Panasonic portable audio; Birdview satellite dishes.

Special Factors: PQ by phone or letter with SASE.

BERNIE'S DISCOUNT CENTER, INC.; 821 Sixth Ave.; New York, NY 10001 (212) 564-8582/ Cat.: $1 & 2-stamp SASE (quarterly)/ **Save:** 20–50%/ **Pay:** C or MO **Sells:** electronics, appliances/ **Shop:** same address; M–F 9–5:30, Sa 11–3:30

$$$/ ✉

Comment: Bernie's was founded in 1948 and sells products at 8% to 12% above dealer cost ("the best cost," Bernie's tell us). One of the city's best sources for discounted electronics and appliances, Bernie's tries to carry at least 3 top buys in each product category.

Sample Goods: Compact and personal audio by Panasonic, Sony, Sharp; TVs and video equipment by Sony, Mitsubishi, Panasonic, Toshiba, Hitachi; phones and machines by Panasonic, Sharp, Sanyo, Phone-Mate; white and brown goods (shipped in NYC area only) by Amana, G.E., Caloric, Gibson,

Hotpoint, KitchenAid, Litton, Magic Chef, Maytag, Rangaire, Tappan, Welbilt, White-Westinghouse, Whirlpool, Airtemp, and Friedrich; small and personal-care appliances (shipped nationwide) by G.E., Hoover, Eureka, Regina, Bionaire, Edison, Corona, Norelco, Oster, Braun, Clairol, Teledyne, Sunbeam, Remington, KitchenAid, Toastmaster, Presto, Proctor-Silex, Norelco, Hamilton Beach, Farberware, Oster, West Bend, Mr. Coffee, Panasonic.

Special Factors: PQ by phone or letter with SASE on items not listed in catalog; closed Saturdays in July and Aug.

BI-RITE PHOTO AND ELECTRONICS; 15 E. 30th St.; New York, NY 10016-7031 (800) 223-1970/ Info: PQ/ Save: to 60%/ Pay: C, MO, MC, V **Sells:** cameras, electronics, audio, video/ **Shop:** same address; M–Th 9–6, F 9–1, Su 10:30–3:30 $$$$/ ✉ / ☎

Comment: Bi-Rite has been comparison-shopped for camera equipment, answering machines, calculators, and VCRs and was found to have the lowest prices among several top New York City discounters on several occasions. Don't order elsewhere until you get a price quote here.

Sample Goods: Cameras, accessories, and darkroom equipment by Olympus, Canon, Nikon, Minolta, Gossen, Hasselblad, Polaroid, Kodak, Ricoh, Vivitar, Mamiya, Tokina, Tamron, Soligor, Pentax, etc.; phone equipment by Panasonic, Uniden, Code-A-Phone, and other firms; personal stereo by Sony, Aiwa, and Panasonic; Canon typewriters; calculators by Canon and Hewlett-Packard; VCRs and video tape by Panasonic, Kodak, TDK, RCA, and Polaroid; and many other goods and manufacturers.

Special Factors: PQ by phone or letter with SASE; trade-ins accepted on cameras; min. order $50 on credit cards.

BONDY EXPORT CORP.; 40 Canal St.; New York, NY 10002 (212) 925-7785/ **Info:** PQ/ **Save:** 30–50%/ **Pay:** C, MO, AE, MC, V **Sells:** electronics, appliances, office machines/ **Shop:** same address; Su–Th 10–6, F 10–3

$$$$/

Comment: Bondy has earned a place on every bargain-hunter's map with its deep discounts and broad range of name-brand goods.

Sample Goods: Appliances, cameras, and projectors; TV and video equipment, vacuum cleaners, phones and answering machines, typewriters, pens, and luggage; small appliances by G.E., Oster, Hoover, SCM, Clairol, Conair, Braun, Panasonic, Krups, Sony, etc.; G.E. and Amana microwave ovens; Samsonite luggage; Parker pens; Seiko and Casio watches; Farberware cookware.

Special Factors: Bondy sells but does not ship large appliances; PQ by phone or letter with SASE.

CRUTCHFIELD; 1 Crutchfield Park; Charlottesville, VA 22906-6020 (800) 336-5566/ **Cat.:** free/ **Save:** to 60%/ **Pay:** C, MO, AE, CB, DC, MC, V **Sells:** audio components, phone equipment/ **Shop:** same address; also 9444 Arlington Expwy., Jacksonville; 72 Blanding Blvd., Orange Park, FL

$$$/

Comment: Crutchfield's lush 100-page catalog of home and auto audio components is a rarity among electronics discounters —loaded with buying tips and product specs on featured goods, sold at up to 40% below list. Est. in 1974.

Sample Goods: Car stereo equipment by such top manufacturers as Sony, Pioneer, Concord, JVC, etc.; home stereo by Advent, Sony, Akai, Pioneer, Infinity, and other firms; name-brand video and telephone equipment. Computer accessories also stocked.

Special Factors: Phone staff can advise on component and equipment selection; shipping included; satisfaction guaranteed; returns accepted within 30 days.

DIAL-A-BRAND, INC.; 110 Bedford Ave.; Bellmore, NY 11710 (718) 978-4400/ Info: PQ/ Save: to 40%/ Pay: MO or cert. check Sells: appliances, TVs, video equipment/ Shop: same address; M–F 9–5

$$$/ /

Comment: Dial-A-Brand has captured the kudos of institutions and individuals with its wide range of appliances and popular electronics, sold at up to 40% below list. Est. in 1967.

Sample Goods: Name-brand air conditioners, TVs, video equipment, microwave ovens, and large appliances by all major manufacturers. Ships chiefly within the New York/New Jersey/Connecticut area, but deliveries are made nationwide. (Note that freight charges may offset savings on outsized or heavy items shipped long distances.)

Special Factors: PQ by phone or letter with SASE; returns accepted for exchange if goods defective or damaged in transit.

E33 TYPEWRITER & ELECTRONICS; 42 E. 33rd St.; New York, NY 10016 (800) 223-3201/ Flyer: free with SASE/ Save: to 60%/ Pay: MO, CC, MC, V Sells: audio, TVs and video, office machines/ Shop: same address

$$$/ ✉ / ☎

Comment: E33 will "meet or beat any advertised price on TVs and VCRs," and that includes Sony! Savings of up to 60% on latest models, top brands.

Sample Goods: TVs and video equipment by Sony, Panasonic, RCA, JVC, Sanyo, Quasar, Mitsubishi, Hitachi, Zenith, Toshiba, Sharp, Fisher, G.E.; audio components and personal stereo by Hitachi, Yamaha, Sony, Marantz, JVC, Denon, Sansui, Akai, Technics, Aiwa, Nakamichi; typewriters by IBM, SCM, Brother, Silver-Reed, Royal, Olympia, Juki, Sharp; computers, peripherals, and software by and for Apple, IBM, Atari, Hayes, NEC, Amdek, Juki, Brother, Silver-Reed, Epson; Sharp and Canon copiers; calculators by Canon, Hewlett-Packard, Casio, Sharp, Sanyo; phones and phone machines by Panasonic, Code-A-Phone, Phone-Mate, Uniden, Record a Call, Sanyo. Casio musical keyboards; microwave ovens by Panasonic and Sharp.

Special Factors: PQ by phone or letter with SASE; service on TVs, video equipment, and typewriters; special orders on foreign-voltage typewriters in all keyboards and typefaces; credit cards accepted on phone orders only; min. order $50.

E.B.A. WHOLESALE CORP.; 2329 Nostrand Ave.; Brooklyn, NY 11210 (718) 252-3400/ Info: PQ/ Save: 10–40%/ Pay: C, MO, cert. check Sells: large appliances, TVs, video equipment/ Shop: same address; M, T, Th 9–8:15, W, F, Sa 9–6

$$$/ ✉ / ☎

Comment: Bargains abound at this Brooklyn discount house, which sets prices based on its cost plus 5%—the savings run from 10% to 40% on list or comparable retail.

Sample Goods: Large appliances by Amana, Caloric, Frigidaire, G.E., Hotpoint, KitchenAid, Jenn-Air, Magic Chef, White-Westinghouse, Whirlpool; air conditioners by Airtemp, Fedders, Carrier, Friedrich; TV and video equipment by Panasonic, Sony, Sanyo, G.E., Zenith, RCA, Quasar, Sylvania, Magnavox.

Special Factors: PQ by phone or letter with SASE; returns accepted; 20% restocking fee.

FOCUS ELECTRONICS, INC.; 4523 13th Ave.; Brooklyn, NY 11219 (800) 223-3411/ Elec. or Photo Cat.: $4 each, ref./ Save: 20–50%/ Pay: C, MO, MC, V **Sells:** electronics, appliances, computers, cameras/ Shop: same address; M–Th 10–7, F 10–2, Su 10–6

$$$/ ✉ / ☎

Comment: Focus has been in the electronics business since 1967, and offers mail-order shoppers a 96-page catalog packed with buys on computers, audio and video equipment, TVs, and appliances. A separate photography catalog is also available.

Sample Goods: Computers and peripherals by Eagle, NEC, Franklin, IBM, Tava, Amdek, Taxan, Zenith, Hayes, Novation, EPD, Epson, Brother, Juki, Okidata, Smith-Corona; TVs and video equipment by Panasonic, Sony, Sharp, JVC, RCA, Kodak, Kiwi, Recoton, Ambico, TeeGee, Vidicraft; audio by Fisher, Aiwa, Sony, Panasonic, G.E., Toshiba; phones and phone machines by top manufacturers; Amana, Thermador, and Sharp microwave ovens; small and personal-care appliances; Anova modular security systems; Canon copiers; Casio keyboards; still, movie, and video cameras and darkroom equipment.

Special Factors: PQ by phone or letter with SASE; returns accepted within 10 days (except software).

FOTO ELECTRIC SUPPLY CO.; 31 Essex St.; New York, NY 10002 (212) 673-5222/ Info: PQ/ Save: 30% +/ Pay: C, MO, MC, V Sells: large appliances, TVs and video, cameras/ Shop: same address; Su–Th 9–7, F 9–2

$$$$/

Comment: Foto has done very little advertising in the 22 years it's been in business because the customers do it all gratis. Foto has been written up in almost every New York shopping guide, and ships to Europe, Israel, South America, and Canada, as well as all over the U.S.

Sample Goods: TVs by Sony, RCA, Zenith, etc.; video equipment and videotape; white goods by G.E., Westinghouse, Amana, Whirlpool, Maytag, Magic Chef, Thermador (ranges), and Sub-Zero (refrigerators). Foto also stocks many other name-brand goods—cameras by all the major manufacturers, plus film by Kodak, Fuji, Agfa, and Polaroid.

Special Factors: PQ by letter only with SASE.

HUNTER AUDIO-PHOTO, INC.; 507 Fifth Ave., New York, NY 10017 (212) 986-1540/ Movie Cat.: free/ Save: 20–60%/ Pay: C, MO, cert. check Sells: audio, electronics, watches, video, movies/ Shop: same address; M–Sa 9–6

$$$/ ✉

Comment: Hunter Audio-Photo has been in business since 1976 and sells a fraction of its large stock of electronics by mail. Flyers are available for each product category (send a SASE).

Sample Goods: Personal audio by G.E., Sony, Panasonic, Sanyo (30–40% below list or comparable retail); Casio, TI, Sharp calculators (30–45% discounts); Parker, Cross, Mont Blanc pens (30–50% discounts); Seiko, Bulova, Timex watches (20–40% discounts); Ray Ban and Porsche Carrera sunglasses (30–40% discounts). The "Video Yesteryear" catalog lists over 600 titles—old movies, TV shows, cartoons, documentaries, and propaganda—in VHS, Beta I and II, and ¾" U-matic formats.

Special Factors: PQ by phone or letter with SASE; some video movies offered on Super-8 film and PAL cassettes.

ILLINOIS AUDIO, INC.; 12 E. Delaware Pl.; Chicago, IL 60611 (800) 621-8042/ Broch.: free (monthly)/ Save: to 40%/ Pay: C, MO, MC, V Sells: audio equipment, components/ Mail order only

$$$/ ✉ / ☎

Comment: Selling top-of-the-line audio components since 1973. This firm's competitive position is summed up on the order form: "See a Better Price? Let Us Know! We Want Your Business!!"

Sample Goods: Components by A.D.C., Acoustic Research, Akai, Altec, Audio Control, Audio Pulse, Audio Technica, BASF, Betamax, D.B.X., Discwasher, Dual, Empire, Fuji, Jensen, JVC, Kenwood, Koss, Marantz, Maxell, MXR, Nortronics, Omnisonic, Aiwa, Onkyo, Audio Research, Pickering, Pioneer, Sansui, Sanyo, Scotch, Sennheiser, Shure, Sony, Stanton, TDK, Teac, Technics, etc.

Special Factors: PQ by phone or letter with SASE; only new goods sold; shipped in factory-sealed cartons; warranted by manufacturers.

INTERNATIONAL SOLGO, INC.; 1745 Hempstead Tpk.; Elmont, NY 11003 (800) 645-8162/ Info: PQ/ Save: to 40%/ Pay: C, MO, cert. check, AE, DC, MC, V Sells: appliances, electronics, cameras/ Shop: same address; M–F 9–6:30, Sa 9–5, Su 10–4 (Sundays during June and holiday season only)
$$$/ ✉ / ☎

Comment: International Solgo is one of the pioneers of discounting, in business since 1933 selling goods at low, low prices. Luggage, office machines, jewelry, and more offered in the Solgo stores. Large catalog of discounted goods is $5, ref.

Sample Goods: TVs and video equipment by Magnavox, Philco, Quasar, G.E., Zenith, Sony, Panasonic, RCA, Hitachi; large, small, and personal-care appliances by Amana, Brown, Eureka, Clairol, Hoover, Charmglo, Garland, Magic Chef, Tappan, Caloric, Hotpoint, Sankyo, Norelco, Mr. Coffee, Maytag, Litton, KitchenAid; Cross and Mont Blanc pens and pencils; cameras by Polaroid, Nikon, Minolta, Canon, Yashica, etc.; audio components by Pioneer, Panasonic, Sankyo, Sanyo, JVC, Audiovox, etc.

Special Factors: PQ by phone or letter with SASE; dual-voltage appliances available; min. order $25, $50 on credit cards.

JEMS SOUNDS, LTD.; 785 Lexington Ave.; New York, NY 10021 (212) 838-4716/ Info: PQ/ Save: 10–40%/ Pay: C,

MO, MC, V **Sells:** audio, video, phones and machines/ **Shop:** same address; also other New York City locations; M–Sa 9:30–7, Sun 11–6

$$$/ ✉

Comment: A wide range of electronics offered here at discounts of up to 40%, and frequent specials on selected items offer further savings.

Sample Goods: Components by Sony, Panasonic, Sanyo, Toshiba, Onkyo, Teac, Akai, Dual, JBL, Technics, Marantz; TVs and video equipment by Sony, Panasonic, Sanyo, Toshiba, RCA, Zenith, JVC; Atari video games; calculators by Sharp, Toshiba, Panasonic, Canon, Texas Instruments, Casio, Hewlett-Packard; phones and phone machines by Phone-Mate, Record a Call, Sanyo, ITT; watches by Bulova, Citizen, Seiko; cameras by major manufacturers.

Special Factors: PQ by letter only with SASE.

LVT PRICE QUOTE HOTLINE, INC.; Box 444; Commack, NY 11725-0444 (800) 645-5010/ Broch.: free/ Save: to 40%/ Pay: C, MO, cert. check **Sells:** appliances, electronics, office machines/ Mail order only

$$$/ ✉ / ☎

Comment: LVT gives you instant access to over 4,000 products from over 200 manufacturers, at savings of up to 40% on suggested list or full retail prices. The brochure lists available brands, and price quotes are given on individual items. Est. in 1976.

Sample Goods: Major appliances, microwave ovens, air conditioners, TVs, video equipment and tapes, phones and phone machines, calculators, typewriters, scanners, radar detectors, cash registers, radios, computers and peripherals.

Special Factors: PQ by phone or letter with SASE; inquiries welcomed on 800 line; shipping, handling, and insurance included; all sales final; all goods warrantied by manufacturers; min. order $50.

LYLE CARTRIDGES; 115 So. Corona Ave.; Valley Stream, NY 11218 (800) 221-0906/ Cat.: free with SASE/ Save: to 75%/ Pay: C, MO, MC, V Sells: stereo cartridges and accessories/ Shop: same address; M–F 9–5:30

$$$$/ ✉/ ☎

Comment: Lyle Cartridges has been in business since 1952 and is one of the best sources around for the cartridges, spindles, drive belts, and diamond styli that help make music in your life.

Sample Goods: Replacement parts for equipment by Garrard, BIC, Thorens, Astatic, Empire, Technics, and similar manufacturers; products by Shure, Stanton, Audio Technica, Dynavector, B & O, ADC, Sonus, Audio Dynamics, Grado, Pickering, and Ortofon. Record-care products by Discwasher and LAST and replacement styli by Signet also available.

Special Factors: PQ by phone or letter with SASE; defective goods replaced; min. order $15 on prepaid orders, $25 on credit cards.

MID AMERICA VACUUM CLEANER SUPPLY CO.; 666 University Ave.; St. Paul, MN 55104-4896 (800) 328-9430/ Cat.: $5, ref./ Save: 15–50%/ Pay: C, MO, MC, V **Sells:** vacuums, floor machines, appliance parts/ **Shop:** same address; M–F 9–5:30

$$$/

Comment: Mid America's 256-page bible of parts and supplies can help when the service center can't, and vacuums and floor machines are also stocked—at up to 50% off. Est. in 1952.

Sample Goods: Parts and accessories for vacuum cleaners, floor machines, blenders, coffee makers, irons, shavers, mixers, pressure cookers, toasters; brand-new vacuum cleaners by Eureka, Hoover, Kirby, MagNuM, Oreck, Panasonic, Progress (Mercedes), Rexair (Rainbow), Royal, Sanitaire, Shop-Vac; central vacuum systems; bags, belts, lights, etc.

Special Factors: PQ by phone or letter with SASE; quantity discounts available; consult appliance manual before attempting repairs; min. order $15.

PERCY'S INC.; 315 Grove St.; Worcester, MA 01605 (617) 755-5334/ Info: PQ/ Save: 30–50%/ Pay: C, MO, MC, V **Sells:** large appliances, TVs, video equipment/ **Shop:** same address; M, W, F 9–9, Tu & Th 9–6, Sa 9–5

$$$/

Comment: Percy's has more than 50 years of experience backing its motto, "The difficult we do immediately. The impossible takes a few minutes longer." No delay for the discounts—prices are 3% above wholesale cost, or up to 50% below list.

Sample Goods: Washers, dryers, dishwashers, refrigerators, ranges, standard and microwave ovens, freezers, TVs and video equipment and tapes, dehumidifiers, disposals, etc., by RCA, Hotpoint, Panasonic, Maytag, Whirlpool, White-Westinghouse, Caloric, Regency, Jenn-Air, Mitsubishi, Zenith, Frigidaire, Magic Chef, KitchenAid, G.E., Litton, Sylvania, Waste King, Quasar, Thermador.

Special Factors: PQ by phone or letter with SASE.

S & S SOUND CITY; 58 W. 45th St.; New York, NY 10036-4280 (800) 223-0360/ Broch.: free (quarterly)/ Save: 20–60%/ Pay: C, MO, MC, V Sells: appliances, audio, TVs, video equipment/ Shop: same address; M–Sa 9–6, Su (in Dec. only) 11–5

$$$/ ✉ / ☎

Comment: S & S has been in business since 1975, selling microwave ovens, air conditioners, audio components, and TVs and video equipment. The owners aim to be "the nicest people in town," and will try to get anything you want.

Sample Goods: TVs, video, and audio by Zenith, Toshiba, Quasar, RCA, Sanyo, Panasonic, Hitachi, JVC, Emerson, Sony, Akai, Fisher, G.E., Smith-Victor, Ambico, Vidicraft; phone machines by Panasonic, Record A Call, Teletender, AT&T, Code-A-Phone; Panasonic tape recorders; Sharp security and surveillance equipment, microwave ovens by Sharp, Samsung, Toshiba, Amana, Litton, etc.

Special Factors: PQ by phone or letter with SASE; returns accepted within 7 days; special orders accepted.

SALES CITI, INC.; 27 Essex St.; New York, NY 10002 (212) 673-8383/ Info: PQ/ Save: 10–40%/ Pay: C, MO, MC, V Sells: appliances, audio, video, luggage, watches/ **Shop:** same address; Su–Th 9–6:30, F 9–2
$$$/ ✉

Comment: This firm, also known as Sam's Sale Citi, is a real bargain emporium that sells a little of everything at savings of up to 40% on list or retail prices.

Sample Goods: Audio components and personal stereo sets by Panasonic and Sony; TVs and video equipment by Panasonic, Sony, Sharp, Zenith; phones and phone machines by Sanyo, Phone-Mate, Code-A-Phone, ITT; video games by Atari; Samsonite attaché cases; Seiko, Pulsar, Bulova, Timex watches; small and personal-care appliances; perfumes and colognes (in store only).

Special Factors: PQ by phone or letter with SASE; min. order $25.

SEWIN' IN VERMONT; 84 Concord Ave.; St. Johnsbury, VT 05819 (802) 748-2165/ Mfr. Broch.: free/ Save: 20–35%/ Pay: C, MO, MC, V Sells: sewing machines and vacuum cleaners/ **Shop:** same address; M–F 9–5, Sat 9–1
$$$/ ✉ / ☎

Comment: If you're shopping for a name-brand sewing machine but don't want to pay top-of-the-line prices, Sewin' in Vermont has the answer. It carries several of the best American and European brands at prices 20% to 35% below list.

Sample Goods: Singer, Pfaff, and Viking sewing machines and replacement parts and accessories; Sewin' also sells vacuum cleaners made by the best-known firm in the U.S. at excellent prices.

Special Factors: PQ by phone or letter with SASE; shipping and insurance included on machine orders; helpful sales staff.

STEREO CORPORATION OF AMERICA; 1629 Flatbush Ave.; Brooklyn, NY 11210 (800) 221-0974/ Cat.: free/ Save: 30–60%/ Pay: C, MO, MC, V **Sells:** audio components/ **Shop:** same address
$$$/ ✉ / ☎

Comment: SCA, aka Stereo Warehouse/Video Warehouse, has been selling audio components at rock-bottom prices since 1951. Prices run from cost to 10% above cost, or 30% to 60% below list.

Sample Goods: Components by Audio Research, Harmon Kardon, Teac, BASF, Bose, Onkyo, Technics, Yamaha, Aiwa, Akai, Shure, Pioneer, Sony, ADC, Sansui, Maxell, and TDK.

Special Factors: PQ by phone or letter with SASE.

THE VIDEOTIME CORP.; 48 Urban Ave.; Westbury, NY 11590 (800) 645-2317/ Broch.: $1, ref./ Save: 20–60%/ Pay: C, MO, MC, V Sells: video equipment and computers/ Shop: same address

$$$$/ ✉/ ☎

Comment: Videotime has been selling by mail since 1976, and publishes a brochure of specials every other month. Corporate and commercial business is welcome—purchase orders are accepted and the terms are 10 days net.

Sample Goods: VCRs, cameras, accessories, and tapes by Sony, Panasonic, JVC, Maganvox, Quasar, Hitachi, Toshiba, Sanyo, RCA, Bogan (tripods); Franklin computers and compatible programs.

Special Factors: PQ by phone or letter with SASE; min. order $50 on credit cards.

WISAN TV & APPLIANCE INC.; 4085 Hylan Blvd.; Staten Island, NY 10308 (718) 356-7700/ Info: PQ/ Save: 10–40%/ Pay: C, MO, MC, V Sells: appliances, TVs, video equipment/ Shop: same address

$$$/ ✉

Comment: Wisan was established in 1946 and has been selling major appliances and TV and video equipment at discount prices by mail for 6 years. "We shoot straight and try to get the best prices," says the owner, who will take special orders for goods not in stock.

Sample Goods: Appliances by Frigidaire, Hotpoint, G.E., Caloric, Whirlpool, Maytag, Magic Chef, White-Westinghouse, Tappan, Sub-Zero, Amana, Chambers, Waste King, Thermador, KitchenAid, Jenn-Air; TV and video equipment by Zenith, Quasar, G.E., RCA, Sony, Hitachi, Toshiba. Service available in the NYC area.

Special Factors: PQ by phone or letter with SASE.

WISCONSIN DISCOUNT STEREO; 2417 W. Badger Rd.; Madison, WI 53713 (800) 356-9514/ Info: PQ/ Save: 15–70%/ Pay: MO, AE, MC, V Sells: audio, video, electronics/ Mail order only

$$$/ ✉/ ☎

Comment: WDS, which began doing business by mail in 1977, told us it carries "every major brand of electronics—the largest selection in the United States, possibly in the world."

Sample Goods: Audio components, portable stereo, video equipment, and tapes by Sony, Jensen, Kenwood, Teac, Pioneer, Marantz, Sanyo, Technics, Aiwa, Koss, Panasonic, Clarion, Maxell, Discwasher, and many other manufacturers.

Special Factors: PQ by phone or letter with SASE; C.O.D. orders accepted.

IRV WOLFSON COMPANY; 3221 W. Irving Park Rd.; Chicago, IL 60618 (800) 621-1468/ Cat.: $4, ref./ Save: 25–

40%/ **Pay:** MO, cert. check, MC, V **Sells:** foreign-voltage appliances, electronics/ **Shop:** same address

$$$/ ✉ / ☎

Comment: Wolfson has been selling 220-volt/50-cycle appliances and electronics since 1952, at prices 7% over cost (25% to 40% below retail prices). Domestic-current goods, as well as some name-brand furnishings, are also offered.

Sample Goods: Foreign-voltage TVs and video equipment, white goods, microwave ovens, air conditioners, audio components, kitchen appliances, vacuum cleaners, personal-care appliances, electric blankets, and power tools by White-Westinghouse, G.E., Amana, Caloric, Roper, Sub-Zero, Thermador, Modern Maid, Gaggenau, Maytag, Zenith, Panasonic, RCA, Sharp, Singer, Black & Decker, Eureka, KitchenAid, Oster, Jenn-Air, JVC; "stepdown" autotransformers, currency converters, and plug adapters also stocked.

Special Factors: PQ by phone or letter with SASE; domestic-current goods available; helpful customer-service department.

SEE ALSO:

American Marine Electronics . . . marine electronics . . . AUTO

Comp-U-Card . . . appliances, electronics . . . GENERAL

E & B Marine, Inc. . . . marine electronics . . . AUTO

Executive Photo & Supply Corp. . . . personal stereo and video . . . CAMERAS

The Finals . . . personal stereo, fitness-related electronics . . . CLOTHING

Fiveson Food Equipment, Inc. . . . commercial restaurant equipment . . . HOME—Kitchen

47st Photo, Inc. . . . microwave ovens, personal stereo, TV, video, etc. . . . CAMERAS

Garden Camera . . . video equipment . . . CAMERAS

Goldberg's Marine . . . marine electronics . . . AUTO

Greater New York Trading Co. . . . appliances, TV, typewriters, vacuum cleaners, etc. . . . HOME—Table Settings

Jilor Discount Office Machines, Inc. . . . phones, phone machines, calculators . . . OFFICE

Kaplan Bros. Blue Flame Corp. . . . Garland commercial stoves . . . HOME—Kitchen

Lamp Warehouse/New York Ceiling Fan Center . . . ceiling fans . . . HOME—Decor

Mast Abeam . . . marine electronics . . . AUTO

Olden Camera & Lens Co., Inc. . . . video equipment . . . CAMERAS

Opticon Laboratories, Inc. . . . film transferred to video cassettes . . . CAMERAS

Pearl Brothers Office Machinery & Equipment . . . typewriters, office machines, repairs . . . OFFICE

Typex Business Machines, Inc. . . . typewriters, calculators, office machines, supplies . . . OFFICE

Warehouse Marine Discount . . . marine electronics . . . AUTO

West Side Camera Inc. . . . video cassettes . . . CAMERAS

Whole Earth Access . . . appliances, electronics . . . GENERAL

ART, ANTIQUES, AND COLLECTIBLES

Fine art, limited editions, antiques, and collectibles.

Since antiques and collectibles can be investments as well as objects of pleasure, it makes sense to buy at wholesale or dealer prices so you can maximize your profits when you resell. Buying expressly for resale is not wise, however, unless you're a genuine expert. There are too many variables contributing to the real market worth of works of art and collectibles to make the field safe for neophytes and wishful thinkers. For example, a Fiestaware pitcher in perfect condition may be $20 to $30 if it's orange or lime green, and twice that in a scarce or highly coveted color. The hopeful who seizes upon a $10 orange pitcher in a junk shop as a "find" may find no dealer willing to purchase the item, or may be offered $10 at most. Even professional repairs and restoration can devalue an otherwise pristine object, especially in high-end collecting. You'll proceed much more happily in assembling a collection if you remember that you can rarely outsmart a dealer, and if you buy only what you like and would enjoy keeping.

Getting to know the market is one of the pleasures of "antiquing" and collecting, and there are hundreds of reference books and guides available to give you the necessary grounding. The indefatigable Kovels compile *Kovels' Antiques & Collectibles Price List* on a regular basis. It will give you an idea of the price spread among items of similar type and vintage. It doesn't include much beyond the one-line descriptions, but it can tell you the going rate for thousands of antiques and collectibles in the U.S. market. Whether you're a seasoned connoisseur or a novice, you'll find *The Kovels' Collectors' Source Book* (374 pp., 1983, $13.95, Crown Publishers) a great help in finding sources for specific types of antiques and collectibles, locating restoration and repair services, assembling a bookshelf of magazines and reference texts on your area of interest, learning about related clubs and societies, and much more. It should be stocked in bookstores.

Once you're somewhat familiar with your field, you'll find you can learn volumes by seeing the objects firsthand. Visit flea markets, antique shops, art galleries, and museums as often as possible; attend the viewings held before auctions of "your" collectible. And don't just look—*talk.* Dealers are usually proud of both their knowledge and their wares, and by demonstrating an appreciation of the latter you should elicit a good deal of the former. Dealers will often point out special attributes of a piece and draw your attention to critical details you might have overlooked. The people who run "junk" shops that carry everything from old postcards to furniture can sometimes spot new collecting trends—what's "walking out of here"—as well as the has-beens that "we just can't move at all, at any price." Avoid the latter unless you love them or don't care a whit about appreciation.

It's best to know what you want when buying by mail, for you're not likely to get more than a photo of the items available. And remember that one-of-a-kind items are subject to prior sale, so order promptly upon receipt of the mailing and give second and third choices if possible. Purchase from firms that accept returns so you can send the piece back if it's not to your liking.

**ANTIQUE IMPORTS UNLIMITED; P.O. Box 2978; Coving-
ton, LA 70434-2978** (504) 892-0014/ PL: see text/ Save:
40–60%/ Pay: C, MO, MC, V **Sells:** antiques and collectibles/
Mail order only

$$$$/ ✉/ ☎

Comment: Formerly known as Gand, Ltd., this firm markets
a range of antiques and ephemera through separate price lists.
Get "dealer" prices here—up to 60% below antique-shop rates.
Est. in 1976.

Sample Goods: Single lists, $1; annual subscription rates
listed as follows: "Antique and Collectible Jewelry" (10–12 issues, $12)—silver sugar tongs, snuff boxes, etc.; "Antiques and
Collectibles" (3–5 issues, $5)—Staffordshire, bisque dolls, lace
collars, clocks, antique bobbins, etc.; "Antique Maps, Prints and
Paintings" (3–5 issues, $5)—maps, many of American geogra-
phy; "Antiquities" (3–5 issues, $5)—ancient Egypt, Greece,
Persia, the Celts, and India; "Old Legal Documents" (3–5 issues,
$5)—indenture papers and wills.

Special Factors: Price lists include detailed descriptions but
no illustrations. All one-of-a-kind items, subject to prior sale;
listing second choices recommended; min. order $30 in each
category.

**GEORGE CHANNING ENTERPRISES; P.O. Box 342; Car-
mel, CA 93921** (408) 372-0873/ Broch.: $2, ref./ Save: 30–
60%/ Pay: C or MO **Sells:** art prints, objets d'art/ Mail order
only

$$$/ ✉

Comment: "Discover the treasure of a bygone era" with Channing's reasonably priced art reprints. Future catalog offerings of Chinese silk embroideries and chinoiserie are planned. Est. in 1976.

Sample Goods: Striking reprints of illustrations that originally appeared over a century ago in *Harper's Weekly:* "The Launch of the Atlanta," celebrating a now-forgotten moment; a montage of illustrations on "Law and Moonshine"; a great boating close-up, "Yacht Racing"; and a fashion review, among others. The prices are $12 a print. Custom-framed Chinese silk embroideries are also sold.

Special Factors: Bonus prints may be offered on orders of 4 or more catalog items; satisfaction guaranteed; returns accepted within 30 days.

DECOR PRINTS; 277 Main St.; P.O. Box 502; Noel, MO 64854 (417) 475-6367/ Cat.: $3, ref./ Save: 50%/ Pay: C or MO Sells: art prints, reproductions/ Shop: same address $$$/

Comment: Reproductions of great art masterpieces sold here for little more than museum admission, plus a variety of nostalgic prints. Est. in 1978.

Sample Goods: Copies of treasures by Gainsborough, Brueghel, Degas, Renoir, and other greats; reproductions of nostalgic turn-of-the-century lithographs, advertising posters, and magazine illustrations, from $1.50 to $6. Deduct 50% on orders of 15 prints or more.

Special Factors: Shipping and insurance included on orders of 10 or more prints; min. order 15 prints for 50% discount.

MISCELLANEOUS MAN; P.O. Box 1776; New Freedom, PA 17349 (717) 235-4766/ Cat.: $3; $5 for 2 issues/ Save: 30%+/ Pay: C, MO, MC, V **Sells:** original memorabilia and ephemera/ Mail order only

$$$/ ✉ / ☎

Comment: George Theofiles, ephemerologist extraordinaire, is the moving force behind Miscellaneous Man. He trades in vintage posters, handbills, graphics, labels, guides, brochures, and other memorabilia, *all* of which are original—no reproductions or reprints.

Sample Goods: Theater posters, publicity photographs, handbills, promotional giveaways, circus posters and broadsides, advertising posters and miscellany, WW II ration books, unused sardine-can labels, old insurance calendars, Army recruiting leaflets, KKK membership applications and other such material, sold here at prices 30% or more below the going rate.

Special Factors: Stock moves quickly—order promptly and list second choices; returns accepted within 3 days; min. order $50 on credit cards.

MUSEUM EDITIONS NEW YORK LTD.; 105 Hudson St.; New York, NY 10013 (800) 221-9576/ Cat.: $4, ref./ Save: 10%+/ Pay: C, MO, MC, V **Sells:** fine contemporary art reprints/ Shop: same address

$$$/ ✉ / ☎

Comment: Museum Editions, est. in 1982, produces a stunning 32-page catalog of reproductions of the posters used to announce exhibits in museums and art galleries. If your taste runs to modern and contemporary art, you'll have a field day deciding what to choose for your walls.

Sample Goods: Modern masterpieces by Klee, Pissarro, O'-Keeffe, Rothko, Hopper, Hockney, Hiroshige, Glaser, and Randy Green, among those in a current catalog. Prices run from about $10 to $30. Custom framing is available; inquire for information.

Special Factors: Catalog free to corporate buyers; shipping included on orders of over 30 prints.

QUILTS UNLIMITED; P.O. Box 1210; Lewisburg, WV 24901 (304) 645-6556/ **Cat. & Photos:** $5; $20, year's subs./ **Save:** to 40%/ **Pay:** C, MO, MC, V **Sells:** new, old, antique quilts/ **Shop:** 124 W. Washington St., Lewisburg, WV; M–Sa 10–5; also The Homestead, Hot Springs, VA; M–Su 10–5 $$$/ ✉ / ☎

Comment: This firm, run by two avid collectors, brings you great buys on vintage quilts through monthly mailings of booklets and color photos. Est. in 1969.

Sample Goods: Patchwork, applique, stuffed work, tops, crib quilts, Amish quilts, etc., many in the $200 to $500 range, about 40% less than prices charged by dealers for quilts of similar age, size, detail, and condition. Descriptions include information on material used, number of stitches per inch, whether the work was done by hand or machine, whether signatures or dates are present, estimated age and provenance, presence of any damage or wear, size, and pattern name. Books, new hand-quilted crib quilts, custom services, and a quilt Teddy bear also offered.

Special Factors: Stock moves quickly—order promptly; quilting supplies offered in future mailings; returns accepted within 3 days.

SEE ALSO:

Dinosaur Catalog . . . collectible pewter and porcelain dinosaurs . . . TOYS

Doll House & Toy Factory Outlet . . . miniatures and collectible toys and dolls . . . TOYS

Dollsville Dolls and Bearsville Bears . . . collectible stuffed bears . . . TOYS

Front Row Photos . . . photos and photo buttons of rock stars . . . BOOKS

Greater New York Trading Co. . . . Lladro, Royal Doulton figurines . . . HOME—Table Settings

Guitar Trader . . . vintage fretted instruments . . . MUSIC

Mandolin Brothers Ltd. . . . vintage fretted instruments . . . MUSIC

Rainbow Music . . . vintage guitars and amps . . . MUSIC

The Renovator's Supply, Inc. . . . reproduction copper weathervanes . . . HOME—Maintenance

Nat Schwartz & Co., Inc. . . . porcelain figurines, collectibles . . . HOME—Table Settings

Albert S. Smyth Co., Inc. . . . porcelain figurines, collectibles . . . HOME—Table Settings

TAI, Inc. . . . silk-screened military insignias . . . CLOTHING

ART MATERIALS

Materials, tools, equipment, and
supplies for fine and applied arts.

Name-brand art materials are seldom discounted more than 10% in retail shops unless they're purchased in quantity. But mail-order firms usually offer savings of twice that, and also sell "proprietary" products. These may be manufactured by lesser-known firms and are much less expensive than their branded equivalents—in fact, we know several working artists who buy nothing but. Private-label goods may also be the products of the same firms manufacturing top brands, but because they're identified as the "house brand," they're usually cheaper.

The firms listed here offer pigments, paper, brushes, canvas, frames, stretchers, pads, studio furniture, vehicles and solvents, silk-screening supplies, carving tools, and many other goods. If you don't know the market and the range of available goods, you'll find the general catalog offered by many distributors quite helpful. You can obtain a copy of the 224-page catalog for $2 from Grand Central Artists Materials; 18 E. 40th St., New York, NY 10016. For detailed information on the properties and uses of almost every type of media available today, see *The Artist's Handbook of Materials and Techniques* (749 pp., Viking Press). It can usually be found in good bookstores, as well as the public library. The Handbook is considered indispensable by many artists, and can introduce you to old techniques that may broaden your artistic horizons.

Last, we are pleased that 35 art-materials manufacturers, representing 90% of the industry, are participating in a voluntary program to include hazard warnings on the labels of their products. The inclusion of certain materials, such as toluene, asbestos, xylene, n-hexane, and benzene, presents a serious, ongoing health risk to schoolchildren, hobbyists, and artists. Many do not use adequate precautions in handling materials, and it's believed that exposure levels in schools, workshops, and studios often exceed the limits set for industrial workers using the same substances. Some of the hazardous materials are linked to nervous disorders and higher rates of miscarriage and fetal damage, respiratory disease, heart attacks, liver and kidney disease, leukemia, and cancer of the bladder, colon, rectum, kidneys, and brain. There should be no need to suspend your creative activities if you learn how to protect your health. Rubber gloves, respirators, and window-exhaust systems can reduce much of what you inhale and may all but eliminate the absorption of chemicals through the skin. Remember that you need to have a *real* air-flow when working with fume-producing materials—not just an open window. (One source cites the definition of "adequate ventilation" as *16 complete air changes per hour.*) Keep children and animals out of the work place, since chemicals reach higher levels of concentration in their systems. And don't be reluctant to ask your child's art teacher what materials are being used and whether protective measures are employed in the classroom.

For information on firms selling related products, see "Crafts and Hobbies."

DICK BLICK CO.; P.O. Box 1267; Galesburg, IL 61401
(800) 477-8192/ Cat.: $2/ Save: to 40%/ Pay: C, MO, MC,
V Sells: name-brand and proprietary art supplies/ Shop: see
Animal Veterinary Products in "Animals" for locations

$$$/ ✉ / ☎

Comment: Dick Blick lists over 20,000 items in its 320-page
catalog of art supplies and equipment, geared to schools but
of interest to all. Founded in 1911. Store locations listed in cata-
log.

Sample Goods: Liquitex paints, Shiva pigments, Crayola
crayons and finger paints, drawing tables, paintbrushes, Alfac
transfer letters, kraft paper, canvas, scissors, adhesives, silk-
screening materials, display lighting, print-making equipment,
wood-carving tools, molding materials, kilns, glazes, copper
enamels, decoupage, lapidary equipment, leather-working kits,
dyes, macrame material, looms, art slides, blackboards, and
much more. Quality house-label goods are real savings.

Special Factors: Quantity discounts available; min. order
$40.

**CROWN ART PRODUCTS CO., INC.; 90 Dayton Ave.,
#18; Passaic, NJ 07055** (201) 777-6010/ Cat.: free/ Save:
to 65%/ Pay: C, MO, MC, V Sells: section frames, silk-screen
supplies/ Shop: same address; Sa 11–4

$$$/ ✉ / ☎

Comment: A well-known source for silk-screening supplies
and equipment and metal section frames, at discounts of up to
65%.

Sample Goods: Silver, gold, and black metal section frames, in lengths up to 40", from $2.86 to $12; foam boards and hand-cut mats. A complete line of silk-screening supplies, from textile inks and dyes to unique screen systems—screens, tools, a special line of inks and colors, and many products not available elsewhere. Workshops and instruction offered as well.

Special Factors: Assembly hardware included with frame sections; PQ by phone or letter with SASE on special sizes.

JERRY'S ARTARAMA, INC.; P.O. Box 1105; New Hyde Park, NY 11040 (800) 221-2323/ Cat.: $2, ref. (5 & 11)/ Save: 10–70%/ Pay: C, MO, MC, V Sells: name-brand and generic art supplies/ Shop: 24B-12 Union Tpk., Bellerose, NY; also 1530 Northern Blvd., Manhasset, NY

$$$$/ ✉ / ☎

Comment: This 154-page compendium of materials, tools, and equipment for crafts and fine arts is inspiration itself—imported goods seldom discounted elsewhere are featured at real savings.

Sample Goods: Pigments, brushes, vehicles and solvents, studio furniture, lighting, visual equipment, canvas and framing materials, papers, film products, airbrushing equipment, clays and moulage supplies, wood-carving tools, books, etc. For sculpture, graphic arts, drafting, calligraphy, printmaking, fabric painting, sumi-e, scratch art, stained glass, etc. Grumbacher, Holbein, Rowney, Blockx, Lefrank & Bourgeois, W & N, Robert Simmons, Isabey, Conte, Koh-I-Noor, Stabilo, Letraset, Chartpak, Stanrite, Neolt, Ledu, X-Acto, Fredrix, D'Arches, Fabriano, Paillard, Deka, Iwata and other brands.

Special Factors: Unconditional guarantee of satisfaction; color charts and product specs available on request; quantity discounts offered; min. order $25, $50 on credit cards.

PEARL PAINT; 308 Canal St.; New York, NY 10013-3086
(800) 221-6845/ Cat.: $1, ref./ Save: 20–60%/ Pay: C, MO,
MC, V Sells: name brand and proprietary art supplies/ Shop:
same address; also East Meadow, Long Island, NY; Woodbridge, Paramus, NJ; Miami, Ft. Lauderdale, FL

$$$/ ✉ / ☎

Comment: Pearl Paint is known throughout New York City as
one of the best discount sources for art and crafts supplies. In busi-
ness for over 50 years, the firm will do its best to fill your needs
—and if it can't, will tell you which other art-supply house can.

Sample Goods: Fine-art materials, tools, equipment and
materials for every possible craft, including pigments, brushes,
vehicles and solvents, stretchers, papers of all kinds, canvas,
manuals, studio furniture, and much more. Brands stocked in-
clude Grumbacher, W & N, Holbein, Bellini, Paasche, Fabriano,
Liquitex, Robert Simmons, and Pelikan, among others.

Special Factors: Quantity discounts available; specials on
selected items; min. order $50.

**STU-ART SUPPLIES, INC.; 2045 Grand Ave.; Baldwin, NY
11510** (800) 645-2855/ Cat. & Samples: free/ Save: to 50%/
Pay: C, MO, MC, V Sells: name-brand section frames and
supplies/ Mail order only

$$$$/ ✉ / ☎

Comment: Framing source nonpareil, which offers all you
need to do a professional job. Stu-Art supplies galleries and

institutions, and offers the best materials, a wide range of sizes, and savings of up to 50% on list prices.

Sample Goods: Nielson metal frames in 3 widths for flat, stretched-canvas, and dimensional-art (deep) mounting; gold, silver and 6 other finishes ($2–$7.50 per pr. standard segments). Reversible duo-color, acid-free and regular mats; nonglare or clear plastic, wood and tenite section frames, and shrink film and dispensers also available.

Special Factors: Returns accepted; shipping included on UPS-delivered orders over $250; catalog requests not accepted on 800 line; min. orders of $15–25 on certain items.

UTRECHT ART AND DRAFTING SUPPLY; 33 35th St.; Brooklyn, NY 11232 (718) 768-2525/ Cat.: free/ Save: 25–50%/ Pay: C or MO **Sells:** name-brand and proprietary art supplies/ **Shop:** same address; M–Sa 9:30–6

$$$/ ✉

Comment: Utrecht has been selling professional art, sculpture, and printmaking supplies and equipment since 1949, and manufactures some of the best-priced oil and acrylic paints on the market.

Sample Goods: Canvas, stretchers, frames, pads, paper, brushes, tools of all kinds, books, easels, tables, pigments, palettes, and much more. In addition to Utrecht's own line, materials by Grumbacher, Eberhard Faber, Chartpak, Strathmore, Pentel, Niji, and other manufacturers are featured in the catalog, which also includes product specs and information.

Special Factors: Quantity discounts of 5–20% available on selected goods. Min. order $40.

SEE ALSO:

AUTO AND MARINE

Parts, supplies, maintenance
products, and services.

If you haven't shopped for mail-order auto parts before, you're in for a pleasant surprise. Savings of 30% to 50% are almost routine, and because many of the firms are located off the beaten track, they can rent their warehouses for less, stock more, and pass savings on to you. Quick shipment is another feature of many of these firms. They know that if they can't provide a part immediately, the customer will go elsewhere for it. These firms sell everything you could possibly need for your auto, motorcycle, RV, truck, or van (with a few exceptions), including mufflers, shocks, tires, batteries, and much more. Some also stock products for vintage cars as well. And look here for one of the best values around on parts: salvaged goods. Expect savings of up to 70% compared to the price of new parts, and note the guarantees of satisfaction offered by most of these firms. (They wouldn't be around long if their goods didn't survive as well.)

If you've spent anywhere from a few hundred to tens of thousands of dollars on a canoe, sailboat, or yacht, you'll want to minimize the upkeep expenses. Save up to 75% on the cost of maintenance products and equipment by buying from these suppliers, who sell every type of coating, tool, and device to keep your vessel afloat. Exhaustive selections of electronics, hardware, instruments, and other goods are offered, as well as galley accoutrements and foul-weather clothing. Even landlubbers should take a look through these catalogs, if they're interested in well-designed slickers and oiled sweaters and the handsome teak bath and kitchen fixtures designed for yacht installations, which are equally useful on terra firma.

If you're interested in purchasing an auto through one of the car-buying services that sell at $125 over dealer price, see the listing for Comp-U-Card in "General Merchandise."

If you decide to negotiate your own bargain at the local lot, you'll need all the help you can get. *Don't Get Taken Every Time* (Penguin Books, 1982), by former car salesman Remar Sutton, is a casebook of the tricks of the trade that's entertaining as well as instructive.

If you do your own mechanical work, you'll find the factory-service manual written for your car an invaluable aid. Manuals for hundreds of models are available for under $15 each from Carbook; 181 Glen Ave.; Sea Cliff, NJ 11579. Request the free catalog, which also lists a range of do-it-yourself books on other topics.

AMERICAN MARINE ELECTRONICS; 2 Wilton Ave.; Norwalk, CT 06851 (800) 243-0264/ Cat.: free (1, 5, 9)/ Save: 40%/ Pay: C, MO, MC, V Sells: marine electronics/ Shop: 900 E. Atlantic Blvd.; Pompano Beach, FL

$$$/ ✉/ ☎

Comment: American Marine has been in business since 1980 selling *everything* in electronics for sailing vessels. It carries products by scores of manufacturers at an average discount of 40%.

Sample Goods: Depth sounders, chart recorders, antennas and mounts, compasses, autopilots, CB radios, battery chargers, VHF radios, lorans, radar equipment, and much more. Brands include ACR, Apelco, Aqua Dynamics, Bausch & Lomb, Belden, Bushnell, Coastal Navigator, Cybernet, Datamarine, Dytek, EMS, Epsco, First Mate, Hull, Intech, Lowrance, Marlin Marine, MDR, Morrow, Navidyne, Ritchie, SMR, Seamaster, Sitex, TI, Wesmar, etc. Specialized equipment for deep-sea fishing also available.

Special Factors: PQ by phone or letter with SASE on models not shown in the catalog; authorized returns accepted.

BELLE TIRE DISTRIBUTORS, INC.; Competition Div.; 12190 Grand River; Detroit, MI 48204 (313) 834-3880/ Info: PQ/ Save: 25–35%/ Pay: C or MO Sells: radial tires/ Mail order only

$$/ ✉

Comment: If you're in the market for tires, Belle can save you up to 35% off list prices.

Sample Goods: Radial tires by Michelin, B.F. Goodrich, Goodyear, Firestone, Pirelli, Uniroyal, and Trans Am.

Special Factors: New tires only, no retreads; PQ by phone or letter with SASE; shipping $5–20 per tire, depending on destination.

CENTRAL MICHIGAN TRACTOR & PARTS; 2713 N. U.S. Hwy. 2; St. Johns, MI 48879 (800) 248-9263/ Info: PQ/ Save: to 50%/ Pay: C, MO, MC, V Sells: used, salvaged tractor parts/ Mail order only

$$$/

Comment: This firm, also known as Tractor Salvage, can save you up to 50% on parts for tractors and combines. It stocks used, reconditioned, and rebuilt parts, all backed by a 30-day guarantee.

Sample Goods: Everything from starters to cylinder blocks for machines made by almost any major manufacturer. Some of the goods are reconditioned, some rebuilt; a rebuilt part is overhauled completely and you can expect it to function as well and for as long as a new one. Want lists are maintained if the part you seek is not in stock.

Special Factors: PQ by phone or letter.

CAPITAL CYCLE CORPORATION; 2328 Champlain St. N.W.; Washington, DC 20009 (202) 387-7360/ Cat.: free/ Save: 20–50%/ Pay: C, MO, MC, V Sells: BMW motorcycle parts/ Shop: same address

$$$/ / ☎

Comment: Capital Cycle is the nation's definitive source for BMW motorcycle spare parts—over 4,000 genuine, original parts are available, at 20% to 50% less than dealer prices. Est. in 1972.

Sample Goods: BMW parts manufactured from 1955 through the current year, including engine parts and electronics, carburetors, fuel tanks, mufflers, pipes, clutches, gears, steering bearings, shocks, springs, handlebars, mirrors, brake linings, tires, rims, fenders, fairings, locks and keys, paint, seats, switches and relays, tachometers, voltmeters, lights, tools, and much more.

Special Factors: Quantity discounts available; shipping included on orders of $250 or more; mail-order repair services; min. order $15, $25 on credit cards.

CHERRY AUTO PARTS; 5650 N. Detroit Ave.; Toledo, OH 43612 (800) 537-8677/ Info.: PQ/ Save: to 70%/ Pay: MO, MC, V Sells: used foreign-car parts/ Mail order only

$$$/ ✉ / ☎

Comment: Why pay top dollar for new car parts if you can get perfectly good ones, used, for up to 70% less? Cherry Auto Parts, "The Midwest's Leading Foreign Car Dismantler," can supply you with used foreign-car parts at up to 70% less than the cost of new parts. Est. in 1946.

Sample Goods: Alfa Romeo, Audi, Austin, BMW, Datsun, Fiat, Honda, Jaguar, Mazda, Mercedes, MG, Peugeot, Porsche, Renault, Saab, Simca, Subaru, Triumph, Toyota, VW, and other auto parts.

Special Factors: PQ by phone or letter with SASE; "all parts are guaranteed in stock at the time of quotation, guaranteed to be the correct part, and in good condition as described."

CLARK'S CORVAIR PARTS, INC.; Rte. 2; Shelburne Falls, MA 01370-9748 (413) 625-9776/ Cat.: $4/ Save: to 50%/ Pay: C or MO **Sells:** Corvair parts/ Mail order only

$$$/

Comment: Clark's lists its inventory of over 4,500 Corvair parts in a 400-page catalog that's published in even-numbered years. Many parts available nowhere else, and savings run up to 50%—an indispensable resource for the Corvair owner. Est. in 1973.

Sample Goods: Original and replacement GM parts, reproductions, and goods by Chevrolet, TRW, Gabriel, Clevite, and over 400 other suppliers; brakes, cables, lights, air filters, body parts and panels, carburetor and engine parts, gauges, gas tanks, manuals, pistons, points, seals, rims, specialty tools, paint, and much more stocked.

Special Factors: Indexed catalog; returns accepted; min. order $7.

CLINTON CYCLE & SALVAGE, INC.; 6709 Old Branch Ave.; Camp Springs, MD 20748 (301) 449-3550/ PL: free/ Save: to 70%/ Pay: C, MO, MC, V **Sells:** used motorcycle parts/ Mail order only

$$$/

Comment: Clinton's salvage operations are a boon to anyone who owns a road bike that's 250cc or larger. Reclaimed parts of every type turn up here, at prices up to 70% less than those of new parts.

Sample Goods: Parts for Honda, Yamaha, Suzuki, and Kawasaki cycles, including large parts, engines, etc. Want lists maintained.

Special Factors: PQ by phone or letter with SASE; satisfaction guaranteed; returns accepted within 14 days.

DEFENDER INDUSTRIES, INC.; 255 Main St.; New Rochelle, NY 10801 (914) 632-3001/ Cat.: $1/ Save: 25–70%/ Pay: C or MO Sells: marine supplies, gear, equipment/ Shop: same address; M–F 9–6, Sa 9–2:45

$$$/

Comment: Defender defends its claim to have "the largest selection in the USA at the very lowest prices" with a 194-page catalog that actually proves it. Defender has earned a reputation for good service and reliability and is known as one of the best marine-supply houses in the business. Est. in 1938.

Sample Goods: Boat maintenance supplies, resins and coatings, winches, windlasses, communications devices, foul-weather gear, books, tools and hardware, optics, galley fittings, navigation equipment, electronics, etc. Excellent selection of hull finishes and goods for the fiberglass boat.

Special Factors: Will not be undersold on any item; no phone orders; returns accepted; restocking fee may be charged; min. order $25.

E & B MARINE, INC.; 980 Gladys Ct.; P.O. Box 747; Edison, NJ 08818 (201) 287-3900/ Cat.: free (2, 6, 10)/ Save: 20–60%/ Pay: C, MO, MC, V Sells: marine supplies, gear, equipment/ Shop: other locations in CT, FL, MD, NJ, RI, VA

$$$/ ✉ / ☎

Comment: E & B Marine, founded in 1956, "consistently maintains the boating industry's lowest discount prices," which has helped establish E & B as "the nation's leading retailer of quality marine supplies."

Sample Goods: Products for sailing, boat maintenance and repair, safety, communications, navigation, etc., by Cybernet, Unimetrics, Apelco, Icom, Boatlife, Woolsey, Interlux, Kohler, Seth Thomas, EMS, Signet, Aqua Meter, Datamarine, Ray Jeff, Si-Tex, Galaxy, Aneroid, Mansfield, Kidde, Intermatic, Achilles, Sand-Piper, Stearns, and many other firms; around 75 new products featured in every catalog; 14 stores nationwide.

Special Factors: Store locations listed in catalog; authorized returns accepted within 10 days; min. order $10.

EASTERN CYCLE SALVAGE, INC.; 87 Park St.; Beverly, MA 01915 (617) 922-3707/ Info: PQ/ Save: to 50%/ Pay: MO, MC, V Sells: used and reconditioned motorcycle parts/ Shop: same address; Tu–Sa 9–5

$$$/ ✉ / ☎

Comment: Eastern Cycle sells used and reconditioned motorcycle parts "at savings of up to 50% retail," or the cost of the same parts if new.

Sample Goods: Engines, fenders, handlebars, kickstands, mufflers, pipes, lights, mirrors, clutches, gears, carburetors, etc.

Special Factors: PQ by letter with SASE or by phone, Tuesday to Saturday, 9–5 EST.

EURO-TIRE, INC.; 567 Rte. 46 W.; P.O. Box 1198; Fairfield, NJ 07006 (800) 631-1143/ Cat.: free/ Save: to 40%/ Pay: C, MO, MC, V Sells: European tires, wheels, shocks/ Shop: same address

$$$/ ✉ / ☎

Comment: Euro-Tire's specialty is European tires and auto components, which are sold at up to 40% off list. The staff is informed and helpful.

Sample Goods: Tires by Michelin, Ceat, Fuida, Dunlop, Conti, Kleber, Pirelli, Phoenix, Uniroyal (European); Hella and Cibie halogen headlamps; Bilstein and Koni shock absorbers; Rial light-alloy wheels.

Special Factors: PQ by phone or letter with SASE; no seconds or retreads are sold; shipping included; min. order $25.

GOLDBERG'S MARINE; 202 Market St.; Philadelphia, PA 19106-2877 (800) 262-8464/ Cat.: free/ Save: to 40%/ Pay. C, MO, AE, DC, MC, V Sells: marine supplies, gear, equipment/ Shop: same address; 40 N. 2nd St., Philadelphia; also 12 W. 37th St., New York, NY

$$$/ ✉ / ☎

Comment: Goldberg's, "where thousands of boaters save millions of dollars," publishes a hefty color catalog yearly with updates every 6 weeks. New items added constantly, many exclusives, discounts of 20% to 40%.

Sample Goods: Everything from anchors to zinc collars—rope, bilge pumps, fishing tackle, rigging, knives, lifeboats, preservers, navigation equipment, boat covers, winches, and even a kitchen sink. Emphasis on pleasure-boat equipment, but much of the boating gear—French fishermen's and oiled-wool sweaters, sunglasses, boots, caps, slickers—would appeal to landlubbers. Selection of stylish galley gear, teak bulkhead racks, and other yacht accessories. Top brands; save 50% and more through sales catalogs.

Special Factors: Authorized returns accepted within 10 days (policy stated in catalog); store hours listed in catalog; min. order $25.

OFFSHORE IMPORTS; 3674 E. Noakes St.; Los Angeles, CA 90023 (800) 421-8561/ Cat.: free/ Save: 20–50%/ Pay: C, MO, MC, V Sells: tires, shocks, exhausts, other auto parts/ Shop: same address

$$$/ ✉ / ☎

Comment: Save up to 50% on name-brand tires and car parts, most by foreign manufacturers, through Offshore. Est. in 1939.

Sample Goods: B.F. Goodrich, Goodyear, Michelin, Pirelli, Yokahama, Semperit, and Kleber tires; wheels by Epsilon, BBS, Carrol Sherby, Ronaz; car shocks by Koni and KYB; exhausts by Monza and Anza; steering wheels, suspensions, springs, stabilizer bars, mag wheels, Mercedes wheel locks, Interpart rear-window louvers.

Special Factors: PQ by phone or letter with SASE; shipping included.

MICKEY THOMPSON TIRES; P.O. Box 227; Cuyahoga Falls, OH 44222 (216) 928-9092/ Cat.: free/ Save: to 50%/ Pay: C, MO, MC, V Sells: high-performance, proprietary tires/ Mail order only

$$$/

Comment: Mickey Thompson designs, engineers, and manufactures a unique line of high-performance tires at up to 50% less than name-brand models.

Sample Goods: Widest tires on market, high-performance radials, 70-60-50 series sizes with matching heights; a complete line of on- and off-road RV tires featuring wraparound tread for extra traction; racing slicks.

Special Factors: Tire materials and workmanship warrantied for tire life; credit or refund on returned tires prorated.

TUGON CHEMICAL CORP.; P.O. Box 31; Cross River, NY 10518 (203) 323-3010/ PL & Lit.: free/ Save: to 35%/ Pay: C or MO Sells: proprietary marine maintenance compounds/ Mail order only

$$$/

Comment: Tugon Chemical manufactures a line of maintenance products for older wooden boats; the compounds are more durable, versatile, and of a higher quality than those sold by other firms and cost up to 35% less.

Sample Goods: Epoxy primer, caulking, decking, sealant, glue, filler, and rotted-wood aid. Many of the products can be used in low temperatures and on damp or wet wood and still cure effectively; formulated to resist water, sun, salt, barnacles, temperature changes, fuel spills.

Special Factors: Shipping included; staff can advise proper product and application.

WAREHOUSE MARINE DISCOUNT; P.O. Box 70348; Seattle, WA 98107 (800) 426-8666/ Cat.: $2/ Save: 20–50%/ Pay: C, MO, MC, V Sells: marine supplies and equipment/ Mail order only

$$$/ ✉ / ☎

Comment: Warehouse Marine sells a 200-page catalog with no-nonsense lines of electronics, hardware, and maintenance products for sailboats and powerboats. Est. in 1973.

Sample Goods: Epoxies and finishes, cordage, anchors, windlasses, buoys, horns, seacocks, winches, electronics, communications devices, navigation instruments, lumber, hardware, kerosene lamps, boating clothes, teak and mahogany furnishings and fittings, and a complete line of galley gear. Top brands, up to 50% off list.

Special Factors: Satisfaction guaranteed; returns accepted within 30 days.

**J.C. WHITNEY & CO.; 1917 Archer Ave.; P.O. Box 8410;
Chicago, IL 60680** (312) 431-6102/ Cat.: $1/ Save: to 60%/
Pay: C, MO, MC, V Sells: auto parts and accessories/ Shop:
same address

$$$/ / ☎

Comment: J. C. Whitney offers just about everything you
could want in equipment in "the world's most complete automo-
tive catalog"—200 pages crammed with parts, supplies, tools,
and more. Est. in 1916.

Sample Goods: Parts, maintenance supplies, accessories, and
manuals for cars foreign and domestic, from antique models to
the latest releases from Detroit; products for recreational vehi-
cles and motorcycles; body-repair and customizing tools and
products.

Special Factors: Orders taken 24 hours a day.

SEE ALSO:

Allyn Air Seat Co. . . . air-filled seat liners for cycles, autos,
    trucks, aircraft seats . . . SPORTS
Annex Outlet Ltd. . . . name-brand auto audio . . .
    APPLIANCES
Caviarteria Inc. . . . vintage cars . . . FOOD
Comp-U-Card . . . car-buying service . . . GENERAL
Crutchfield . . . name-brand auto audio . . . APPLIANCES
Danley's . . . marine binoculars . . . CAMERAS
The Finals . . . board sailer . . . CLOTHING
LVT Price Quote Hotline, Inc. . . . name-brand scanners,
    radar detectors . . . APPLIANCES

Pagano Gloves . . . deerskin motorcycle jackets . . .
   CLOTHING
Ruvel and Co., Inc. . . . government-surplus dinghies, etc. . . .
   SURPLUS
S & S Sound City . . . name-brand auto audio
   . . . APPLIANCES

BOOKS, MAGAZINES, RECORDS, AND TAPES

Publications of every sort,
cards and stationery,
films, and services.

There's simply no point in paying the cover price for any book, or full rates for magazine subscriptions, when you can get most of them by mail at discounts of 30% to 80%. If you buy only one book a month, you could be saving over $100 per year from these sources—and much more if you're currently buying your favorite magazines from the newsstand.

You can make the most of these sources by keeping a file of book reviews, recommendations, and similar notes. Refer to it whenever you receive a new catalog, and you'll run a better chance of finding that elusive volume. If you're searching for a rare or out-of-print publication, check with a firm that deals in such material. (Consult *Books in Print,* in any library, to see whether the book is still being published or has been reissued.) The Strand Book Store will maintain want lists, and although you can't expect "discount" prices on such books, Strand usually prices them competitively.

Although they're listed in the "Office" chapter, computer programs are also publications. And there are tens of thousands of programs now in the public domain, which means they can be copied without infringement of copyright (hence the term "free programs"). They're sold at very low prices—often $10 and under—and can be as valuable as protected programs that cost $300 to $900 each. The definitive reference to locating sources and evaluating what's available is Alfred Glossbrenner's *How to Get Free Software,* available in bookstores nationwide.

In addition to books and magazines, you'll find firms listed in this chapter that sell stationery, cards, gift wrapping and ribbon, records and tapes, library embossers, and photos of rock stars.

AMERICAN FAMILY PUBLISHERS; P.O. Box 4824; Chicago, IL 60680 (312) 527-4088/ **Info:** inquire/ **Save:** to 50%/ **Pay:** C or MO **Sells:** magazine subscriptions/ Mail order only
$$$$/ ✉

Comment: American Family Publishers is one of several magazine clearinghouses offering subscriptions to dozens of popular periodicals at rates that are usually much better than those offered by the publishers themselves.

Sample Goods: Subscriptions to *Car and Driver, Popular Science, The Atlantic, TV Guide, Esquire, Bowling Digest, Time, Savvy, Jet,* and *The Family Handyman* offered in past mailings; bonuses, premiums, and sweepstakes featured.

Special Factors: Inquire for information; satisfaction guaranteed; installment plan available.

THE AMERICAN STATIONERY CO., INC.; P.O. Box 207; Peru, IN 46970-9989 (317) 473-4438/ **Cat.:** free (1 & 7) **Save:** to 50%/ **Pay:** C, MO, MC, V **Sells:** custom-printed stationery/ **Shop:** same address; M–F 8–5
$$$/ ✉ / ☎

Comment: American Stationery, founded in 1919, offers a good assortment of tasteful personalized stationery at savings of up to 50% on the prices of comparable goods and printing.

Sample Goods: Deckle-edge and plain sheets and envelopes in white, ivory, and pale blue; heavyweight Monarch sheets; erasable sheets; business envelopes; "executive" stationery of heavy, chain-laid paper; personalized memo pads; bill-paying envelopes; bordered postcards; stationery sets; gummed and self-sticking return-address labels.

Special Factors: Satisfaction guaranteed; returns accepted for replacement or refund.

BARNES & NOBLE BOOKSTORES, INC.; 126 Fifth Ave.; New York, NY 10011 (201) 440-3336/ Cat.: free/ Save: to 94%/ Pay: C, MO, AE, MC, V Sells: books, records, tapes, video cassettes/Shop: same address; M–F 9:45–6:15, Sa 9:-45–6, Su 10–5; also other locations nationwide.

$$$$/

Comment: Barnes & Noble, founded in 1873, is "committed to a policy of offering you hundreds of new and exciting books at inflation-fighting prices." In addition, the regular catalog mailings feature hundreds of records, tapes, and video cassettes at discounts of up to 50% and even more on sales and specials.

Sample Goods: Best sellers, paperbacks, reprints, and publishers' overstock; topics include cooking, mystery, chemistry, literature, film, medicine, satire, juvenilia, current fiction, linguistics, religion, reference, crafts, photography, etc.; recordings of classical music, jazz, old radio programs; vintage movies in Beta and VHS, from *Birth of a Nation* to World War II newsreel footage; collapsible beechwood bookshelves; book embossers, art prints; cassette cases and cabinets; the Zelco book light.

Special factors: Satisfaction guaranteed; returns accepted within 30 days; institutional accounts; min. order $15 on credit cards.

CHESTERFIELD MUSIC SHOPS, INC.; 226 Washington St.; Mt. Vernon, NY 10553 (914) 667-6200/ Cat.: free (quarterly)/ Save: 30–70%/ Pay: C, MO, MC, V Sells: musical recordings/ Mail order only

$$$/ ✉ / ☎

Comment: Chesterfield has done business by mail since 1946 and is regarded as an excellent source for esoteric recording of every type at up to 70% below list price.

Sample Goods: Classical, jazz, popular, and folk LPs and cassettes, from medieval carols to the classic children's songs rendered by Tom Glazer. Over 100 labels are represented, including Asylum, Caedmon, Delos, Dictation Disc, Erato, Kicking Mule, Motown, Orion, Painted Smiles, Spoken Arts, and Yazoo.

Special Factors: PQ by letter only with SASE; returns accepted on records or tapes that have been played only once for replacement or catalog credit.

CURRENT, INC.; The Current Building; Colorado Springs, CO 80901 (303) 593-5990/ Cat.: free/ Save: to 45%/ Pay: C or MO Sells: stationery, cards, gifts/ Mail order only

$$$/ ✉

Comment: Current, a family-owned business begun in 1950, publishes a 64-page catalog of stationery and cards in appealing designs, ranging from animal and nature scenes to quilt motifs and other Americana.

Sample Goods: All-occasion and holiday cards, notes, stationery, gift wrapping, ribbon, recipe cards and files, toys, games, home organizers, calendars, memo boards, note pads, canning labels, and gifts.

Special Factors: Discount of about 20% on 8 or more items; 40–45% on 16 or more; satisfaction guaranteed; returns accepted.

DAEDALUS BOOKS, INC.; 2260 25th Pl. N.E.; Washington, DC 20018 (202) 526-0058/ Cat.: free/ Save: 50–95%/ Pay: C, MO, AE, MC, V Sells: remaindered books/ Shop: 3424 Connecticut Ave. N.W.; Washington, DC; M–Sa 11–11, Su 12–7

$$$$/ 📧/ ☎

Comment: Daedalus, founded in 1980, offers fine books from trade publishers and university presses at 50% to 95% off the publisher's prices. These remainders, culled from thousands, will appeal to the literary reader looking for culture on the cheap.

Sample Goods: Ronald Steel's *Walter Lippmann and the American Century* ($4.98 from $19.95); *A Visit with Magritte,* photographs by Duane Michals ($1.98 from $15); Ruskin's *The Stones of Venice,* edited by Jan Morris; and *Night and Day,* by Tom Stoppard, among past offerings; categories include literature and general interest, visual and performing arts, philosophy, history, feminism, politics, and social sciences.

Special Factors: Institutional accounts available; stock moves quickly.

FRONT ROW PHOTOS; Box 484; Nesconset, NY 11767
(516) 585-8297/ Cat.: $2, ref./ Save: 30–50%/ Pay: C, MO,
cert. check Sells: rock-star photos and buttons/ Mail order
only

$$$/ ✉

Comment: Front Row offers serious rock fans and photo col-
lectors an easy way to get the shots they missed at the concert,
without hazarding camera confiscation. Thousands of photos
available, plus photo buttons, at up to 50% less than charged
elsewhere for similar goods. Est. in 1979.

Sample Goods: Rock-concert photos of the top rock, new
wave, and heavy metal groups of the 60s through today, from
ACDC to ZZ Top. Photos are $1.25 for the 3½″ size, $5.50 for
an 8″ × 10″, and photo buttons are also available.

Special Factors: Satisfaction guaranteed; undamaged returns
accepted within 10 days; bonuses offered on large orders; min.
order $5.

EDWARD R. HAMILTON, BOOKSELLER; Falls Village, CT
06031 Cat.: free/ Save: to 90%/ Pay: C or MO Sells: closeout
and remaindered books/ Mail order only

$$$$/ ✉

Comment: Mr. Hamilton's 36-page tabloid catalog, pub. 8 to
10 times yearly, lists *thousands* of bargain books in every con-
ceivable category, at an average of 50% to 70% off the published
prices. An old favorite among bargain-hunting bookworms.

Sample Goods: Art, humor, poetry, fiction, literature, photography, self-help, reference, business, crafts, psychology, history, film, science, cooking, sports, biography, and other categories. Past best sellers show up here frequently.

Special Factors: Satisfaction guaranteed; returns accepted; prepaid institutional orders welcomed.

L & D PRESS; P.O. Box 629; Lynbrook, NY 11563 (516) 593-5058/ PL: free/ Save: to 45%/ Pay: C or MO Sells: custom-printed stationery/ Shop: same address

$$$/ /

Comment: L & D, founded in 1960, sells printed business cards, envelopes, and stationery, plus several Sentry safes. The stock might not be extensive at L & D, but the values are great. Prices on *small* orders of stationery are much better than those charged by similar firms.

Sample Goods: Business cards in flat and raised thermographic print ($7.95 for 500), colored stock and inks and 18 typefaces available; business letterhead, envelopes in a variety of styles and sizes; imprinted reply messages at up to 40% savings; personal stationery in Princess and Monarch sizes in ivory, white, or pale blue; Embassy informals and notepads with self-sealing envelopes; Sentry safes; full-suspension lateral files in all sizes, 6 colors, at about 40% below list prices.

Special Factors: Accuracy guaranteed on all printing.

PUBLISHERS CENTRAL BUREAU; One Champion Ave.; Avenel, NJ 07001 (201) 382-7600/ Cat.: free (monthly)/ Save: to 93%/ Pay: C, MO, MC, V Sells: video cassettes, records, tapes, books/ Mail order only

$$$$/

Comment: Publishers Central Bureau is one of the nation's largest clearinghouses for publishers and video cassette and record producers. Everything seems to turn up here, and first-rate bargains abound—savings run up to 93%. Almost 50 years of reliable service.

Sample Goods: A wide range of video cassettes—from classic Hitchcock to M-G-M musicals. Books on every topic— Americana, art and architecture, boating, computers, boxing, trivia, occult and magic, animals, film, humor, crafts, erotica, gardening, diet and beauty, cuisine, etc. Pop-up books for children, trivia games, posters, library embossers, self-inking stampers, and similar goods have appeared in past catalogs. Records and tapes—classical, golden oldies, old radio shows, opera—also featured.

Special Factors: Sweepstakes featured; all items unconditionally guaranteed; min. order $10 on credit cards.

PUBLISHERS CLEARING HOUSE; 382 Channel Drive; Port Washington, NY 11050 (516) 883-5432/ Info: inquire/ Save: to 50%/ Pay: C or MO Sells: magazine subscriptions/ Mail order only

$$$$/

Comment: Publishers Clearing House acts as an agent for magazine publishers, offering *scores* of subscriptions to popular and special-interest magazines at savings of up to 50% on regular rates. Excellent service; guarantees lowest to-the-public prices.

Sample Goods: Subscriptions to *Reader's Digest, Gambling Times, Tax Hotline, Vanity Fair, Working Mother, Gifted Children Newsletter, Ms., Playboy, Time, Bestways Magazine,* and *Audio* among "129 unbeatable magazine values" offered in past mailings; bonuses, premiums, and sweepstakes featured.

Special Factors: Inquire for information; satisfaction guaranteed; installment plan available.

ROCKY MOUNTAIN STATIONERY; 11725 Co. Rd. 27.3; Dolores, CO 81323 (303) 565-8230/ Broch, Samples, PL: free with SASE/ **Save:** to 50%/ **Pay:** C or MO **Sells:** handmade note cards/ Mail order only

$$$/ ✉

Comment: This business is run by Rose Ruland, an artist who presses flowers and leaves from her garden and the surrounding wilds of the Rockies and uses them to create note cards. Small oil paintings on notes also available.

Sample Goods: "Nature" and "Just a Note" series, sold in collections of 12 in assorted colors, with envelopes. Prices are $7.95 for the "Nature" card collection, compared to $2 each for similar items sold in gift shops.

Special Factors: Shipping included; SASE required for literature.

STRAND BOOK STORE, INC.; 828 Broadway; New York, NY 10003 (212) 473-1452/ Cat.: free/ Save: to 80%/ Pay: C, MO, AE, MC, V Sells: new and used books/ Shop: same address; M–Sa 9:30–6:30, Su 11–5; also 159 John St., New York City

$$$$/ / ☎

Comment: NYC's legendary Strand Book Store boasts 8 miles of books—2,000,000 volumes—and is the largest dealer of used and out-of-print books in the U.S. Catalogs show a fraction of the inventory. Est. in 1928.

Sample Goods: The catalog of "Specials" lists 900 titles of works of every sort, from *Coming of Age in Samoa* to Quentin Bell's *Ruskin* to *British Cut and Thrust Weapons*—critique and commentary, biographies, books on art, architecture, philosophy, crafts, politics, food, drama, etc., including a selection of classic children's books. "Review Specials" catalog lists new releases at 50% off publishers' prices; "Art Books" and "Rare and Unusual Art Books" list rare, out-of-print, and used editions at excellent savings.

Special Factors: Specify catalog desired; catalog requests on postcards only; want lists maintained; book collections purchased; institutional accounts; returns accepted.

TARTAN BOOK SALES; 500 Arch St.; Williamsport, PA 17705 (800) 233-8467/ Cat. & Broch.: free (monthly)/ Save: 66%+/ Pay: C, MO, MC, V Sells: used books/ Shop: same address; Th & F 12–7:30

$$$$/ / ☎

Comment: Tartan sells library books that have had short-term use. Only undamaged, unsoiled, popular adult fiction and nonfiction books are offered—no paperbacks, juvenile titles, or reference texts.

Sample Goods: Shirley MacLaine's *Out on a Limb,* published at $15.95, sells here for $4.98 (the paperback edition lists for $3.95); *Life Extension,* $5.49; Mary Lee Settle's *The Killing Ground,* $4.49; the *Richard Simmons Never-Say-Diet Cookbook* and *Edie,* $4.98 each, among over 200 titles in general fiction, nonfiction, mystery, romance, science fiction, and Western categories. All books available in durable "Flexiweld" binding for $5.98. Institutional catalog (for libraries, bookstores, etc.) lists 2,500 titles at 80% and 90% discounts.

Special Factors: Returns accepted only if error made in filling order; request institutional catalog on company letterhead.

SEE ALSO:

Amity Hallmark, Ltd. . . . offset printing, typesetting . . . OFFICE
Animal City Wholesale . . . books on animals and pet care . . . ANIMAL
Animal Veterinary Products, Inc. . . . . books on animals and pet care . . . ANIMAL
Sam Ash Music Corp. . . . . classical and popular records . . . MUSIC
Bike Nashbar . . . manuals on bicycle repairs . . . SPORTS
Bruce Medical Supply . . . small selection of books on health care . . . MEDICAL
Buy Direct, Inc. . . . . printed business stationery, forms, labels, etc. . . . OFFICE
Campmor . . . books on camping, survival . . . SPORTS
Custom Golf Clubs, Inc. . . . . manuals on golf-club repair . . . SPORTS

Dinosaur Catalog . . . juvenile and adult reference works on prehistoric animals . . . TOYS

Walter Drake & Sons, Inc. . . . stationery, address labels, etc. . . . GENERAL

Envelope Sales Company . . . printed business stationery . . . OFFICE

Erewhon Trading Co. . . . books on natural foods and health . . . FOOD

Glorybee Honey, Inc. . . . books on cooking with honey . . . FOOD

Gohn Bros. . . . Amish cookbooks, quilting books . . . CLOTHING

Hunter Audio-Photo, Inc. . . . vintage video movies, TV shows, etc. . . . APPLIANCES

Jerry's Artarama, Inc. . . . books on fine arts, crafts . . . ART MATERIALS

E.C. Kraus . . . books on wine- and beer-making . . . CRAFTS

Lincoln House, Inc. . . . stationery, calendars, cards, etc. . . . GENERAL

Lyle Cartridges . . . record-care products . . . APPLIANCES

The Mexican Kitchen . . . Mexican and Tex-Mex cookbooks . . . FOOD

Paradise Products, Inc. . . . huge selection of party goods . . . TOYS

PBS Livestock Drugs . . . books on livestock care . . . ANIMAL

Regal Greetings & Gifts, Inc. . . . gift wrapping, cards, calendars, stationery, etc. . . . GENERAL

S & C Huber, Accoutrements . . . books on early American crafts . . . GENERAL

Soccer International, Inc. . . . books on soccer . . . SPORTS

Straw Into Gold, Inc. . . . books on textile and other crafts . . . CRAFTS

Sultan's Delight Inc. . . . Greek, Lebanese, Syrian, and Mid-East cookbooks . . . FOOD

Terminal Musical Supply, Inc. . . . guitar manuals . . . MUSIC

Turnbaugh Printers Supply Co. . . . comprehensive manual on printing; envelopes, paper stock . . . OFFICE

United Pharmacal Company, Inc. . . . books on animals and pet care . . . ANIMAL

Whole Earth Access . . . books on a wide range of topics . . . GENERAL

Wholesale Veterinary Supply, Inc. . . . large selection books on livestock and pet care . . . ANIMAL

CAMERAS, PHOTOGRAPHIC AND DARKROOM EQUIPMENT, OPTICS, FILM AND SERVICES

Equipment, supplies, and services.

Contrary to popular belief, prices on cameras and photographic equipment are, for the most part, better here in the United States than they are in Hong Kong. Even major electronics outlets with small camera departments can probably offer discounts of up to 40% off list prices. The large camera houses carry much more than cameras, bulbs, and film. Some of the specialized goods available include lighting equipment, screens, film editors, splicers, batteries, projection tables, lenses, filters, adapters, cases, darkroom outfits, chemicals, and film-processing services—and they're all sold at substantial discounts.

Even if you don't need custom work done, you can have your film processed, enlargements made, slides duplicated, and other services performed by a discount mail-order lab at about half the price a drugstore or retail outlet would charge. One of the firms listed here can also put your movie film on a video cassette, complete with sound track, at competitive prices.

We'd like to make one strong suggestion regarding camera purchases: buy American. A foreign-made camera may have been manufactured under different quality-control standards than those used by the U.S. division of the same company, and it usually carries a warranty that is not honored by the U.S. firm. Should the item need repair, it may have to be sent back to its point of manufacture—which could be Hong Kong or Singapore. Add the expense of mailing to the frustration of waiting what could be months for its return, and the sum total is often a negative experience. Make it a habit to ask whether the product you're pricing is U.S.-made, and whether the warranty will be honored in this country. Consider the risks if you do decide to buy the foreign model.

Beware also the "strip-and-requip" gambit, in which a camera seller takes the outfit as supplied by the manufacturer and *removes* the extra lenses, case, lens covers, flash attachment, and other accessories in the original package. The seller then replaces the lenses with inferior models (usually termed "famous make" in the ad) and offers the stripped outfit at a very low price. The lens covers, case, and attachments are sold separately and the original lenses are also offered at a surcharge, and the price of the original package winds up much closer to list when the shopper is through with the "extras" and "improvements." We've seen far fewer examples of this practice in the last few years since it's been given wide publicity, and many firms now make a point of stating that they sell cameras "as outfitted by the manufacturers." The repackaging maneuver and several other less-than-ethical business practices are detailed in the BBB booklet, "Buying Photographic Equipment by Mail." If your local office doesn't have copies, you can order one through the Council's headquarters in Virginia. See the chapter introduction of "Appliances" for the address.

AD-LIBS ASTRONOMICS; 2701 Tee Circle, Suite 106; Norman, OK 73069 (405) 364-0858/ Cat.: $1/ Save: 10–35%/ Pay: C, MO, AE, MC, V Sells: telescopes and optics/ Shop: same address; M–F 9:30–5:30

$$$/ 📫/ ☎

Comment: Ad-Libs sells telescopes and astronomical equipment made by the best firms in the business at up to 35% below list, and its stock includes complete lines for astronomical photography. The catalog is quite informative and well worth the price. Est. in 1979.

Sample Goods: Over 80 telescopes and 500 accessories by Edmund, Meade, Bausch & Lomb, Coulter, Celestron, Questar, Televue, Unitron, etc.; lenses, eyepieces, tripods, cameras, visual and photographic filters, and other items. Catalog includes guides to buying the appropriate telescope for your needs, choosing eyepieces and photographic accessories, and complete lists of specifications. Send a SASE for the one-page list of current specials.

Special Factors: PQ by phone or letter with SASE; shipping included on prepaid orders delivered within continental U.S.

B & H PHOTO; 119 W. 17th St.; New York, NY 10011 (800) 221-5662/ Info : PQ/ Save: to 40%/ Pay: C, MO, MC, V Sells: photo supplies/ Shop: same address; M–Th 9–6, F 9–1, Su 10–4

$$$/ 📫/ ☎

Comment: B & H, "The Professional's Source," sells supplies, equipment, and accessories for still, movie, and underwater photography at to 40% below list. Extensive selection; some hard-to-find items.

Sample Goods: Cameras and lenses, darkroom equipment and supplies, bags, projectors, lighting, etc. by Nikon, Canon, Olympus, Minolta, Konica, Yashica, Novoflex, Lumedyne, Durst, Eseco, Quad-Matic, Sigma, Bushnell, Pentax, Hanimex, Kiron, Cokin, Vivitar, Kodak, Agfa, Ilford, LowePro, Domke, Slik, Bronica, Hasselblad, Sinar, Omega, Metz, Chimera, Smith-Victor, Beseler, Unicolor, etc.

Special Factors: PQ by phone or letter with SASE; "all items are complete with all accessories as supplied by manufacturer"; returns accepted within 14 days.

CAMERA WORLD OF OREGON; 500 S.W. 5th Ave.; Portland, OR 97204 (800) 222-6262/ Cat.: $1/ Save: 25–50%/ Pay: C, MO, MC, V Sells: photo supplies/ Shop: same address

$$$/

Comment: Camera World of Oregon stocks a wide range of still, move, video, and underwater photo supplies and equipment, at discounts of up to 50%. "All merchandise supplied with U.S.A. warranty."

Sample Goods: Cameras, lenses, accessories, and darkroom equipment by Canon, Nikon, Pentax, Olympus, Tamron, Kiron, Hansa, Tokina, Ricoh, Vivitar, Cokin, Kodak, Leitz, Hanimex, Meade, Beseler, Ilford, Agfa, Domke, LowePro, Tenba, etc. Binoculars also available.

Special Factors: PQ by phone or letter with SASE; "all items are complete with accessories as shipped by manufacturer"; returns accepted within 14 days with original wrapping and inserts, in "original unaltered condition"; restocking fee may be charged.

COLORCHROME; P.O. Box 25009; Seattle, WA 98125
(206) 364-2485/ Broch.: free/ Save: to 40%/ Pay: C, MO, AE, MC, V Sells: 35mm film services/ Mail order only

$$$/

Comment: Colorchrome, founded in 1975, is the mail-order division of a large lab that processes film for professional photographers and can offer you the same quality services at to 40% below list or comparable retail.

Sample Goods: 35mm color film and slide processing; full-frame enlargements from 3″ × 5″ to 20″ × 30″ in matte, silk, and canvas textures; photo calendars; flush (borderless) mounting on acid-free board; flush-framed, unmounted prints in gold, silver, black, oak, and walnut "floater" frames; and jigsaw puzzles. Postpaid mailers included with brochure.

Special Factors: Quarterly specials flyers sent to customers; monthly specials in *Modern Photography* and *Popular Photography;* liability limited to replacement of lost or damaged film with a like quantity of unexposed film.

DANLEY'S; Div. of Sporting Optics, Inc.; P.O. Box 1-WMU; Ft. Johnson, NY 12070 (518) 842-7853/ Info : PQ/ Save: to 50%/ Pay: C, MO, cert. check Sells: optics and accessories/ Mail order only

$$$/ ▨/ ☎

Comment: Danley's carries one of the best selections of top-of-the-line optics for sports, marine use, and other specialized functions at up to 50% off list. A real find for the stargazer, spectator, and hunter.

Sample Goods: Sporting optics by Bushnell, Bausch & Lomb, Swift, Celestron, Leitz, Zeiss, Nikon, and HPM-Optolyth; every type of binocular made by these firms, including standard and compact models, sports binocs, armored models for field work, giant models, waterproof styles for marine use, zoom lenses, and folding models; theater glasses, telescopes, and rifle scopes (available from certain companies); Welt and Flip-lock tripods, and more.

Special Factors: PQ by phone or letter with SASE; layaway plan available; authorized returns accepted.

EXECUTIVE PHOTO & SUPPLY CORP.; 120 W. 31st St.; New York, NY 10001-3485 (800) 223-7323/ Info : PQ/ Save: to 50%/ **Pay:** C, MO, AE, MC, V **Sells:** photo supplies/ **Shop:** same address; M–Th 9–6, F 9–2, Su 10–5

$$$/ ✉ / ☎

Comment: Popular brands and latest models in cameras, video equipment, computers, phone machines, and other electronics are sold here at up to 50% below list or retail prices.

Sample Goods: Photography and darkroom equipment by Nikon, Canon, Hasselblad, Minolta, Olympus, Konica, Vivitar, Tokina, Sigma, Kiron, Pentax, Yashica, Polaroid, Kodak, Contax, etc.; personal stereo from Sony, Aiwa, Panasonic, Toshiba, Sanyo, Olympus; video equipment by Panasonic, RCA, Sanyo, JVC; computers, peripherals, and software by IBM, Compaq, Sanyo, Apple, AT&T, Columbia, Eagle, Epson, Zenith, Juki, TI,

Silver-Reed, NEC, Toshiba, Okidata, Gemini, Brothers, Hayes, Taxan, Amdec, etc.; calculators, phones and machines, typewriters, copiers, and telescopes also available.

Special Factors: PQ by phone or letter with SASE; returns accepted within 10 days on defective goods with original wrappings, invoice, and blank warranty card for exchanges; for computer information and price quotes, call (800) 882-2802.

47ST. PHOTO, INC.; 36 E. 19th St.; New York, NY 10003
(800) 221-7774/ Photo Cat.: $2/ Save: to 70%/ Pay: C, MO, AE, MC, V Sells: photo supplies/ Shop: 115 W. 45th St., 116 Nassau St., New York City; M–Th 9–6, F 9–2, Su 10–4

$$$/

Comment: 47st. Photo is a circus of audio, video, office, and home electronics, and cameras and photo equipment. The stores are usually mobbed, but the discounts—usually 30% to 50%, and up to 70% on specials—are given on mail purchases, too. Est. in 1965.

Sample Goods: Cameras, lenses, tripods, film, light meters, darkroom equipment and supplies, lighting, etc. by Nikon, Leica, Mamiya, Canon, Eumig, Yashica, Zeiss, Rollei, Minox, Hasselblad, Minolta, Pentax, Konica, Ricoh, Smith-Victor, Beseler, Leitz, Omega, Soligar, Kiron, Vivitar, LowePro, Tamron, Sigma, etc.; binoculars by Leica, Zeiss, Celestron, Nikon; Cometron and Celestron telescopes; name-brand TV and video equipment, microwave ovens, typewriters, phones and machines, etc.

Special Factors: PQ by phone or letter with SASE; general electronics cat. $1; returns accepted (except photo paper, tapes, and film) within 15 days with original wrappings and blank warranty card; min. order $35.

FRANK'S HIGHLAND PARK CAMERA; 5715 N. Figueroa St.; Los Angeles, CA 90042 (800) 421-8230/ Cat.: $2/ Save: to 50%/ Pay: C, MO, MC, V Sells: photo supplies/ Shop: same address

$$$/ ✉/ ☎

Comment: There's a real "Frank" behind this family-run business, which is a franchised dealer for many top manufacturers. Recommended as reliable by customers. Est. in 1965.

Sample Goods: Cameras, photo and darkroom equipment, and supplies by Pentax, Nikon, Canon, Vivitar, Olympus, Kodak, Hasselblad, etc. Will try to beat your best price if you call for a quote; use the catalog as a guide to available brands and lines.

Special Factors: PQ by phone or letter with SASE; C.O.D. and purchase orders accepted; min. order $10.

MARDIRON OPTICS; 37 Holloway St.; Malden, MA 02148-5901 (617) 322-8733/ Broch.: free/ Save: to 45%/ Pay: C, MO, cert. check Sells: optics, binoculars, telescopes/ Mail order only

$$$/ ✉

Comment: Mardiron sells optics—binoculars and telescopes

—from a select group of manufacturers at savings of up to 45% below list. Est. in 1982.

Sample Goods: Steiner binoculars, which are used extensively by 41 military forces; binoculars and telescopes by Optolyth; the full range of Swift optics; Hertel & Reuss binoculars (on a par with Steiner) may also be available. The price lists and brochures include Mardiron's recommendations of different models for specific purposes. Telescopes and binocular accessories also available.

Special Factors: PQ by phone or letter with SASE; shipping included.

OLDEN CAMERA & LENS CO., INC.; 1265 Broadway; New York, NY 10001 (800) 221-3160/ Cat.: 50¢/ Save: 20–60% / Pay: C, MO, MC, V Sells: photo supplies and electronics/ Shop: same address; M–W 9–7, Th 9–8, F–Sa 9–7, Su 10–5 $$$$/ ✉ / ☎

Comment: Olden has one of the most extensive inventories of new and used photographic equipment in New York. Patronized by many professional photographers. Est. in 1937.

Sample Goods: Cameras, accessories, and darkroom supplies and equipment by Konica, Canon, Minolta, Fuji, Omega, Yashica, Hasselblad, Leica, Chinon, Pentax, Mamiya, Hanimex, Kodak, Bronica, Minox, Olympus, Nikon, Rollei, Bogen, Contax, Praktica, Ricoh, Samigon, etc.; collectors' cameras, underwater photographic equipment and cameras, and books. Video cameras and VCRs by RCA, JVC, Elmo, Panasonic, Quasar, Sharp, Magnavox, Vidicraft, etc.; and name-brand computers, typewriters, and phones and machines also featured.

Special Factors: PQ by phone or letter with SASE; satisfaction guaranteed; returns accepted within 7 days with original packing materials and blank warranty card; trade-ins accepted by mail; min. order $50 on credit cards.

OPTICON LABORATORIES, INC.; 806 Hastings; P.O. Box 2160; Traverse City, MI 49685-2160 (616) 947-4355/ Broch. & PL: free/ Save: 10–20%/ Pay: C, MO, MC, V Sells: film-conversion service/ Mail order only

$$$/ ✉

Comment: Opticon will take your Super-8, 8mm, and 16mm films and transfer them to Beta or VHS videocassettes—a great way to enjoy old home movies and short films without projector, screen, and hassles. Est. in 1983.

Sample Goods: Films converted to Beta or VHS videocassettes; original unharmed in process; "bar" images eliminated on copy; sound recorded if sound present on the original. Opticon offers its services at prices up to 20% less than those of its competitors.

Special Factors: Satisfaction guaranteed; orders reprocessed at no additional fee if not acceptable; min. order $50.

ORION TELESCOPE CENTER; P.O. Box 1158; Santa Cruz, CA 95061 (800) 447-1001/ Cat.: free/ Save: to 35%/ Pay: C, MO, cert. check Sells: telescopes and accessories/ Shop: 2215 41st Ave., Capitola, CA

$$/ ✉ / ☎

Comment: Orion can give you the moon at stellar savings of up to 35%—especially good discounts on top-quality telescopes and accessories. Est. in 1975.

Sample Goods: Astronomical and terrestrial telescopes, including spotting, reflector, refractor, guide, finder, "deep sky," and other scopes; camera adaptors, filters, lenses, optical tubes, eyepieces, star charts, books, and other accessories stocked; brands include Meade, Celestron, Schmidt, Bushnell, etc

Special Factors: PQ by phone or letter with SASE; complete Meade catalog $3.

SOLAR CINE PRODUCTS, INC.; 4247-49 South Kedzie Ave.; Chicago, IL 60632-2890 (800) 621-8796/ Cat.: free/ Save: to 40%/ Pay: C, MO, DC, MC, V Sells: photo supplies/ Shop: same address; M–F 8:30–5, Sa 9–1

$$$/ ✉ / ☎

Comment: Solar Cine's catalog is packed cover to cover with all kinds of photographic equipment and accessories by a large number of manufacturers. Excellent source for professionals and serious amateurs. Est. in 1937.

Sample Goods: Cameras, lenses, studio lights, light meters, tripods, and darkroom equipment from Yashica, Kodak, Canon, Elmo, Bell & Howell, Minolta, Sylvania, Smith-Victor, Praktica, Olympus, Pentax, Konica, Nikon, Hanimex, Ciro, Soligar, Gossen, etc.; scores of books on photography for beginners and professionals; electronics; and processing (movies, slides, reprints, prints).

Special Factors: PQ by phone or letter with SASE; min. order $10.

THE WORLD OF 35MM; P.O. Box 2945; Paterson, NJ 07509 PL: free/ Save: to 50%/ Pay: C, MO, cert. check Sells: film-processing services/ Mail order only

$$$$/ ✉

Comment: When The World of 35mm was independently tested with 11 other film-processing services, it was found to offer among the best work in color quality and value and in proper handling of prints and negatives.

Sample Goods: Developing and printing 35mm negatives and slides; enlargements; slide duplications; other custom services. Prices up to 50% less than those charged by camera stores and other processors. Kodak papers used; film mailers sent on request.

Special Factors: Liability for lost or damaged film limited to replacement with an equal amount of unexposed film.

SEE ALSO:

Annex Outlet Ltd. . . . name-brand video equipment, blank tapes . . . APPLIANCES
Berry Scuba Co. . . . name-brand underwater cameras . . . SPORTS
Bondy Export Corp. . . . name-brand still and video cameras, projectors . . . APPLIANCES
Central Skindivers of Nassau, Inc. . . . name-brand underwater cameras . . . SPORTS
Focus Electronics, Inc. . . . name-brand cameras, darkroom equipment, photography supplies . . . APPLIANCES
Foto Electric Supply Co. . . . name-brand cameras, film, video tape . . . APPLIANCES

International Solgo, Inc. . . . name-brand cameras . . .
   APPLIANCES
Jems Sounds, Ltd. . . . name-brand cameras . . .
   APPLIANCES
S & S Sound City . . . name-brand blank video tapes . . .
   APPLIANCES

CIGARS, PIPES, TOBACCO, AND OTHER SMOKING NEEDS

Cigars, chewing tobacco, cigarette tobacco, snuff, pipes, and smoking accessories.

It's not easy being a smoker today, and if you're going to light up and enjoy, you might was well do it at a discount. The companies listed here sell cigars, chewing tobacco, shredded tobacco for cigarette rolling, pipes, and other smoking accessories at savings of up to 75%. If your current smoke is a name-brand cigar, look here for off-brand versions sold at a fraction of the price of their inspirations, as well as the famous labels themselves, which are often available at off-price.

You probably know that your right to smoke is being threatened on several levels. The Surgeon General's objective of a "smoke-free society by the year 2000" may never be realized, but local ordinances are being passed all over the country to limit the right to smoke in public places. While debates on the ethics of such actions rage on, know that one fact can't be argued: smoking poses serious hazards to your long-term health. Millions have quit, aided by everything from hypnosis to nicotine-impregnated gum, but most have done it with something that doesn't cost a cent: sheer willpower. If you want to overcome nicotine addiction, help is available from many sources. One of the most frequently cited is the American Cancer Society, whose local chapters run "Quit Smoking Clinics." Some chapters charge a small fee for the program, but most offer it free of cost. Contact your chapter or write to the American Cancer Society; 777 Third Ave.; New York, NY 10017 for information. The American Lung Association publishes two booklets, "Freedom from Smoking in 20 Days" and "A Lifetime of Freedom from Smoking," which are available from local chapters or by writing to the American Lung Association; 1740 Broadway; New York, NY 10019.

As a final note, please remember that tobacco is quite toxic and the residue left in cigarette filters and cigar stubs is potent.

Children have been known to eat the contents of ashtrays—with disastrous results. Keep tobacco products out of the reach of children and omnivorous pets, and make sure ashtrays can't be reached by either.

FAMOUS SMOKE SHOP, INC.; 55 W. 39th St.; New York, NY 10018 (800) 672-5544/ Cat.: free/ Save: to 50%/ Pay: C or MO Sells: cigars, tobacco/ **Shop:** same address; M–F 7–6, Sa 8–2

$$$/ ✉ / ☎

Comment: Super selection of name-brand and generic cigars and tobacco. Famous has served finicky New Yorkers since 1939 and can offer you the same privilege the firm's faithful enjoy: a private charge account.

Sample Goods: Dunhill, Macanudo, Partagas, Perfecto Garcia, Cuesta Rey, and other makers represented in fine, hand-rolled cigars of every taste, length, size, and shape. Unbranded house cigars, equivalent in quality to their famous counterparts, sold at savings of up to 50% on the brand-name versions; pipe tobaccos also stocked. Specials featured regularly.

Special Factors: Catalog includes many valuable tips on choosing cigars; satisfaction guaranteed; returns accepted.

WALLY FRANK LTD.; 63-25 69th St.; Middle Village, NY 11379 (800) 221-0638/ Cat.: free (4 & 10)/ Save: 30%/ Pay: C, MO, MC, V Sells: cigars and tobacco/ **Shop:** also 344 Madison Ave., New York, NY; Roosevelt Field Mall, Garden City, NY

$$$/ ✉ / ☎

Comment: Wally Frank has been delighting cigar and pipe smokers since 1930 with savings of 30% and more on famous-label cigars, tobacco, and privately produced smoke-alikes.

Sample Goods: Cigars by Don Diego, Martinez, Lancer, Montecruz, Dunhill, Te-Amo, Partagas, H. Upmann, etc., and Frank's generic equivalents; "irregulars" and closeout specials; humidors, cutters, holders, and accessories; briar pipes in every bowl shape and stem style from under $5; corn cob and meerschaum pipes; Colibri lightes, pipe-cleaning tools, pouches, racks, and tobacco humidors; name-brand pipe tobaccos and generic blends; loose and plug chewing and pinch ("spitless") tobaccos.

Special Factors: Satisfaction guaranteed; returns accepted; pipe service and repairs; shipping included on orders over $40.

J-R TOBACCO CO.; 100 Sterling Mine Rd.; Sloatsburg, NY 10974 (800) 431-2380/ Cat.: free (quarterly)/ Save: to 75%/ Pay: C, MO, AE, MC, V Sells: cigars and tobacco/ Shop: 11 other store locations in NY, DC, MI, NJ, PA, Tel-Aviv

$$$$/ ✉ / ☎

Comment: Owner Lew Rothman has been selling fine cigars at a discount since 1971. Half the 72-page catalog is packed with J-R's own cigars, at up to 75% less than name-brand prices.

Sample Goods: Cigars from Canaria D'Oro, Don Diego, Don Marcos, Excalibur, Fuente, Fundadore, H. Upmann, Montecruz, Partagas, Primo Del Rey, Pride of Jamaica, Rey Del Mundo, etc.—both J-R Alternatives and the name-brand cigars. All are handmade, long-leaf cigars; country of import, ring size, length, and relative body and strength of smoke (very mild to heavy) listed. Pipe tobacco from Dunhill, Sobranie, Lane's English, MacBarrens, etc., offered in a choice of blends and package sizes.

Special Factors: Satisfaction guaranteed; store locations listed in catalog; min. order $10.

FRED STOKER FARMS; Rte. 1, P.O. Box 707; Dresden, TN 38225 (901) 364-5419/ Broch.: free/ Save: to 70%/ Pay: C, MO, cert. check Sells: pipe, cigarette, chewing tobacco/ Mail order only

$$$/

Comment: Mr. Fred "Famous Since 1940" Stoker sells home-grown at down-home prices. He raises tobacco and sells forms and flavors for chewing, smoking, and snuffing at prices up to 70% lower than those of his competitors.

Sample Goods: Flake and chewing tobacco in peach, cherry-apple, wild cherry, wintergreen, mint, cigar, and other flavors in 1½–20 lb. containers; long shredded tobacco for cigarettes, clipping cigar tobacco, and domestic and imported pipe tobacco blends ($8–$10 per 1½ lbs.); plain, sweet, and flavored snuff; tobacco seeds ($3–$4 per teaspoonful); 16 varieties of sweet potato plants.

Special Factors: Inquire for information on quantity discounts; shipping included on local deliveries and all plant orders; plants shipped Apr. 15–July 15.

CLOTHING

Clothing, furs, and accessories
for men, women, and children.

You can buy just about anything to wear by mail today, from just about any part of the country—Amish clothing from Indiana, stock underthings and silk lingerie from New York's Lower East Side, swimsuits that have qualified for the Olympics, T-shirts printed with anything you'd like to say, bridal gowns, large sizes, executive suiting for both sexes, kid's clothes and infants' basics, army surplus, custom-made deerskin coats and jackets, and much more—at savings of up to 90%.

Clothing manufactured in the U.S. is now required to bear care labels that provide specific information on washing, dry cleaning, ironing, drying, etc. The FTC has prepared a booklet that defines all the terms used in the new labeling and answers a number of hypothetical questions. For a copy, request "What's New About Care Labels" from the Federal Trade Commission; Public Reference Office; Washington, DC 20580.

Learning what goes into quality construction and a well-made garment is vital if you're going to shop for name-brand goods by mail. Do your homework while store shopping and identify which manufacturers and designers maintain high standards of workmanship, and then you'll feel confident about buying those goods without having examined them in person. At least two books can be recommended for the person who wants to get the most out of the least: *Dress Better for Less*, by Vicki Audette (Meadowbrook Press, 1981), and *Good Garb*, by William Dasheff and Laura Dearborn (Delta Publishing Company, Inc., 1980). Both should be available at local libraries.

CHARLIE'S PLACE; 61 Orchard St.; New York, NY 10002
(212) 431-8880/ Info: PQ/ Save: 20–35%/ Pay: C, MO, MC,
V Sells: men's clothing/ Shop: same address; M–F, Su 9–5
$$$/ ✉/ ☎

Comment: The Lower East Side of New York is jammed with
dozens of shops selling name-brand goods at off-price. Charlie's
Place specializes in popular menswear, at discounts of up to
35%.

Sample Goods: Shirts, jerseys, raincoats, sportswear, outer-
wear, and other apparel by Gant, Arrow, Pierre Cardin (robes),
Puritan, Izod, Aquascutum, Christian Dior, London Fog, Misty
Harbor, and other firms. Sizes on many lines run from 34S to
54L; women's raincoats available.

Special Factors: PQ by phone or letter with SASE: returns
accepted with garment tags attached for exchange only.

**CHOCK CATALOG CORP.; 74 Orchard St.; New York, NY
10002-4594** (212) 473-1929/ Cat.: $1 (4 & 9)/ Save: 25–
35%/ Pay: C, MO, cert. check, MC, V Sells: hosiery, under-
wear, baby clothing/ Shop: same address; Su–Th 9–5, F 9–1
$$$/ ✉/ ☎

Comment: It is not easy to find underwear, sleepwear, and
hosiery for the entire family at a discount, but Louis Chock has
it all. Well-produced 72-page catalog. Est. in 1921.

Sample Goods: Women's stockings and pantyhose by Berk-
shire and Hanes; underpants by Vassarette, Jockey For Her,

Lollipop; Vassarette slips; Louis Chock sleepwear. Men's underwear by Hanes, Jockey, Munsingwear, BVD; pajamas from Knothe, Botany, Oscar de la Renta, Yves St. Laurent; socks by Interwoven, Burlington, Dior, Supp-Hose. XXXX sizes for large men. Layettes and nursery needs, kids' pajamas, socks, undies.

Special Factors: PQ by phone or letter with SASE; returns accepted within 30 days if package unopened.

CUSTOM COAT COMPANY, INC.; P.O. Box 69; Berlin, WI 54923-0069 (414) 361-0900/ Cat.: free/ Save: 50% +/ Pay: C, MO, cert. check, MC, V **Sells:** deerskin clothing, tanning services/ **Shop:** 227 N. Washington St.; M–F 8–5, Sa 8–9 $$$$/ ✉ / ☎

Comment: Custom Coat will tan your green hides, color them, and create custom clothing and accessories from the leather. The same items available in the company's deerskin. Low prices. Est. in 1938.

Sample Goods: Deerskin vests, town-and-country jackets and coats, classic wrap coats, safari and bush jackets, fringed and Western models, sports coats; riding, motorcycle, and bomber jackets; bags; driving, shooting, hunting, children's, and dress gloves for men and women; change purses, key cases, billfolds, cigarette cases, golf-club covers, and smooth-soled moccasins. Custom sizes, lengths, details, and linings available. Green deer, elk, and moose hides cured and colored. No fur work.

Special Factors: Tanning rates, guides to shipment of skins, number of hides needed per garment, etc., listed in catalog; deerskin samples provided with PL.

D & A MERCHANDISE CO., INC.; 22 Orchard St.; New York, NY 10002 (212) 925-4766/ Cat.: free/ Save: to 33%/ Pay: C, MO, MC, V Sells: underwear and hosiery/ Shop: same address; Su–F 9–5

$$$/ ✉/ ☎

Comment: D & A, home of "The Underwear King," sells name-brand lingerie, socks, hosiery, and underwear for men, women, and boys. Solid discounts on first-quality goods. Est. in 1946.

Sample Goods: Men's underwear by Jockey, Munsingwear, B.V.D., Camp, duofold; socks by Burlington, Interwoven, Dior, Camp, Wigwam; women's underwear by Bali, Carnival, Christian Dior, Do All, Chicas, Lollipop, Exquisite Form, Flexnit, Formfit Rogers, Lillyette, Lily of France, Maidenform, Olga, Playtex, Poirette, Smoothie, Surprise, Vassarette, Warner's, Danskin; hosiery by Burlington, Bonnie Doon, Camp, Trimfit, Hanes; Hanes and B.V.D. underwear in boys' sizes.

Special Factors: PQ by phone or letter with SASE.

THE DEERSKIN PLACE; 283 Akron Rd.; Ephrata, PA 17522 (717) 733-7624/ Broch.: free/ Save: to 50%/ Pay: C, MO, MC, V Sells: deerskin clothing and accessories/ Shop: same address; M–F 9–9, Sa 9–7

$$/ ✉/ ☎

Comment: The brochure from this firm shows clothing and accessories of deerskin, cowhide, and sheepskin at prices up to

50% less than those charged elsewhere for comparable goods. Est. in 1969.

Sample Goods: Fingertip-length shearling jacket with full collar and patch pockets, $225; fringed buckskin-suede jackets, $125; sporty deerskin handbags, $50–80; moccasins and casual shoes, chukka boots, and crepe-soled slip-ons for men and women (under $40); deerskin wallets, clutches, coin purses, and key cases ($2.95–$22); mittens and gloves for the whole family; beaded belts ($3.95); many other accessories.

Special Factors: Color chart not included with brochure; inquire before ordering if unsure of color, size, etc.; satisfaction guaranteed; returns accepted; C.O.D. orders accepted.

EISNER BROS.; 76 Orchard St.; New York, NY 10002 (212) 475-6868/ **Cat.:** free/ **Save:** 30–50%/ **Pay:** MO or cert. check **Sells:** T-shirts and sportswear/ **Shop:** same address; M–Th 9–6:30, F 9–1:30, Su 8:30–5
$$$$/ ✉

Comment: The Eisners have established themselves as major distributors of T-shirts, which they sell to stores, schools, athletic teams, and consumers worldwide. Est. in 1971.

Sample Goods: T-shirts, including "punk" cutoffs, midriff-baring "shimmel" shirts, muscle, long-sleeved, tank, V-neck, French-cut, camisole-style, and children's shirts shown in 28-page catalog; sizes run from 6 months to XXXX (58 to 60). Hanes, Russell, and Eisner's label. Sweatshirts, pants, football and baseball jerseys, polo and soccer shirts, extra-long sweatshirts, nightshirts, halter tops, athletic shorts, baseball and coaching jackets, and sporting caps and jackets also available.

Special Factors: Printing available; min. order one dozen items (same size and color) on most lines, 6 items on sweats and some athletic apparel.

THE FINALS; 21 Minisink Ave.; Port Jervis, NY 12771 (800) 431-9111/ Cat.: free (3 & 8)/ Save: 50% +/ Pay: C, MO, MC, V Sells: swimwear and athletic apparel/ Shop: 149 Mercer St., New York, NY; also Gayley Ave., Los Angeles, CA $$$$/ /

Comment: The Finals outfits many American swim teams, and once you've seen its catalog, you'll know why. It offers an unbeatable combination of style, comfort, practicality, and price. Est. in 1976.

Sample Goods: Swimsuits of Dupont's Antron nylon, Lycra, and other materials designed for competition use; sleek, form-fitting tank suits for women ($12–$25) and men's trunks ($7–$12); shirts, suits, and coverups for lifeguards and surfers; racquetball clothing and shoes; running and track gear; standard shirts, shorts, warmups, and sweats. Singlets and shorts ($5–$7) in "junior" unisex sizes; Accusplit and Cronus timepieces; swimming goggles, caps, fins, buoys, tubes, kickboards, etc.

Special Factors: Satisfaction guaranteed; returns accepted within 30 days (90 days on defective goods); min. order $25 on credit cards.

F.R. KNITTING MILLS, INC.; 69 Alden St.; Fall River, MA 02723 (800) 343-3383/ Cat.: free/ Save: 35–50%/ Pay: C,

MO, MC, V **Sells:** sweaters/ **Shop:** other locations in MA, ME, NH, RI, VT

$$$/ ✉ / ☎

Comment: Fall River Knitting Mills was founded in 1911, when Fall River was a thriving textile center. Buy through the 16-page catalog or from one of the factory outlets and save up to 50% on department-store prices for the *same* sweaters.

Sample Goods: Turtlenecks, crews, V-necks, cardigans, rugby styles, and vests for the whole family; classic Shetland/Orlon crew, in children's size 6 to men's XL, 26 colors, is under $12; styles in acrylic, Wintuk, and Orlon; cotton crews ($12.95), argyles, snowflake patterns, collegiate stripes, jacquard designs, all-wool, cable-front pullovers for men and women ($19), and much more. Monogramming in 24 thread colors and 9 styles available.

Special Factors: Satisfaction guaranteed; returns accepted; factory-outlet locations listed in catalog; min. order $20 on credit cards.

GOHN BROS.; P.O. Box 111; Middlebury, IN 46540-0111
(219) 825-2400/ **Cat.:** free/ **Save:** 20–60%/ **Pay:** C, MO, cert. check **Sells:** general merchandise and Amish specialties/ **Shop:** same address; M–Sa 8–5:30

$$$$/ ✉ / ☎

Comment: Reading the Gohn Bros. catalog takes you back into a world where bonnet board and frock coats were stock items in the general store. Prices—up to 60% below comparable retail—recall better days. Est. in 1906.

Sample Goods: 100% cotton Sanforized blue denim in 10 and 13¾ oz. weights ($3.29–$4.69/yd.), muslin ($1.39), chambray ($1.59), quilting thread (79¢); work-tailored, sturdy Amish clothing; men's cotton chambray work shirts ($7.39), denim broadfall pants ($12.99), men's underwear, cotton dress socks (79¢), Red Wing shoes (20% off suggested retail), rubber galoshes and footwear by LaCrosse and Tingley, work gloves, felt hats, and handkerchiefs; diapers and Gerber baby clothing; cotton percale and quilting prints, pillow tubing, 100% cotton sheeting, tailor's canvas, haircloth, mosquito netting, embroidery floss (17¢ a skein), wool overcoating (under $11/yd.), etc.

Special Factors: Satisfaction guaranteed; orders filled and shipped the day they're received; catalog pub. 8 times yearly; C.O.D. orders accepted.

GOLDMAN & COHEN INC.; 54 Orchard St.; New York, NY 11598-5052 (212) 966-0737/ Info: PQ/ Save: 20–60%/ Pay: C, MO, MC, V Sells: women's underwear/ Shop: same address; M–Th 9–5:30, F 9–4, Su 9–5:30

$$$/ /

Comment: Goldman & Cohen sells no hosiery and doesn't publish a catalog, but that hasn't diminished its reputation among its store and mail customers. Top lingerie lines offered here at sizable savings. Est. in 1958.

Sample Goods: Women's intimate apparel by Bali, Maidenform, Warner's, Playtex, Lily of France, Vanity Fair, Christian Dior, Olga, and other top manufacturers and designers; loungewear by these names; hard-to-find sizes.

Special Factors: PQ by phone or letter with SASE; no phone orders or inquiries on Sunday.

THE MAIL ORDER BRIDE, INC.; P.O. Box 160; Stilwell, KS 66085 Info: PQ/ Save: to 30%/ Pay: cert. check Sells: bridal gowns, dresses, accessories/ Mail order only

$$/

Comment: The Mail Order Bride offers savings of up to 30% on the cost of gowns and dresses for the entire wedding party. No alterations, but no bridal-salon hassles either.

Sample Goods: Gowns and accessories shown in *Bride's* and *Modern Bride*. Send the pages showing your selections for a PQ. Measurements and deposit of 50% of gown's retail price required. Examining actual gowns in local bridal shops is recommended. Delivery approx. 12 weeks from order date; sent C.O.D.

Special Factors: PQ by letter with SASE; no alterations; deposits not refundable.

NATIONAL WHOLESALE COMPANY, INC.; 400 National Blvd.; Lexington, NC 27292 (704) 249-0211/ Cat.: free (2, 4, 5, 7, 9, 10, 12) **Save:** 30–50%/ **Pay:** C, MO, MC, V **Sells:** women's hosiery and underwear/ **Shop:** same address

$$$/ / ☎

Comment: National Wholesale offers virtually every woman, regardless of height (from 5') or girth (to 60" hips), savings of up to 50% on pantyhose compared to similar name-brand products. Est. in 1952; endorsed by the Lexington Chamber of Commerce.

Sample Goods: Control-top styles, support, sheer mesh, cotton-soled, and other pantyhose; stockings (support, sheer, garterless) and knee-highs; bras, girdles, and body shapers by Glamorise, Sarong, Kayser, Exquisite Form, and Playtex; cotton-knit vests, briefs, long-leg pants, thermal underwear, pants liners; slips by Pinehurst, Barbizon, and Figurefit; dusters by Swirl. Larger sizes available. Hosiery sold by the box (3–6 pairs).

Special Factors: Satisfaction guaranteed; returns accepted.

PAGANO GLOVES, INC.; 3-5 Church St.; Johnstown, NY 12095 (518) 762-8425/ Cat.: $1.75, ref./ Save: 50–75%/ Pay: C, MO, cert. check, MC, V **Sells:** deerskin clothing and accessories/ **Shop:** same address; M–F 8–5, Sa 9–3 **$$$**/ /

Comment: Pagano Gloves has been selling its deerskin clothing, gloves, and footwear since 1946 and offers a large part of its inventory in a 32-page color catalog. Great buys; custom services.

Sample Goods: Gored and belted coats, tailored and fringed Western models, motorcycle jackets, etc. for men and women; chukka boots, moccasins, travel slippers, etc.; billfolds, keycases, tobacco pouches, handbags; mitts, dress gloves, golfing and driving gloves, and specialty gloves for shooting, archery, and bow-hunting. Custom sizes, lengths, and linings.

Special Factors: Include measurements when ordering; guide included in catalog.

RACHEL'S FOR KIDS; 4218 13th Ave.; Brooklyn, NY 11219 (718) 435-6875/ Info : PQ/ Save: 20–35%/ Pay: C, MO, MC, V Sells: children's clothing/ Shop: same address $$$/

Comment: Here's the answer to every parent's prayer—a source for first-quality, name-brand clothes for kids, at up to 35% below list. Order as early as possible in season, since stock moves quickly.

Sample Goods: Clothing by Oshkosh, Carter's, Billy the Kid, Izod, Dijon, Cutecumber, and Absorba; sizes from infant to youth on full lines of separates and activewear. Specify alternate color choices when ordering.

Special Factors: PQ by phone or letter with SASE.

REBORN MATERNITY; 1449 Third Ave.; New York, NY 10028 (212) 737-8817/ Cat.: $2/ Save: 10–50%/ Pay: C, MO, AE, MC, V Sells: maternity clothing/ Shop: 7 other locations in CT, NJ, NY
$$$/

Comment: You can look your best while at your biggest without dipping into Baby's trust fund if you buy your clothes from Reborn Maternity. Savings of up to 50% on top brands; 8 retail stores.

Sample Goods: Sasson, J. G. Hook, Belle France, Jordache, Regina Kravitz, and other famous labels featured; full range of seasonal apparel, including swimwear, sportswear, office and dressy clothing, and evening outfits. Sizes run up to 18. Comfortable materials; styles chosen to complement all stages of pregnancy.

Special Factors: Returns accepted for credit; min. order $20.

REIN FURS; 32 New York Ave.; Freeport, NY 11520 (516) 379-6421/ Lit.: free with SASE/ Save: 10% (see text)/ Pay: C, MO, cert. check Sells: furs for men and women/ Shop: New York City showroom; hours by appt.

$$$/ ✉

Comment: *"You can't WEAR high overhead . . .* so why PAY for it?" asks Arthur Rein, who sells furs at 10% below his competitors' prices—even advertised *sale* prices. That's equal to 50% to 60% discounts. Est. in 1967.

Sample Goods: Garments and accessories from any furs legal in the U.S.: Russian sable, lynx, fisher, marten, fox (red, Norwegian blue, silver, etc.), chinchilla, beaver, muskrat, opossum, raccoon, nutria, otter, ermine, coyote, Blackglama, Emba, and other ranch mink; any item made to order; fur remodeling, lengthening, color darkening, relining, etc.; used furs bought and sold. Copies of Revillon, Ben Kahn, Perry Ellis, and other designer furs at 30% below list.

Special Factors: Information on PQ and discount terms in literature; satisfaction guaranteed; returns accepted within 3 days for refund; all goods warrantied for 1 year against defects in workmanship and materials.

ROYAL SILK, LTD.; Royal Silk Plaza; Clifton, NJ 07011
(800) 227-6925/ Cat.: $1 (pub. monthly)/ Save: 40–60%/
Pay: C, MO, AE, DC, MC, V Sells: silk clothing/ Shop: 79 Fifth
Ave., New York City; also Freeport, ME; Clifton, NJ; Greensboro, NC

$$$/ /

Comment: Royal Silk offers good-quality silk and silk-blend clothing and accessories for men and women at great prices. A booklet on caring for silk is included with the year of catalogs —all for $1. Est. in 1978.

Sample Goods: The 50-page catalog features a wide range of silk and silk-blend apparel: shirts, dresses, and accessories for women; work-into-evening dresses; men's shirts and separates; silk and angora sweaters; evening wear for women, etc. Items include safari shirts, bikinis, robes, jewelry, scarves, sashes, jackets, etc. Sizes 4–20; some petite styles.

Special Factors: Satisfaction guaranteed; returns accepted within 10 days.

RUBENS BABYWEAR FACTORY; Rubens & Marble, Inc.;
P.O. Box 14900A; Chicago, IL 60614 (312) 348-6200/
Broch.: free with SASE/ Save: 20–60%/ Pay: C, MO, cert.

check **Sells:** infants' clothing and bedding/ **Shop:** 2340 N. Racine Ave.; M–F 9–3:30

$$$/

Comment: Rubens & Marble has been supplying hospitals with infants' clothing since 1890 and offers the same goods to you through Rubens Babywear Factory at up to 60% less than comparable list prices. Good stock of basics.

Sample Goods: Baby shirts in sizes from newborn to 36 months; short, long, and mitten-cuff sleeves; snap, tie, plain, and double-breasted slipover styles (many are seconds, with small knitting flaws); first-quality cotton/wool blend and preemie-sized cotton shirts; fitted bassinet and crib sheets (repaired seconds at half the cost of first quality); training and waterproof pants, kimonos, drawstring-bottom baby gowns, and terry bibs.

Special Factors: Seconds clearly marked; min. order 1 package (varying number per type of item).

SAINT LAURIE LTD.; 897 Broadway; New York, NY 10003
(800) 221-8660/ Cat.: $2 (3 & 8)/ Save: 33%/ Pay: C, MO, AE, DC, MC, V **Sells:** business clothing/ **Shop:** same address; M–W 9–6, Th 9–7:30, F & Sa 9–6, Su 12–5

$$$/

Comment: Saint Laurie has been manufacturing better suits since 1913 and made its mail-order debut in 1979. The $2 catalog charge brings 2 issues; $10 brings the 2 catalogs plus 2 swatch brochures with 80 samples.

Sample Goods: Conservatively styled suits, jackets, skirts, and trousers in fine fabrics: all-wool worsted and blends, Italian and Moygashel linen, hand-woven silk, gabardine, sharkskin, pinstripes, cotton seersucker, glen plaids, etc. Men's suits in short, regular, long, and extra-long; petite, regular, and tall for women. Tailoring details (belt-loop length, width of trouser legs, type of shoulder, vents, pockets, lapels, etc.) described; all jackets lined; pants sent unhemmed.

Special Factors: Returns on unworn, unaltered garments accepted within 14 days; showroom closed Sundays in July and Aug.

7TH HEAVEN FASHIONS, INC.; 12125 Rockville Pike; Rockville, MD 20852 (301) 231-9077/ Cat.: free/ Save: 20–40%/ Pay: C, MO, MC, V Sells: children's clothing/ Shop: same address

$$$/

Comment: The glossy, 16-page color catalog from 7th Heaven should make shopping for children's playwear and school clothing a breeze—the latest fashions in eye-popping colors and patterns, most discounted 20% to 25%.

Sample Goods: Separates for boys and girls by Jet Set, Oshkosh, Levi's, Gitano, Calabash, French Toast, Pierre Cardin, Billy the Kid, and Diane Von Furstenburg; button-down Oxford shirts, corduroy pants, Shetland crews, and other classics available. Hosiery by Bonnie Doon, underwear by Hanes and Wundies, and corduroy shoulderbags, lunch totes, backpacks, and umbrellas.

Special Factors: Will beat lower advertised prices by 10%; satisfaction guaranteed; returns accepted within 30 days.

16 PLUS MAIL ORDER; 3250 S. 76th St.; Philadelphia, PA 19153 (215) 492-9619/ Cat.: free (1, 4, 7, 10)/ Save: 30%+/ Pay: C, MO, MC, V Sells: larger women's clothing/ Mail order only

$$$/ ✉ / ☎

Comment: If you're between size 16 and 52 and have been searching for stylish clothing at affordable prices, 16 Plus is the answer. This season's colors and fashion accents, at prices 30% and more below list prices. Est. in 1972.

Sample Goods: Swimsuits, intimate apparel, nightwear, jeans, sportswear, and dresses by Bonjour, Gitano, Cap Ferrat, Levi's Womenswear, David Tracy, Movie Star, Sasson, etc. Queen-sized Berkshire pantyhose, belts, and other accessories. Clothing modeled by larger women.

Special Factors: Satisfaction guaranteed; returns accepted; include measurements when ordering.

SUNCO PRODUCTS CORP.; P.O. Box 535; Hampstead, NC 28443 (919) 270-3435/ Broch. and PL: free/ Save: 30–70%/ Pay: C, MO, cert. check Sells: work gloves/ Mail order only

$$$/ ✉

Comment: Sunco, established in 1983, offers great savings on work gloves and T-shirts and baseball-style caps that can be printed or embroidered with slogans or logos.

Sample Goods: Flock-lined rubber gloves (about 90¢ a pair, compared to $1.50 for similar gloves sold elsewhere); PVC-impregnated gloves with "pebble" finish ($1.35, compared to $4.95); suede gloves with elasticized wrists ($2.95–$5.95, compared to up to $14.95); neoprene-coated, acid-resistant gloves ($2.95, compared to $8.95); canvas, terrycloth, and brown jersey gloves; white knit "inspection" gloves (30¢, compared to up to $1); disposable polyethylene and leather-palmed work gloves.

Special Factors: PQ by phone or letter with SASE; quantity discounts available; min. order 12 pairs same size and style.

SUSSEX CLOTHES, LTD.; 302 Fifth Ave.; New York, NY 10001 (212) 279-4610/ Swatch and Style Broch.: $2/ Save: 40–45%/ Pay: MO, cert. check, MC, V **Sells:** men's business clothing/ **Shop:** same address; M–W 9:30–6, Th 9:30–7, F & Sa 9:30–6, Su 11–4

$$$/

Comment: Sussex has been manufacturing suits for prominent retailers since 1929 and now offers the same suits directly to consumers through a swatch/style booklet at savings of up to 45%.

Sample Goods: Conservatively styled men's suits (2-button jacket with natural shoulder, center vent, flap pockets, moderate lapels, horn buttons; straight-leg trousers) in wool worsteds, pinstripes, glen plaids, tick weaves, wool/polyester blends, and silks. Two-piece suits from $179, pants from $55; a single-breasted navy worsted blazer with gold buttons is $169. Choice of 40 seasonal fabrics, 4 sizes (to fit 5′ 4″ to 6′ 6″), and fine tailoring.

Special Factors: Returns accepted on unaltered, unworn garments sent with tickets attached within 14 days.

WEAR-GUARD WORK CLOTHES; Norwell, MA 02061-1609 (800) 343-4817/ **Cat.:** $1/ **Save:** 10–30%/ **Pay:** C, MO, AE, MC, V **Sells:** work clothing and accessories/ **Shop:** other locations in DE, MA, ME, PA, RI

$$$/ ✉ / ☎

Comment: Wear-Guard supplies more than a million U.S. companies and consumers with work clothing at 10% to 30% below regular and comparable retail prices. The free "Weekend Editions" catalog features New England–style casual separates for men and women, also reasonably priced. Est. in 1950.

Sample Goods: Men's work shirts in 18 colors and patterns, long or short sleeves, S–XXXXXL, at $12.99–$17.99; T-shirts, polo shirts, chambray shirts, turtlenecks, Western and flannel shirts, jeans, Timberland western boots, Durango Wellingtons, work shoes, gloves, thermal underwear and union suits; jumpsuits, coveralls, gabardine jackets, boat moccasins, varsity-style jackets, and windbreakers. Comparable items for women. Custom designs on patches, emblems, T-shirts, and work shirts available; stock logos and lettering. Wide range of items for truckers and enforcement personnel: money changers, holsters, tow straps, etc.

Special Factors: Satisfaction guaranteed: returns accepted; quantity discounts available.

CHARLES WEISS & SONS, INC.; 38 Orchard St.; New York, NY 10002 (212) 226-1717/ Cat.: free with SASE/ Save: 20–50%/ Pay: C, MO, MC, V Sells: women's underwear and lingerie/ Shop: same address; Su–Th 9–5:30

$$$/ ✉/ ☎

Comment: The Weiss family has been running what may be the largest lingerie emporium in New York City for 40 years. Top goods, solid discounts, pleasant shop and salespeople.

Sample Goods: Underwear, lingerie, and loungewear by Playtex, Dior, Vassarette, Formfit Rogers, Maidenform, Bali, Lily of France, Lilyette, Warner's, Kayser, John Kloss, Barbizon, Olga, Pucci, Halston, etc. Catalog shows a fraction of the stock.

Special Factors: PQ by phone or letter with SASE; satisfaction guaranteed; returns accepted on unworn items with tags attached; no phone inquiries or orders on Sundays.

WORKMEN'S GARMENT CO.; 15205 Wyoming Ave.; Detroit, MI 48238 (313) 834-7236/ Cat.: $1, ref./ Save: to 80%/ Pay: C, MO, MC, V Sells: new, used, reconditioned work clothing/ Shop: same address; also Warren, Pontiac, MI

$$$/ ✉/ ☎

Comment: Workmen's Garment, in business for over 30 years, can save you up to 80% on the cost of work clothing. New, used, and reconditioned goods available.

Sample Goods: New blue and green denim jeans, shop coats (to size 52), coveralls, zippered work jackets, shirts, pants, T-shirts, bandannas, towels, cotton and leather work gloves, tube socks, and shop aprons; Carhartt work clothes, brown duck, blue denim, white sail cloth, coveralls, painters' pants, etc. "Wear-Again" reconditioned clothing (washed, pressed, and sterilized): coveralls from $4, leather-palmed work gloves ($2), pants and shirts ($4; large sizes to 50 and XXXL, $5); work jackets, lab coats, etc. "Economy line" of serviceable clothing: cleaned and pressed shirts and pants from $2.17.

Special Factors: Satisfaction guaranteed on new and "Wear-Again" clothing; economy line sold as is; returns accepted within 10 days; shipping included; min. order $15, $20 on credit cards.

SEE ALSO:

Ace Leather Products, Inc. . . . name-brand handbags, attaché cases, small-leather goods . . . LEATHER

Altman's Luggage . . . name-brand attaché cases . . . LEATHER

Athlete's Corner . . . name-brand court, running shoes . . . SPORTS

The Austad Company . . . golf and sporting apparel . . . SPORTS

Beitman Co., Inc. . . . custom-covered buttons, belts, buckles . . . CRAFTS

The Best Choice . . . name-brand apparel, shoes for sports . . . SPORTS

Bettinger's Leather Shop . . . name-brand attaché cases . . . LEATHER

Bike Nashbar . . . bicycling clothing . . . SPORTS

Bowhunters Discount Warehouse . . . camouflage clothing . . . SPORTS

Campmor . . . name-brand outdoor clothing, footwear . . . SPORTS

Clothcrafters, Inc. . . . aprons, garment bags, tote bags . . .
GENERAL

The Company Store, Inc. . . . name-brand down-filled
outerwear . . . HOME—Linen

Custom Golf Clubs, Inc. . . . golf clothing, footwear . . .
SPORTS

Cycle Goods Corp. . . . cycling apparel . . . SPORTS

Defender Industries, Inc. . . . foul-weather wear . . . AUTO

The Down Outlet . . . small selection down-filled outerwear
. . . HOME—Linen

Dyker Heights Sports Shop, Inc. . . . football jerseys . . .
SPORTS

E & B Marine, Inc. . . . foul-weather wear . . . AUTO

Goldberg's Marine . . . foul-weather wear . . . AUTO

Golf Haus . . . name-brand golf shoes . . . SPORTS

Gurian Fabrics Inc. . . . crewel tote bags . . . HOME—decor

Holabird Sports Discounters . . . name-brand court shoes,
warmups . . . SPORTS

Hunter Audio-Photo, Inc. . . . Porsche Carrera, Ray Ban
sunglasses . . . APPLIANCES

Innovation Luggage . . . name-brand handbags, small-leather
goods . . . LEATHER

Las Vegas Discount Golf & Tennis . . . name-brand tennis
and golf clothing, footwear . . . SPORTS

Mass Army & Navy Store . . . new and used military surplus
clothing . . . SURPLUS

Omaha Vaccine Co., Inc. . . . work gloves and shoes . . .
ANIMAL

PBS Livestock Drugs . . . work gloves and boots . . .
ANIMAL

Pedal Pushers, Inc. . . . cycling apparel . . . SPORTS

Professional Golf & Tennis Suppliers, Inc. . . . name-brand
golf, tennis, running shoes, apparel . . . SPORTS

Road Runner Sports . . . name-brand running shoes . . .
SPORTS

Ruvel and Company, Inc. . . . surplus military clothing . . .
SURPLUS

Shama Imports, Inc. . . . crewel tote bags . . . HOME—decor

Soccer International, Inc. . . . soccer jerseys, shorts . . . SPORTS

Spiegel, Inc. . . . name-brand clothing for men, women, children . . . GENERAL

Sports America, Inc. . . . name-brand tennis, court shoes . . . SPORTS

Squash Services, Inc. . . . name-brand court shoes . . . SPORTS

Sultan's Delight Inc. . . . belly-dancing outfits, Arab headdresses . . . FOOD

Thai Silks . . . embroidered Chinese blouses . . . CRAFTS

Warehouse Marine Discount . . . foul-weather gear . . . AUTO

Weiss & Mahoney . . . new and military surplus clothing . . . SURPLUS

Whole Earth Access . . . name-brand work, functional clothing . . . GENERAL

CRAFTS AND HOBBIES

Materials, supplies, tools, and equipment
for every sort of craft and hobby.

If the high price of crafts supplies is blocking your creative instincts, you'll find this chapter positively inspiring. We've rounded up suppliers for virtually every craft imaginable, including all the needle arts, marquetry, miniatures, quilting, stenciling, wine-making, basketry, clock-making, wheat weaving, quilling, wood carving, spinning and weaving, batiking, decoy-painting, jewelry-making, and many more—and all of them sell at a discount. Greek and Icelandic yarns can be purchased from the source at a fraction of the prices charged by U.S. firms. Some of these companies have been in business for generations and specialize in avocations that your local crafts shop may not even know exist. If you have a problem with a material or technique, most can help you solve it by phone or letter. And if your interests run to model trains, cars, planes, and boats, look here for savings of up to 40%. Placing an order from these firms usually guarantees you a spot on the mailing list, and that means you'll receive the sales flyers with savings of up to 70%. Do remember to save your catalogs—they're invaluable for comparison-shopping and may also be necessary if the company runs promotions or clearances and sends you a leaflet reading "deduct 50% from winter catalog prices on items FA1001 through FX5934," as some do.

For related products that may be of interest, see the listings in "Art Materials" and "Tools."

AMERICA'S HOBBY CENTER, INC.; 146 W. 22nd St.; New York, NY 10011-2466 (212) 675-8922/ Cat.: $2/ Save: 10–40%/ Pay: C or MO Sells: model planes, boats, and trains/ Shop: same address; M–F 8:30–5:30, Sa 8:30–3:30

$$$/ ✉ / ☎

Comment: The Center has been in business since 1931 and is staffed by avid hobbyists who can offer advice and answer just about any question you may have. "Every known hobby item by every brand name."

Sample Goods: Model airplanes, cars, trains, ships, and boats, as well as the tools, materials, and supplies needed to build and run them, at discounts of 10% to 40% (figured on a legitimate list price and not an exaggerated figure); 160-page catalog consolidates the specialty books America's used to publish; bulletins published on a subscription basis.

Special Factors: Bulletin subscriptions offered through catalog.

BEITMAN CO., INC.; P.O. Box 1541; Bridgeport, CT 06601 (203) 333-7738/ Cat.: free/ Save: 10–30%/ Pay: C or MO Sells: custom-covered buttons and belts/ Mail order only

$$$/ ✉

Comment: Beitman has been supplying home sewers with garment and upholstery buttons, belts, and buckles since 1950, and prices are up to 30% less than other services. You send the firm your fabric, specify size and style from the many available, and Beitman does the rest.

Sample Goods: Buttons from a ⅓″ ball to a 2⅛″ half-ball; belts from ½–4″ wide; dozens of buckles in coordinating sizes; screwback earrings and French cufflinks with covered faces; upholstery buttons in a variety of backing styles—an open nylon hook, standard wire eye shank, nail, prong, threaded nail with washer, and pivot back with tack; Beitman's synthetic leather covering available in 7 colors.

Special Factors: Prices in catalog may be outdated and rate of increase printed on order form; include return-address label or facsimile with catalog request; min. order $5.

BELL YARN CO., INC.; 10 Box St.; Brooklyn, NY 11222
(718) 389-1904/ PL: free with SASE/ Save: to 50%/ Pay: C or MO Sells: yarn and needlework supplies/ Shop: also New York, Rego Park, Lake Grove, NY; Woodbridge, Wayne, NJ
$$$/

Comment: Bell has served the nimble-fingered since 1917, and is renowned for its extensive stock of hand-painted French needlepoint canvases. Salespeople are all avid needleworkers, and advice is given in the store.

Sample Goods: Yarn and floss by Columbia, Minerva, Bucilla, DMC, Wonoco, Coronation, Fox, Reynolds, Coats & Clark, Dimension, Pingoin, Paragon, Margot, Bernat, etc., at up to 50% off list prices; materials and supplies for knitting, needlepoint, crewel, embroidery, macrame, quilting, rug hooking, cross-stitch; needlework finished, blocked, and framed.

Special Factors: PQ by phone or letter with SASE; sales flyers mailed to customers; yarn cards $2.

BOYCAN'S CRAFT, ART, NEEDLEWORK & FLORAL SUPPLIES; P.O. Box 897; Sharon, PA 16146 (412) 346-5534/ Cat.: $2/ Save: to 20%/ Pay: C, MO, MC, V **Sells:** art and craft supplies/ Mail order only

$$$/ / ☎

Comment: The 104-page catalog from Boycan's lists everything from adhesives to X-Acto knives for scores of arts, crafts, and hobbies, at discounts of up to 32%. Est. in 1952.

Sample Goods: Tools and materials for egg decorating, tole and paper tole, "Shrink Art," glass staining and engraving, drawing, oil and acrylic painting, wheat weaving, quilling, macrame, crewel, cross-stitch (stamped and counted), knitting, crocheting, flower drying, decoupage, wood-burning, potpourri, stenciling, corn-husk and other dolls, silk flowers, basketry, candles, rug hooking, etc.; full range of general crafts supplies; many books and manuals.

Special Factors: Quantity discounts available; authorized returns accepted within 10 days; min. order $10.

CRAFT PRODUCTS COMPANY; 2200 Dean St.; St. Charles, IL 60174-1098 (312) 584-9600/ Clock Kit Cat.: free/ Save: to 50%/ Pay: C, MO, MC, V **Sells:** clock and music-box kits, components/ **Shop:** Rte. 83, Elmhurst; also 1519 N. Main St., St. Charles, IL

$/ ▨ / ☎

Comment: Craft Products began its business in 1940 with the publication of woodworking patterns and added clock kits in 1950. Fine components, a wide range of clock styles, and a separate catalog of clock and cabinetry parts make this a top source.

Sample Goods: "Regulator" models, Gothic wooden-wheel clocks, tambour, mantel, steeple, bracket, school, gallery styles; grandfather clocks; music-box kits; clamps, music and clock movements, flat and bezel dials, hardware, numerals, hands, clock patterns, etc. Save up to 50% on cost of comparable finished goods.

Special Factors: "Clock Components" catalog $2, ref.; satisfaction guaranteed; returns accepted within 20 days for refund or credit.

CRAFTSMAN WOOD SERVICE CO.; 1735 W. Cortland Ct.; Addison, IL 60101 (312) 629-3100/ Cat.: $1/ Save: to 40%/ Pay: C, MO, MC, V Sells: woodworking tools and supplies/ Shop: same address; M–F 8:30–4:45, Sa 8:30–12:45

$$$/ ✉ / ☎

Comment: The Craftsman catalog is 144 pages jammed with the kind of specialty tools and hardware, lumber, veneers, finishes, books, plans, and related products that inspire long workshop retreats. Serving woodworkers since 1930.

Sample Goods: Materials and equipment for marquetry, cabinetry, picture-framing, decoys, clock-making, wood-burning, upholstery, lamp refurbishing, toy-making, etc.; wide range of veneers and cabinetry-grade lumber; stains and finishes; routers, table saws, lathes, honers and sharpeners, clamps, jointers and planers, engravers, etc., by Dremel, Stanley, Wen, Arco, Rockwell, American Machine & Tool, Surform.

Special Factors: Satisfaction guaranteed; returns accepted within 30 days; min. order $10, $15 on credit cards.

GETTINGER FEATHER CORP.; 16 W. 36th St.; New York, NY 10018 (212) 695-9470/ PL & Samples: $1.75/ Save: 40–75%/ Pay: MO or cert. check **Sells:** feathers/ **Shop:** same address

$$$/

Comment: Gettinger has been serving New York City's milliners and craftspeople since 1915 with its marvelous stock of exotic and common feathers.

Sample Goods: Raw and dyed pheasant, turkey, duck, goose, rooster, and peacock feathers; available loose or sewn (lined up in a continuous row of even length), by the ounce and pound, $3.50 (loose) and $6 (sewn) per ounce and up; pheasant tail feathers, 6"–8" long, 100 for $13; 25" peacock feathers, 100 for $19; pheasant hides, $6.50 per skin. Feather boas also sold, by the yard.

Special Factors: PQ by phone or letter with SASE.

GREAT TRACERS; 3 Schoenbeck Rd.; Prospect Heights, IL 60070 (312) 255-0436/ Broch.: 50¢ and SASE/ Save: to 50%/ Pay: C, MO, cert. check **Sells:** custom-made stencils/ Mail order only

$$$/

Comment: Great Tracers is a growing firm founded in 1983 in classic mail-order tradition: it's family-run, offers one product, and sells at low prices. That one product is something everyone can use: a hand-cut, personalized stencil.

Sample Goods: Stencils featuring name and address, organization or company name, slogan, or other message, cut in ⅝″ letters from stiff oil board; maximum of 20 characters per line, 3-line limit (up to 50% less than other firms charge for custom stencils).

Special Factors: Paints, applicators, and supplies to be offered in future brochures; min. order $5.

E.C. KRAUS; P.O. Box 7850; Independence, MO 64053
(816) 254-7448/ Cat.: free (quarterly)/ Save: to 50%/ Pay: C, MO, MC, V Sells: wine- and beer-making supplies/ Shop: 9001 E. 24 Hwy., Independence, MO; M–F 9–5:30

$$$/ / ☎

Comment: E.C. Kraus publishes an illustrated, 16-page catalog of supplies and equipment for making your own beer, wine, and liqueurs. Save up to half the cost of wine and even more on liqueurs by producing them yourself. Est. in 1964.

Sample Goods: Yeasts, additives, clarifiers, purifiers and preservatives, fruit acids, acidity indicators, hydrometers, bottle caps, rubber stoppers, corks and corkscrews, barrel spigots and liners, oak kegs, tubing and siphons, the Saftborn steam juicer, fermenters, fruit presses, Virginia Dare's "Messina" and T. Noiret extracts, dried botanicals, books and manuals, etc.

Special Factors: Local ordinances may regulate production of alcoholic beverages; min. order $5 on credit cards.

LHL ENTERPRISES; Box 241; Solebury, PA 18963 (215) 345-4749/ Cat.: $3, ref./ Save: 30–40%/ Pay: C, MO, AE, MC, V **Sells:** arts and crafts supplies/ Mail order only

$$$/ ✉ / ☎

Comment: LHL Enterprises sells supplies and equipment for a broad range of crafts and hobbies, at prices that make experimenting with a new interest—or exploring an old favorite—even more appealing. Est. in 1982.

Sample Goods: Materials for embroidery, cross-stitch, candlewicking, macrame, stenciling, painting, quilling, decoy decoration, wood-burning, clock-making, basketry, wheat-weaving, potpourri, fabric flowers, jewelry, etc., including DMC embroidery floss, Charles Craft cross-stitch fabric, Grumbacher pigments and brushes, Liquitex acrylic paints, Stanrite easels, Illinois Bronze spray paints and stains, Adele Bishop stencils, X-Acto implements, Aunt Lydia's rug yarn, Elephant macrame cord, etc.; large range of books and manuals.

Special Factors: PQ by phone or letter with SASE; shipping included on orders over $100; min. order $10.

NEWARK DRESSMAKER SUPPLY, INC.; P.O. Box 2448, Dept. WBM-U; Lehigh Valley, PA 18001 (215) 837-7500/ Cat.: free/ Save: to 50%/ Pay: C, MO, MC, V **Sells:** sewing notions/ Mail order only

$$$$/ ✉ / ☎

Comment: Newark Dressmaker carries anything and everything a home sewer needs, from glass-headed pins to the material itself. The 44-page catalog features many hard-to-find goods. Est. in 1930.

Sample Goods: Trims, appliqués, scissors, piping, lace, braid, twill, zippers, gadgets to make the sewing easier, name tapes and woven labels, buttons, thread, floss, bias tape, rhinestones, doll and stuffed bear supplies, some fabric, and much more. Uncommon sewing notions, silk thread, and other specialty items.

Special Factors: Satisfaction guaranteed.

S & C HUBER, ACCOUTREMENTS; 82 Plants Dam Rd.; East Lyme, CT 06333 (203) 739-0772/ Cat.: $1.50/ Save: to 30%/ Pay: C or MO **Sells:** Early American crafts supplies, finished goods/ **Shop:** same address; hours by appt.
$/

Comment: The Hubers run a center for "early country arts" from their farm, which predates the Revolutionary War. The 32-page catalog features a range of products for Early American crafts as well as finished goods.

Sample Goods: Tools for spinning and weaving: castle spinning wheels, table looms, niddy-noddies, carders, shuttles, spindles, etc.; sheep's fleece, flax, cotton, silk cashmere, camel's hair, llama tops, and other fibers; natural dyes and mordants. Wool, cotton, linen, and silk yarns; reproduction sample kits, yard goods, floor cloths, herbs, potpourri, reproduction redware and combware, woodenware, beeswax candles and tin lighting fixtures, period stencils and supplies, basketry materials, bandboxes, reproduction Shaker baskets and boxes, and books on related topics.

Special Factors: Many goods not discounted; workshops held at the farm.

STRAW INTO GOLD, INC.; 3006 San Pablo Ave.; Berkeley, CA 94702 (415) 548-5247/ Cat.: SASE/ Save: to 70%/ Pay: C, MO, MC, V Sells: textile crafts supplies/ **Shop:** same address; M–Sa 9:30–5:30

$$$/ ✉

Comment: Straw Into Gold is a highly regarded mail-order source for textile crafts supplies and equipment. Specials on fibers, yarns, books, and other goods appear regularly in flyers, at savings of up to 70%. Send 4 double-stamped SASEs for catalog updates and flyers. Est. in 1971.

Sample Goods: Spinning fibers, including silk, cotton, flax, wool, mohair, camel's hair, goat's hair, etc.; Ashford spinning wheels and tools (not discounted); natural and synthetic dyes, thickeners, additives, fabric-painting supplies, etc. Chatelaine yarns from France, Crystal Palace goods, and yarns from Japan and Europe available. Basketry materials, Folkwear patterns, books, and rubber stamps offered. Good source for weavers and machine knitters.

Special Factors: Fiber samples and yarn cards available; quantity discounts; helpful, informed staff; min. order $20 on credit cards.

THAI SILKS; 252 State St.; Los Altos, CA 94022 (415) 948-8611/ Broch.: 50¢ (2 & 10)/ Save: 30–50%/ Pay: C, MO,

MC, V **Sells:** imported silks/ **Shop:** same address; M–Sa 9–5:30

$$$/

Comments: Beautiful, comfortable silk is also affordable at Thai Silks, where the home sewer, decorator, and artist can save 30% to 50% on yardage and piece goods, compared to retail prices. Just 2% of the stock comes from Thailand. Est. in 1964.

Sample Goods: Jacquard weaves, crepe de Chine, bouclé knits, pongee, cotton-backed silk corduroy, China silk, silk satin, raw silk, brocades and tapestry weaves, silk taffeta, woven plaids, Dupioni silk, upholstery weights, etc., from China, India, Italy, and Japan. Hemmed scarves for painting and batik, batiked cotton and cotton shirting, Chinese embroidered handkerchiefs, blouses, tablecloths, placemats, and napkins also available.

Special Factors: PQ by phone or letter with SASE; quantity discounts to firms and professionals; samples available, details in brochure; satisfaction guaranteed; returns accepted; min. order ½ yd. fabric.

UTEX TRADING ENTERPRISES; 710 Ninth St.; Suite 5; Niagara Falls, NY 14301 (716) 282-4887; ext. 18/ PL: free with SASE/ **Save:** to 50%/ **Pay:** MO or cert. check **Sells:** imported silks/ Mail order only

$$$/

Comment: Utex trades in silk yard goods and sewing supplies, imported directly from China. Of interest to textile artists, designers, and home sewers—Utex stocks over 100 weights, weaves, and widths. Est. in 1980.

Sample Goods: Silk yardage, including shantung, pongee, taffeta, twill, Habotai, peau de soie, lamé, suiting, etc.; unprinted scarves, silk thread, floss, and yarn available. Roster of specific fabrics recommended for wedding dresses, blouses, lingerie, kimonos, and other apparel included in brochure.

Special Factors: Quantity discounts available; min. order $20.

SEE ALSO:

A.E.S. . . . Makita power tools . . . TOOLS

The Airborne Sales Co. . . . surplus hobby and crafts supplies . . . TOOLS

American Discount Wallcoverings . . . name-brand decorator fabrics . . . HOME—Decor

American Vacuum & Sewing Machine Corp. . . . name-brand sewing machines and attachments . . . APPLIANCES

Dick Blick Co. . . . wide range of crafts supplies . . . ART MATERIALS

Crown Art Products Co., Inc. . . . silk-screening materials . . . ART MATERIALS

Del-Mar Co. . . . resin-embedded gold cabochons . . . JEWELRY

Doll House & Toy Factory Outlet . . . dollhouse kits and assembly supplies . . . TOYS

The Fabric Center . . . name-brand decorator fabrics . . . HOME—Decor

Gohn Bros. . . . hard-to-find, natural-fiber yardage, thread, floss, notions, quilt frames . . . CLOTHING

Gold N' Stones . . . jewelry findings . . . JEWELRY

Good 'N' Lucky Promotions . . . closeout crafts supplies . . . JEWELRY

Gurian Fabrics Inc. . . . crewel fabric . . . HOME—Decor

Hong Kong Lapidaries . . . gemstones . . . JEWELRY

International Import Co. . . . cut precious, semiprecious gemstones . . . JEWELRY

Kountry Bear Company . . . stuffed bears in kits, patterns . . . TOYS

Plastic BagMart . . . zip-top plastic bags . . . HOME— Maintenance

Protecto-Pak . . . zip-top plastic bags . . . HOME— Maintenance

Rein Furs . . . mink scraps . . . CLOTHING

Robinson's Wallcoverings . . . decorator fabrics . . . HOME— Decor

S & C Huber, Accoutrements . . . American period crafts supplies, equipment . . . GENERAL

Sanz International, Inc. . . . name-brand decorator fabrics . . . HOME—Decor

Ginger Schlote . . . jewelry findings . . . JEWELRY

Sewin' in Vermont . . . name-brand sewing machines, attachments . . . APPLIANCES

Shama Imports, Inc. . . . crewel fabric . . . HOME—Decor

FARM AND GARDEN

Seeds, bulbs, live plants,
supplies, tools, and equipment.

If you buy your plants at the local florist or nursery, you're probably going to find the same varieties everywhere, and the prices will be about the same across the board. But if you go the mail-order route, you'll have your choice of rare varieties of bulbs, plants, flowers, herbs, and other growing things. And plants and seed packages make lovely gifts for your horticultural friends. But do make sure when you're ordering that the plant will survive in your climate or home environment—a delicate woods flower specimen will not last long in an eastern exposure or an overheated house.

Although we're interested in saving you money, improvements in your landscaping can also *make* you money. A well-planned investment of $50 to $100 in "environmental improvement" can increase the value of your property by as much as $500, especially if you've got something unusual for your locality. But remember that the same cautions about plant survival apply here, perhaps more strongly. "Hostile" soil often takes many tolls until the gardener gets wise and has it tested, to find that it can support only certain types of growth. Investigate *before* you order and you'll save yourself time, labor, and money.

For related products, see the listings in "Tools."

**BEAR MEADOW FARM; 23 Wall St.; North Adams, MA
01247** (413) 663-9241/ Cat.: $1, ref. (3 & 10)/ Save: 20%/
Pay: C, MO, MC, V Sells: live herbs and plants, food, country
gifts/ **Shop:** same address; May 1–Oct. 31, W–Su 12–4

$$$/ /

Comment: The Shays, who run Bear Meadow, promote
"healthful, wholesome living" and offer organically grown
houseplants, herbs, and flowers. Foods and country gifts also
featured; details on services offered to visitors given in catalog.
Est. in 1974.

Sample Goods: Live herbs, geraniums, and "exotic house
plants" in 3″ and 5″ pots, from agrimony to Yerba Buena at
$1.85 and $2.75 each; dried cooking and medicinal herbs, from
alder buckthorn bark to zahtar, 9¢ (sea salt) to $5.49 (powdered
goldenseal) per ounce; tea, decaffeinated coffee, potpourri, essen-
tial oils, pomander balls, spice ropes, sachets, herb wreaths,
herbal vinegars, chutneys, marmalades, pickles, relishes, honey,
maple syrup; herbal and fruit jams, jellies, butters; books on
herbs and gardening.

Special Factors: Wholesale catalog available (request on
company letterhead); plants sent Apr. 15 to mid-Oct.

BRECK'S; 6523 N. Galena Rd.; Peoria, IL 61632 (309) 691-
4616/ Cat.: $1/ Save: to 50%/ Pay: C, MO, MC, V Sells:
Dutch flower bulbs/ Mail order only

$$/

Comment: Breck's has been "serving American gardeners
since 1818" with a fine selection of flower bulbs imported di-

rectly from Holland, at discounts of up to 50% on orders placed by July 31 for fall delivery and planting.

Sample Goods: Tulip, crocus, daffodil, hyacinth, iris, anemone, delphinium, and windflower bulbs; all specifications—blooming period, height, color and markings, petal formation, and scent—are given in the catalog description.

Special Factors: Early-order discounts; bonus bulbs with large orders; satisfaction guaranteed; returns accepted for exchange, replacement, or refund.

DE JAGER BULBS, INC.; 188 Asbury St.; South Hamilton, MA 01982 (617) 468-1622/ Cat.: free/ Save: to 50%/ Pay: C, MO, MC, V Sells: Dutch flower bulbs, seeds, tubers/ Mail order only

$$/

Comment: De Jager imports its bulbs directly from nurseries in Holland, so it's able to offer them at excellent prices—almost 50% below garden-center prices, if you order by July 1. Est. in 1870.

Sample Goods: Over 400 varieties of tulip, narcissus, hyacinth, daffodil, amaryllis, crocus, and other flower bulbs in every possible color and petal formation. The catalog gives both common and botanical names of the flowers, describes the color, scent, optimum growing conditions, blooming period, and approximate height of the mature plant. Tubers and seeds for begonias, dahlias, ground cover, peonies, African violets, berries, vegetables, fruits, and roses also sold.

Special Factors: Bulbs shipped mid-Sept. through Dec.; satisfaction guaranteed on bulbs; returns accepted.

**DUTCH GARDENS INC.; P.O. Box 400; Montvale, NJ
07645-0400** (201) 391-4366/ Cat. & PL: free (4 & 12)/ Save:
to 60%/ Pay: C, MO, MC, V **Sells:** Dutch flower bulbs/ Mail
order only

$$$$/ /

Comment: Dutch Gardens publishes one of the most beautiful
bulb catalogs around—over 60 color pages of breathtaking
flower "head shots" that approximate perfection. The prices are
some of the lowest charged anywhere—up to 60% less than
other mail-order firms and garden-supply houses. Excellent rep-
utation among gardeners. Est. in 1961.

Sample Goods: Tulip, hyacinth, daffodil, narcissus, crocus,
anemone, iris, snowdrop, allium, amaryllis, and other spring-
flower bulbs; tulips alone include single, double, fringed, parrot,
lily, and peony types. The catalog gives the size of the bulb and
the common and botanical name, height, planting zones, blooming period, and appropriate growing situations of each variety;
a zone chart, guide to planting depth, hints on naturalizing, rock
gardening, terrace planting, indoor growing, and forcing included.

Special Factors: Orders accepted up to Oct. 15 (deadlines
given in catalog); 10% goods bonus or discount on orders over
$70; shipping included; bulbs guaranteed to bloom (conditions
in catalog); min. order $20 on credit cards.

**GLORYBEE BEE BOX, INC.; 1015 Arrow St.; Eugene, OR
97402** (503) 584-1649/ Broch.: free/ Save: 30%/ Pay: C,
MO, MC, V **Sells:** beekeeping supplies/ **Shop:** same address

$$$/ /

Comment: Glorybee answers every apiarist's needs with a complete line of equipment and supplies for keeping bees, including live bees and assembled hives. Courses are given covering the essentials of beginning beekeeping; "the highest prices" paid for beeswax. Helpful sales staff. Est. in 1975.

Sample Goods: Foundations, hive frames, hardware, extracting equipment, an observation hive, queen and drone traps, honey dabbers, veils, gloves, tools, smokers, escapes, excluders, repellants, bee feed and stimulants, and honey pumps at about 30% less than prices charged by retail outlets.

Special Factors: Honey and edibles sold by "Glorybee Honey" division of firm, listed in "Food" chapter.

GREENLAND FLOWER SHOP; RD 1, Box 52; Port Matilda, PA 16870 (814) 692-8308/ Cat.: 50¢/ Save: 25–40%/ Pay: C or MO Sells: live houseplants/ **Shop:** same address $$$/ ✉

Comment: When your family name is Greenland, perhaps it's natural that horticulture is your business. The Greenlands have been propagating and selling healthy houseplants, perennials, and other live plants since 1968 and plan to offer shrubbery, evergreens, shade trees, and bulbs in the future.

Sample Goods: Over 100 kinds of plants, including jade plants, Boston and asparagus ferns, baby tears, Irish moss, fuchsia, coleus, wandering Jew, begonias, heather, hibiscus, indoor oats, and more. Plants sent in 2¼" grow pots. Catalog lists botanical names, proper culture, and appropriate environments for each plant, and zones and blooming period for flowering plants.

Special Factors: Quantity discounts available; delivery by UPS only; CA and AZ regulations may prohibit delivery of some species to those states; plants guaranteed to be live upon delivery.

OREGON BULB FARMS; 39391 S.E. Lusted Rd.; Sandy, OR 97055-9595 (503) 663-3133/ Cat.: $2, ref./ Save: 30%/ Pay: C, MO, MC, V Sells: Jagra hybrid lily bulbs/ Mail order only

$$/ ✉ / ☎

Comment: Oregon Bulb Farms, founded in 1929, develops and sells the lovely Jan de Graaff (Jagra) hybrid lilies—as stunning as orchids, but easier to cultivate and guaranteed to bloom. Prices are about 30% lower here than those charged elsewhere for similar blooms.

Sample Goods: Over 70 varieties of Asiatic and Oriental hybrids in upright-flowering, outward-facing, pendant, and trumpet formations; plain, freckled, and color-streaked varieties in white, every shade of pink and orange, yellows, and combinations. Most are scented; blossoms up to 20″ across on some varieties. Orgeon has developed a line of genetic dwarf lilies especially for indoor cultivation, which can be transplanted to the garden where they should flower for years.

Special Factors: Quantity discounts; bonus bulbs with large orders; min. order $25 on credit cards.

PRENTISS COURT GROUND COVERS; P.O. Box 8662; Greenville, SC 29604-8662 (803) 277-4037/ Broch.: 25¢/

Save: 30–40%/ Pay: C, MO, MC, V Sells: live ground-cover plants/ Mail order only

$$$/ ✉ / ☎

Comment: Prentiss Court offers an attractive, labor-efficient alternative to a conventional lawn: ground cover. A wide range of plants is offered, at to 40% below nursery prices. Spacing and planting guides included in the brochure; minimal illustrations. Est. in 1979.

Sample Goods: Ajuga, crownvetch, day lilies, Boston ivy, Euonymous fortunei, fig vine, English ivy and other Hedera helix, Japanese honeysuckle, St. Johnswort, jasmine, phlox, liriope and sedum, Vinca major; sold bare-root and/or potted. Average price 50¢ per plant.

Special Factors: Shipping included; min. order 50 plants of the same variety.

ROYAL GARDENS INC.; P.O. Box 588; Farmingdale, NJ 07727 (201) 780-2713/ Cat.: free/ Save: to 40%/ Pay: C, MO, MC, V Sells: Dutch flower bulbs/ Mail order only

$$$/ ✉ / ☎

Comment: Royal Gardens publishes a gorgeous 64-page catalog literally blooming with glorious color shots of its Dutch-grown flower bulbs, all of which are sold at up to 40% less than regular prices if ordered by July 31. Extensive stock, including varieties not seen in other such catalogs.

Sample Goods: Tulips, daffodils, giant bearded irises (sold as plants), fragrant double peonies, bleeding hearts, "snowflakes," narcissus, amaryllis, lilies, giant allium, anemones, grape and giant hyacinths, fritillaria, etc.; dwarfs and miniatures, hybrids, and varieties suitable for naturalizing, rock gardens, and forcing are available.

Special Factors: Early-order, quantity discounts; bonus bulbs with large orders; bulbs and plants guaranteed to grow and bloom; returns accepted; min. order $15 on credit cards.

VAN BOURGONDIEN BROS.; 245 Farmingdale Rd.; P.O. Box A; Babylon, NY 11702 (800) 645-5830/ Cat.: free/ Save: to 40%/ Pay: C, MO, MC, V Sells: Dutch and domestic flower bulbs, plants/ Mail order only

$$$/ /

Comment: The spring and fall catalogs from Van Bourgondien supply a wealth of vegetation for home, lawn, and garden at up to 40% less than other suppliers. Both 64-page editions offer Hosta and hybrid lilies, ground cover, a wide range of flowers, and supplies and tools. Well-respected firm, est. in 1918.

Sample Goods: Tulip, daffodil, hyacinth, crocus; narcissus, anemone, allium, fritillaria, and other bulbs; perennials, geraniums, delphiniums, shasta daisies, lavender, flowering house plants, foxtails, black-eyed Susans, etc., in fall catalog. House plants, herbs, carnivorous plants, begonias, dwarf fruit trees, shade trees and shrubbery, berries, grapes, nut trees, rhubarb, shallots, artichokes, cranberries, etc., in spring catalog.

Special Factors: Early-order, quantity discounts; bonuses with large orders; goods guaranteed to be "as described" and delivered in perfect condition; returns accepted.

SEE ALSO:

Arctic Glass Supply, Inc. . . . passive solar greenhouse panes
. . . HOME—Maintenance

Central Michigan Tractor and Parts . . . salvaged, rebuilt,
reconditioned tractor and combine parts . . . AUTO

Clothcrafters, Inc. . . . knee pads, gardening aprons . . .
GENERAL

Southeastern Insulated Glass . . . passive solar greenhouse
panels . . . HOME—Maintenance

Fred Stokes Farms . . . sweet potato plants, tobacco seeds . . .
CIGARS

Sunco Products Corp. . . . protective gloves . . . CLOTHING

Whole Earth Access . . . gardening tools, rototillers, etc. . . .
GENERAL

FOOD AND DRINK

Foods, beverages, and condiments.

Herbs, spices, coffee, and tea are mail-order naturals, and all are available through the firms listed here. But these sources also offer you the best buys in cheese to be found in New York City, freshly baked whole-grain breads, caviar and Italian truffles, Mexican and Syrian foods, giant pistachio nuts, Vermont maple syrup at below-supermarket prices, and much more—at savings that run to 80%.

Most of the mail-order food purveyors listed here cater to gourmet and exotic tastes, but one cannot live by lotus-flavored tea and four-alarm chili alone. It's a good idea to learn about fundamental nutritional needs and what types of foods can best fill them, since nourishment cannot be compromised by epicurean pleasures on a regular basis. We recommend reading *The Complete Food Handbook,* by Roger P. Doyle and James L. Redding (Grove Press, 1979). This is a comprehensive guide that, unlike most consumer-oriented publications, is a model of balanced research and reporting on the food industry.

Those who'd like to know more about the emulsifiers, binders, maturing agents, flavor enhancers, dyes, stabilizers, antioxidants, and similar goods found in most foods will find *The Food Additives Book,* by Nicholas Freydberg and Willis A. Gortner (Bantam Books, 1982), a fascinating volume. Hundreds of additives are discussed and rated in terms of safety; additives present in name-brand foods are identified as well. (Note that this information dates easily, since many foods are reformulated on a regular basis. The book is recommended for its information on the functions and possible hazards of the additives themselves.)

Cheese, a product of milk, provides a valuable source of nutrients. If you're unfamiliar with the many forms and flavors offered in gourmet shops and the deli departments of supermarkets, turn to the listing for "Cheese of All Nations" in this book. This firm's catalog lists the origins of over 1,000 different types of cheese with a brief description of each, a guide to storing cheese, selecting complementing wines, recipes, cheese lore and history, and even a cheese trivia quiz.

If, like millions of Americans, you begin your day with a steaming cup of java or enjoy a tall glass of iced tea on a hot summer afternoon, don't miss *The Book of Coffee and Tea* by Joel, David, and Karl Schapira (St. Martin's Press, 1982). The Schapiras started their coffee and tea business in 1903 and are experts on both beverages. In addition to a stimulating account of the history, cultivation, and processing of each, the book includes a guide to the common and exotic varieties available, brewing and serving tips, and recipes. The book is listed in the firm's brochure, along with a superb selection of coffee and tea. Send a SASE to Schapira Coffee Company; 117 W. 10th St.; New York, NY 10011.

When ordering foods, be mindful of the weather. Don't purchase such highly perishable or temperature-sensitive items as chocolate, soft cheeses, fruits, vegetables, and uncured meats during the summer unless you have them shipped by an express service and plan to eat them immediately. (Most catalogs include caveats to this effect, and some firms will not ship certain goods during warm weather under any circumstances.) Don't overlook the firms listed here when making out gift lists—whether it's rare herbs or a year of gustatory delights provided by an "of-the-month" program, you can choose presents that will be remembered long after they're consumed, and many of these companies offer the convenience of direct shipment to the fortunate friend or relative.

CAVIARTERIA INC.; 29 E. 60th St., New York, NY 10022
(800) 221-1020/ Cat.: free/ Save: to 50%/ Pay: C, MO, MC
Sells: caviar and gourmet foods/ Shop: same address; M–Sa
9–6

$$$/ / ☎

Comment: Caviarteria, established in 1950, is the largest distributor of caviar in the U.S. Take advantage of its super prices on all grades, and a great lineup of other gourmet fare, through the descriptive 14-page catalog (updated quarterly with newsletters). Friendly salespeople.

Sample Goods: Several grades of Caspian Beluga and Sevruga caviar, and American sturgeon, whitefish, and salmon caviars; $7.95 per oz. for Kamkatcha bottom-of-the-barrel vacuum-packed to $100 for 3½ oz. Imperial Beluga. Whole sides smoked Scottish salmon, Norwegian gravlax, fresh pâtés, fresh foie gras, tinned white and black Italian truffles, morels, and cepes; French glacé fruits, candied chestnuts, Belgian Lèonidas crème fraîche; chocolates, etc.

Special Factors: PQ by phone or letter with SASE; shipping included on some items; antique and collectors' cars also marketed through catalog; min. order $25 on credit cards.

CHEESE OF ALL NATIONS; 153 Chambers St.; New York, NY 10007 (212) 732-0752/ Cat.: $1 (4 & 9)/ Save: 20–40%/ Pay: C, MO, AE Sells: cheese/ Shop: same address; M–Sa 8–5:30

$$$/ / ☎

Comment: Cheese of all nations (from Africa to Wales) is sold here at up to 40% below comparable retail. Fresh stock, handled and shipped professionally; excellent, knowledgeable salespeople. Est. in 1947.

Sample Goods: Over 1,000 types of fromage, including Tafi (Argentina), Darlag (Armenia), Bushman (Australia), Rahmkäse (Austria), Herve (Belgium), Rejueijao (Brazil), Tao-Foo (China), Queso de Crema (Costa Rica), Karise (Denmark), Telemme (Greece), Dacca (India), Eishel (Israel), Jalapeño (Mexico), Bola (Portugal), Hasandach (Turkey), and Pago (Yugoslavia); hundreds from Italy, France, Germany, Switzerland, the British Isles, and the U.S. Cheese spreads, low fat and salt, Kosher cheese, crackers, etc. Recipes, cheese facts and lore, and storage guide in catalog.

Special Factors: Products guaranteed to arrive in perfect condition; min. order 1 lb. cut cheese or $5 package cheese.

EREWHON TRADING CO.; Erewhon Mail Order; 236 Washington St.; Brookline, MA 02146 (800) 222-8028/ Cat.: free/ Save: 10%/ Pay: C, MO, MC, V Sells: natural foods, toiletries, housewares/ Shop: same address; also 342 Newbury St., Boston; 3 East St., Cambridge, MA; all open 7 days

$$$/ /

Comment: Erewhon is one of the best-known names in the health-food business, since it distributes all over the U.S. Virtually every natural-food store in the country has at least a few Erewhon products on its shelves. Est. in 1963.

Sample Goods: Nut butters, oils, grains, beans, seeds, nuts, flours, Japanese goods, pasta, granola, natural cosmetics, toiletries, cooking utensils, books, etc., by Erewhon, Dr. Bronner, Nature's Gate, Hain, Health Valley, Kendall, Arrowhead Mills,

Pure & Simple, Chico-San, Del Verde, Marusan, Essene, Baldwin Hill, and other firms. Kosher products available. All goods free of sugar, fructose, chemical preservatives, additives, colors.

Special Factors: Quantity discounts available on case and bulk purchases; min. order $25 on credit cards.

GLORYBEE HONEY, INC.; 1006 Arrowsmith St.; Eugene, OR 97402-9121 (503) 584-1649/ Broch.: free (quarterly)/ Save: 30%/ Pay: C, MO, MC, V Sells: honey-based foods/ Shop: same address

$$$/ ✉ / ☎

Comment: This firm is the food division of Glorybee Bee Box (see the "Farm" chapter), and it offers a gourmet line of honey-based edibles and related goods. Prices average 30% below retail.

Sample Goods: Honey, beeswax candles, honey pots, honey candy, recipe boxes, honey and spice racks, cook books (including a guide to canning with honey), bee pollen, propolis, etc.

Special Factors: Quantity discounts available.

LYNN DAIRY, INC.; Rte. 1, Box 177; Granton, WI 54436 (715) 238-7129/ PL: free with SASE/ Save: to 50%/ Pay: C or MO Sells: Wisconsin cheese/ Mail order only

$$$/ ✉

Comment: Lynn Dairy manufactures several types of cheese and sells them by mail at prices up to 50% less than those charged at the supermarket; savings are greater on cheese-shop prices. Gift boxes available.

Sample Goods: Cheddar, Colby, and mozzarella cheese, including flavored varieties (caraway, salami, onion, etc.); 12-oz. jars of cheese spread offered in 11 flavors (including plain, jalapeño pepper, brandy, and garlic). Beef summer sausage available in 12-oz. sticks.

Special Factors: No shipments to AK or HI.

THE MEXICAN KITCHEN/ LA COCINA MEXICANA; P.O. Box 213; Brownsville, TX 78520-0213 (512) 544-6028/ PL: free (1 & 7)/ Save: to 50%/ Pay: C, MO, cert. check Sells: Mexican, Tex-Mex foods, cookware, seasonings/ Mail order only

$$$/

Comment: The Mexican Kitchen sells authentic ingredients, hard-to-find seasonings, and cookbooks full of recipes for Mexican and Tex-Mex favorites at savings of up to 50%.

Sample Goods: El Comal dried whole chile pods, ground chile powders, herbs and spices for Mexican cooking, prepared seasonings (including chorizo and taco flavorings), canned chiles, piloncillos (brown-sugar cones), Ibarra chocolate (with almonds and cinnamon), achiote, Bueno mole poblano, nopalitos (diced cactus pads), dried corn husks, chile chipotle (smoke-dried jalapeño peppers), etc. Cookware includes tortilla presses, flan molds, wooden molinillos (chocolate beaters), tortilla baskets, etc.

Special Factors: Use caution when handling chile pods and powders.

MR. SPICEMAN; 615 Palmer Rd.; Yonkers, NY 10701 (914) 576-1222/ Cat.: $1, ref. (2, 6, 10)/ Save: to 94%/ Pay: C, MO, MC, V **Sells:** herbs, spices, seasonings, kitchen gadgets/ **Shop:** 227 Union Ave., New Rochelle; W & F 8:30–4:30 $$$$/ /

Comment: Mr. Spiceman publishes a catalog that runs from soup to nuts but is best known for great buys on seasonings. Supplier to restaurants, delis, fine food outlets, and consumers.

Sample Goods: Over 130 herbs and spices in small and bulk packaging, including ground allspice, cayenne pepper, ground cumin, curry powder, paprika, and other basics; unusual and hard-to-find seasonings such as achiote, guaram masala, juniper berries, pâté spices, and freeze-dried shallots. Mon Cheri chocolates, Tic Tac mints, crystallized ginger, hard candies, Sun Giant California Snacks, Combos, Knorr boullion, Gravy Master flavoring, Panni mixes, 4C products, French's mixes, Virginia Dare extracts and flavorings, and teas available. A wide selection of food-preparation tools also offered.

Special Factors: Call before visiting retail location; meat products cannot be shipped to Canada; min. order $10, $25 on credit cards.

SULTAN'S DELIGHT INC.; P.O. Box 253; Staten Island, NY 10314-0253 (718) 720-1557/ Cat.: free (1 & 7)/ Save: to

50%/ **Pay:** C, MO, MC, V **Sells:** Middle Eastern foods, gifts/
Mail order only

$$$/ / ☎

Comment: Middle Eastern food specialties are sold here at
excellent prices—to 50% below comparable goods in gourmet
food stores. Est. in 1980.

Sample Goods: Near East and Sahadi products; canned
tahini, cous cous, tabouleh, fig and quince jams, stuffed grape-
vine leaves, bulghur, semolina, green wheat, orzo, fava beans,
Turkish figs, pickled okra, stuffed eggplant, olives, herbs and
spices, jumbo pistachios and other nuts, roasted chick peas, hal-
vah, Turkish delight, marzipan paste, olive oil, Turkish coffee,
fruit leather, filo, feta cheese, Syrian breads, etc. Cookbooks for
Greek, Lebanese, Syrian, and Middle Eastern cuisine offered,
and gifts, belly-dancing clothing, musical instruments, cook-
ware, and related items.

Special Factors: PQ by phone or letter with SASE; min. order
$5.

ZABAR'S; 2245 Broadway; New York, NY 10024 (800)
221-3347/ **Cat.:** free/ **Save:** to 50%/ **Pay:** C, MO, AE, DC,
MC, V **Sells:** gourmet food, cookware/ **Shop:** same address;
Su–Th 8–7:30, F 8AM–10PM, Sa 8AM–midnight

$$$/ / ☎

Comment: Zabar's, characterized as New York City's ulti-
mate deli, offers a sumptuous sampling from its famed counters
to the whole nation via a 48-page catalog. Savings run to 50%
on some items and lines.

Sample Goods: Smoked Scottish salmon, plum pudding, peppercorns, brie, Bahlsen cookies and confections, pâtés, mustards, crackers, escargot, Lindt and Ghiradelli chocolate, Tiptree preserves, Dresden stöllen, olive oil, proscuitto and other deli meats, and other foods available in past catalogs. Cookware selections include Mauviel hotel-weight copper pots and pans; Le Creuset, Farberware, and Revere Ware cookware; Krups and Simac machines, Braun coffee-makers, Robot Coupe food processors, Mouli kitchen tools, etc.

Special Factors: Catalog published in Oct. for holiday orders; PQ by phone or letter with SASE on cookware; min. order $5.

SEE ALSO:

E.C. Kraus . . . wine- and beer-making supplies, flavorings
    . . . CRAFTS
Protecto-Pak . . . zip-top food-storage bags . . . HOME—
    Maintenance
Puritan's Pride, Inc. . . . herbal teas . . . HEALTH
RSP Distributing Co. . . . survival foods . . . GENERAL
Star Pharmaceutical, Inc. . . . herbal tea . . . HEALTH
Sunburst Biorganics . . . small selection herbal tea, natural
    foods . . . HEALTH
Vitamin Specialties . . . herbal tea . . . HEALTH

GENERAL MERCHANDISE, GIFTS, AND BUYING CLUBS

Buying clubs and firms offering a wide
range of goods and services.

This is, as usual, a potpourri of firms selling everything from toweling to silver fox jackets. Some of the companies are here because they are buying clubs and general merchandisers, and others because they resisted easy classification. All offer excellent savings, including the three mail-order giants, Best Products, Spiegel, and Sears. Only Best Products can be considered a discount house in the strictest sense of the term, but if you place regular orders with Spiegel and Sears you'll receive sales catalogs with savings of up to 60% on many of the goods they carry. Their service departments are first-rate, so buying and delivery are a breeze. Go through the other listings carefully—there are some real finds here and countless answers to the question of what to give for Christmas, birthdays, anniversaries, Mother's Day. . . .

BEST PRODUCTS CO., INC.; P.O. Box 25031; Richmond, VA 23260 (800) 446-9827/ Cat.: $1/ Save: to 50%/ Pay: C, MO, MC, V Sells: appliances, electronics, gifts, etc./ Shop: showrooms nationwide

$$$/ ✉ / ☎

Comment: Best Products is a catalog showroom operation with over 100 outlets across the country. Over 8,000 items are shown in the hefty catalog. Good service; discount prices. Est. in 1957.

Sample Goods: Complete range of items, including name-brand appliances, electronics, home accessories, jewelry, toys, tools, etc.

Special Factors: Min. order on some items.

CLOTHCRAFTERS, INC.; Elkhart Lake, WI 53020 (414) 876-2112/ Cat.: free/ Save: to 40%/ Pay: C, MO, MC, V Sells: home textiles/ Mail order only

$$$/ ✉ / ☎

Comment: This firm sells "plain vanilla" textile goods of every sort, from cheesecloth by the yard to flannel gun-cleaning patches. No logos or mottos. Many useful, inexpensive items. Est. in 1936.

Sample Goods: Pot holders and pan handlers (50¢ each), taffeta toaster covers ($1), dish towels, chefs' hats, bouquet garni bags ($2 for 12), salad greens bags, denim placemats, cotton napkins, hot pads, aprons, cotton duck shower curtains, laundry bags, tote bags, shoe totes, woodpile covers, firewood carriers, garment bags, cider-press liners, mosquito netting, lightweight cotton terry towels, Portuguese cotton flannel sheets, pillowcases, sleeping-bag liners, etc.

Special Factors: Satisfaction guaranteed; shipping, insurance included; returns accepted for exchange, refund, or credit.

COMP-U-CARD; 777 Summer St.; Stamford, CT 06901 (800) 252-4100/ Broch.: free/ Save: to 50%/ Pay: C, MO, MC, V Sells: appliances, electronics, furnishings, etc./ Mail order only

$$$$/ ✉ / ☎

Comment: For $30, you get a year's membership in Comp-U-Store and can join over a million shoppers saving up to 50% on a wide range of name-brand products and services.

Sample Goods: Membership includes a year of unlimited toll-free calls for price quotes on Comp-U-Card's database of more than 60,000 name-brand items—appliances, VCRs, tableware, computers, jewelry, furniture, etc.; "Best Buys" newsletter and catalogs sent, which feature specials and buying tips; access to the CUC car-buying service (autos for as little as $50 over dealer cost); discounts on National and Avis car rentals; discount pharmacy service.

Special Factors: WATS line may be used to charge a membership; modem-accessible database; satisfaction guaranteed on membership; shipping, handling, insurance included.

**WALTER DRAKE & SONS, INC.; Drake Building; Colorado
Springs, CO 80940** (303) 596-3854/ Cat.: 25¢/ Save: to
40%/ Pay: C, MO, MC, V Sells: stationery, notions, household
gadgets/ Shop: same address; M–S 9–5

$$$$/ ✉

Comment: Walter Drake publishes a catalog with a wide variety of goods at very low prices. The firm's products are usually
of a better quality than those sold by comparable firms; delivery
and service are quite good.

Sample Goods: The return-address labels are one of the all-
time bargains—$1.29 for 1,000. The stationery line includes
other well-priced labels, notepads, business cards, correspondence paper and envelopes, and other useful goods for the home
office. Kitchen gadgets, Christmas decorations, personalized accessories, grooming tools, toys, party goods and novelties, pet
products, household organizers, energy savers, and other items
available.

Special Factors: Do not request discounts on catalog prices.

**GRAND FINALE; P.O. Box 819027; Farmers Branch, TX
75381** (214) 934-9777/ Cat.: $2, year's subscr./ Save: to
70%/ Pay: C, MO, AE, MC, V Sells: closeouts from upmarket
catalogs/ Mail order only

$$$$/ ✉ / ☎

Comment: This affiliate of The Horchow Collection publishes
a 32-page catalog stocked with clearances and closeouts from

Horchow catalogs and other gift houses and manufacturers. Save to 75% on original or list prices.

Sample Goods: Diamond earrings, hand-embroidered nightgowns, leather desk sets, cashmere mufflers, electric pasta machines, Christmas decorations, antique chinoiserie, personalized stationery, side tables, toys, sheets, Mikasa china, silk ties, and Halston bags featured in past catalogs.

Special Factors: Quantities may be limited; order promptly.

LINCOLN HOUSE, INC.; 2015 Grand Ave.; Kansas City, MO 64141 (816) 842-3225/ Cat.: free/ Save: 30%/ Pay: C, MO, MC, V **Sells:** stationery, gifts/ Mail order only

$$$/ ✉ / ☎

Comment: Lincoln House publishes a 96-page catalog of candles, gifts, and stationery items, offered at savings to 30% on comparable retail.

Sample Goods: Fabric magazine racks, brass candlesticks, terra-cotta bread baskets, auto organizers, spice-scented draft stoppers, recipe files, stationery, gift wrappings, etc., featured in past catalogs. Fall mailing includes holiday items: Christmas ornaments, decorations, candles, decorated cookie tins, gift bags, and related goods.

Special Factors: Satisfaction guaranteed, shipping, insurance included; returns accepted.

**REGAL GREETINGS & GIFTS, INC.; 2221 Niagara Falls
Blvd.; Niagara Falls, NY 14304** (716) 731-9001/ Cat.: free/
Save: to 30%/ Pay: C, MO, MC, V Sells: gifts, stationery/ Mail
order only

$$$/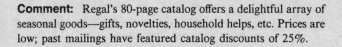

Comment: Regal's 80-page catalog offers a delightful array of
seasonal goods—gifts, novelties, household helps, etc. Prices are
low; past mailings have featured catalog discounts of 25%.

Sample Goods: Wrapping-paper collections, cards, address
labels, stationery; household organizers, kitchen gadgets, vases
and candlesticks, napkin rings and table linens, bathroom acces-
sories, candles, jewelry boxes, and toys usually offered. Revolv-
ing spice racks, gingerbread house kits, crib activity centers and
playthings, letter racks, perfume atomizers, clothing hampers,
Christmas wreaths and ornaments, drawer liners, garment bags,
wooden alphabet blocks, book lights, shower caddies, and model
cars shown in past catalogs.

Special Features: Satisfaction guaranteed; returns accepted
(except personalized items) within 30 days for exchange, refund,
or credit.

**RSP DISTRIBUTING CO.; P.O. Box 2345; Redondo Beach,
CA 90278** (213) 542-0431/ Cat.: $1, ref./ Save: 40–90%/
Pay: C, MO, cert. check Sells: closeout merchandise/ Mail
order only

$$$/

Comment: The photocopied pages from RSP Distributing are real eye-openers: items featured in current gift catalogs are sold here at up to 90% less.

Sample Goods: Book lights and boxed sets of burner covers ($4 each), cloisonné hair clips ($2.25 from $5.95), stuffed animals, sterling rings set with semiprecious stones (under $8), die-cast model sports cars ($13.80 a dozen), and a similar range of products shown in past mailings. "Plain-label food products with shelf lives of up to 10 years, also available in #10 cans: peanut butter powder, beans and rice, vegetable stew, green beans, corn, mashed potato granules, nonfat milk, etc."

Special Factors: PQ by phone or letter with SASE/ quantity discounts; min. order $25.

SEARS, ROEBUCK AND CO.; 925 S. Homan Ave.; Chicago, IL 60607; also 4640 Roosevelt Blvd.; Philadelphia, PA 19132 General Cat.: $4, ref./ **Save:** to 60% (see text)/ **Pay:** C, MO, SearsCharge **Sells:** clothing, furnishings, appliances, etc./ **Shop:** outlets nationwide

$$$$/ /

Comment: Does a direct-mail legend whose annual sales account for over 1% of the GNP really *need* an introduction? Your $4 brings you one of the Big Books (1,514 pages); there are 19 "Specialogs" that feature different lines.

Sample Goods: Everything imaginable, including the kitchen sink. Financial services, insurance, etc. Sales run on a frequent basis; sales catalogs sent to customers placing 2 orders of $30 or more every 6 months. Savings run to 60% during the sales; obtain Big Book and Specialogs (which can be ordered from the Big Book) as a guide to items featured in sales catalogs.

Special Factors: Specialogs available free of charge in Sears stores.

SPIEGEL, INC.; 1515 W. 22nd St.; Oak Brook, IL 60521
(800) 345-4500/ Cat.: $3, ref./ Save: to 50%/ Pay: C, MO,
AE, MC, V Sells: fashions, home furnishings, electronics/
Shop: also Chicago, Villa Park, Countryside, Arlington, Downers Grove, IL

$$$/ / ☎

Comment: The once-dowdy Spiegel catalog has been given a head-to-toe makeover and now sets the pace for fashion trends in middle America. Like Sears, it runs frequent sales and sends sales catalogs to recent customers.

Sample Goods: Stylish clothing and accessories for men, women, and children; up-to-date home furnishings and decorative accents; appliances and electronics. Le Creuset cookware, cashmere sweaters, Bally shoes, French lingerie, name-brand linens, custom window treatments, apartment-sized appliances, and toys among the offerings in a recent catalog.

Special Factors: Ordering from the "big book" helps ensure later mailings of sales catalogs.

WHOLE EARTH ACCESS; 2950 7th St.; Berkeley, CA 94710 (415) 845-3000/ Cat.: $7/ Save: to 60%/ Pay: C, MO, MC, V Sells: appliances, clothing, home maintenance supplies, etc./ Shop: same address; 401 Bayshore, San Francisco; 863 E. Francisco Blvd., San Rafael, CA; M–Sa 10–6, Su 11–5, all locations

$$$/ / ☎

Comment: The Whole Earth Access catalog is a 460-page general-store-by-mail that offers a wide range of goods chosen for performance and durability; savings run to 60% on some items. No affiliation with Stewart Brand's firms and publications. Est. in 1969.

Sample Goods: Items for food preparation, health, energy, outdoor living and recreation, gardening and homesteading, carpentry, and construction; products by Cuisinart, KitchenAid, Hamilton Beach, Henckels, Melior, Melitta, Vollrath, Wolf, and other firms; Levi's and Lee clothing, Oshkosh and Carhartt overalls, Frye and Timberline boots, water stills and filters, Fuchs brushes, Homelite chain saws, Aladdin oil lamps, Hunter ceiling fans, Sea Eagle inflatable rafts, Gerber sports knives, Celestron and Nikon optics, rototillers, hand and power tools, and books all available.

Special Factors: Sales flyers sent to customers; authorized returns accepted; min. order $20.

SEE ALSO:

HEALTH AND BEAUTY

Cosmetics, perfumes, and toiletries;
vitamins and dietary supplements;
and wigs and hairpieces.

You can save up to 90% on your cosmetic and beauty needs and still get the name brands featured in beauty emporiums and department stores. You can also save on imported luxury fragrances by importing them yourself, directly from France. And "copycat" scents are manufactured by three firms listed here—shop them all to see whose version comes closest to the real thing, and save up to 90% on the cost of the original.

Beauty comes from within, which is why you'll find firms selling vitamins and dietary supplements listed here. What you should take to augment your diet (if anything) is a question that's the focus of countless books and magazines. Many are fonts of unscientific advice and undocumented claims, and tend to pander to the universal fears of aging and cancer and the unrealistic belief that there's one product or exercise that can guarantee good health and sex appeal in 24 hours to 30 days.

For this reason, we can recommend no single publication. We advise you to research the topic that interests you thoroughly, in both popular "consumer" magazines and books and scientific or medical journals (bibliographies and abstracts of articles can be obtained through computer services). Don't miss the government pamphlets available through local departments of health and the common-sense health guides published by Consumers Union. Last but not least, consult a physician about specific health problems or before embarking on an experimental course of treatment for an existing condition.

For more firms selling related products, see the listings in "Medical and Scientific."

BEAUTIFUL BEGINNINGS; Spencer Building; Atlantic City, NJ 08411 (800) 222-0053/ Cat.: free/ Save: 50–85%/ Pay: C, MO, AE, MC, V Sells: cosmetics and toiletries/ Mail order only

$$$$/ ✉ / ☎

Comment: Beautiful Beginnings is a division of Spencer Gifts, which has been in business since 1947. The 80-page catalog packed with real buys on cosmetics, perfumes, and toiletries is published 3 times a year.

Sample Goods: Cosmetics, skin treatments, bath products, perfumes, etc., by Coty, Lanvin, Revlon, Frances Denney, Diane Von Furstenberg, Yves St. Laurent, Germaine Monteil, Jōvan, Village, Elizabeth Arden, Hermès, Stagelight, Dana, Scandia, Stendhal, Bonne Bell, Orlane, and others; grooming aids, vanity organizers, costume jewelry, and bath products for children.

Special Factors: Satisfaction guaranteed; returns accepted for refund or credit; min. order $2, $10 on credit cards.

BEAUTIFUL VISIONS, INC.; 810 Hicksville Rd., C.S. 4001; Hicksville, NY 11802-9877 Cat.: free/ Save: 40–85%/ Pay: C, MO, MC, V Sells: cosmetics and toiletries/ Mail order only

$$$/ ✉

Comment: Imagine hundred of name-brand beauty products —at up to 85% off list prices! The Beautiful Visions catalog, pub. every other month, offers almost 50 pages of beauty essentials from top manufacturers. Est in 1978.

Sample Goods: Cosmetics, skin-care products, perfumes, etc., by L'Oreal, Aziza, Barielle, Revlon, Almay, Lancôme, Elizabeth Arden, Vidal Sassoon, Jōvan, Courrēges, Dana, Max Factor, and other manufacturers; current fashion shades; surprise packages offered from $3.95 for a $15-plus value to $19.95 for an assortment worth $150.

Special Factors: Satisfaction guaranteed; returns accepted.

BEAUTY BUY BOOK; 65 E. SouthWater; Chicago, IL 60601 (312) 977-3740/ Cat.: free (1, 7, 9) Save: 30–90%/ Pay: C, MO, AE, MC, V Sells: cosmetics and toiletries/ Mail order only

$$$$/ ✉

Comment: Before paying top dollar for cosmetics and perfumes, see the 40-page, full-color Beauty Buy Book—you'll save up to 90%. Beauty Buy Book's parent company, GRI Corp., has been in business since 1958. Excellent service.

Sample Goods: Cosmetics, toiletries, perfumes, etc. by Prince Matchabelli, Max Factor, Germaine Monteil, Jōvan, Yves St. Laurent, Bonne Bell, Lancaster, Halston, Diane Von Furstenberg, Orlane, Yardley, Countess Isserlyn, Charles of the Ritz, Aziza, Rachel Perry, Elizabeth Arden, etc.; cosmetic sponges, powder puffs, cosmetic cases and vanity organizers, totes, atomizers, makeup brushes; surprise packages of cosmetics at 75% less than the regular retail prices.

Special Factors: Satisfaction guaranteed; returns accepted.

BEAUTY BY SPECTOR, INC.; McKeesport, PA 15134-0502 (412) 673-3259/ Cat.: free (quarterly)/ Save: to 50%/ Pay: C, MO, MC, V Sells: wigs and hairpieces/ Mail order only

$$/ / ☎

Comment: Beauty by Spector offers stylish wigs and hairpieces at savings of up to 50% on salon prices. Helpful sales staff; full-color catalog planned featuring designer styles for women, "unisex" styles, and "celebrity toupees." Est. in 1958.

Sample Goods: Wiglets, cascades, and falls ideal for dressy or special occasions; full wigs for women ranging from neat, softly curled heads to 24"-long "Showgirl"; hairpieces for men with thermal-conductive and mesh bases. Wigs and pieces made of frizz-free modacrylic fiber or human hair; available in a choice of 54 colors; items matched to closest shade if hair sample provided.

Special Factors: Inquiries may be made by phone between 8 and 10 P.M., EST.

ESSENTIAL PRODUCTS CO., INC.; 90 Water St.; New York, NY 10005-3501 (212) 344-4288/ PL & Sample Cards: free with SASE/ Save: to 90%/ Pay: C, MO, cert. check Sells: "copycat" fragrances/ Shop: same address; M–F 9–6, Sa (in Dec.) 10–4

$$$$/ ✉

Comment: "We offer our versions of the world's most treasured and expensive ladies' perfumes and men's colognes, selling them at a small fraction of the original prices." Reproductions of famous perfumes, marketed under the brand name "Naudet." Est. in 1895.

Sample Goods: 43 different copies of such costly perfumes as L'Air du Temps, Arpege, Opium, and Joy; 14 "copycat" colognes for men, from Aramis to Zizanie. A 1-oz. bottle of perfume is $18 (½ oz., $10.50); 4 oz. of any men's cologne cost $9. Sample cards give an idea of how closely the Naudet version replicates the original, but product should be tried by individual to evaluate properly.

Special Factors: Satisfaction guaranteed; returns accepted within 30 days for refund; min. order $18.

HARVEST OF VALUES; HILLESTAD CORP.; 1545 Berger Dr.; San Jose, CA 95112 (408) 298-0998/ Cat.: free (1 & 7)/ Save: 20–40%/ Pay: C, MO, MC, V **Sells:** nutritional supplements/ Mail order only

$$$$/

Comment: Get "factory-direct" prices on vitamins, minerals, and other supplements by ordering from the manufacturer. Complete label data included for most products. Est. in 1959.

Sample Goods: Multi-vitamin and mineral formulations for adults, chewable versions for children; vitamins E, A, C, and B-complex; a "stress" formula, chelated iron, bone meal, lecithin, and alfalfa; "Pick-A-Pill" cylinder with 7 compartments that dispenses your selection gumball-style ($11.49). Vitamin E cream with aloe vera ($2.95 for 2 oz.); pH-balanced cream rinse, conditioning shampoos, liquid "soapless" soap, and a biodegradable, phosphate-free cleanser for dishes, hand-washables, and general cleaning.

Special Factors: Satisfaction guaranteed; returns accepted within 30 days; all goods guaranteed against defects in manufacturing; shipping included.

PURITAN'S PRIDE, INC.; 105 Orville Dr.; Bohemia, NY 11716 (800) 645-1030/ Cat.: free/ Save: to 75%/ Pay: C, MO, MC, V Sells: nutritional supplements/ Mail order only $$$/ ✉ / ☎

Comment: You'll find hundreds of nutritional supplements in the 72 pages of the Puritan's Pride catalog, at prices up to 75% less than comparable products. Most listings include complete label disclosures. Est. in 1962.

Sample Goods: Vitamins, minerals, amino acids, natural diet aids, glandular extracts, and related miscellany—brewer's yeast, alfalfa tablets, herbal tea, ginseng, bee pollen—in a choice of potencies and formulations; synthetic and naturally derived supplements offered; most are free of starch and sugars. Special formulations for geriatric needs, stressful living, pets, children, men, women, and hair available. Toiletries, analgesic balms, thermometers, heating pads, electric foot massagers, and sphygmomanometers are also shown.

Special Factors: Satisfaction guaranteed; returns accepted; shipping included; min. order $12 on credit cards.

J. RICHELLE PARFUMS LTD.; 603 Bedford Ave.; Brooklyn, NY 11211 (718) 387-7961/ Broch.: free/ Save: to 90%/ Pay: C, MO, cert. check Sells: "copycat" fragrances/ Shop: by appt.

$$$/ ✉

Comment: Established in 1982, J. Richelle is one of the most recent entries in the flourishing "copycat" fragrance industry. If you like the house version as much as the genuine article, you'll save up to 90% by buying Richelle's product.

Sample Goods: Copies of Bal à Versaille, Chanel No. 5, Chloé, Halston, Joy, L'Air du Temps, Opium, Oscar de la Renta, Shalimar, Youth Dew, Anais Anais, Armani, First, and Ivoire for women; "interpretations" of Aramis, Eau Savage, Paco Rabanne, and Polo for men; $9.50 per ½-oz. bottle of women's perfume or 2 oz. men's eau de toilette; samples of the scents sold in sets of .75ml vials.

Special Factors: Satisfaction guaranteed.

STAR PHARMACEUTICAL, INC.; 11 Basin St.; Plainview, NY 11803 (800) 262-7827/ Cat.: free (1, 4, 6, 9)/ Save: to 60%/ Pay: C, MO, MC, V Sells: nutritional supplements, toiletries, and health products/ Mail order only

$$$/ ✉/ ☎

Comment: Star manufactures its own line of nutritional supplements, including many formula-equivalents of name-brand goods. Also OTC health products. Great buys. Est. in 1954.

Sample Goods: Vitamins for athletes, women, children, senior citizens, dogs, and cats; single vitamins and minerals, trace elements, formula-equivalents comparable to Theragran-Z, Micebrin-T, Chocks, etc.; national brands; toiletries, diet aids, pet grooming products, Celestial Seasonings teas; cold, cough, and allergy remedies; laxatives, deodorants, shaving products, contact-lens solutions, dentrifices, contraceptives, acne medications, bandages, sleeping pills, rubs and liniments, etc.; Clinistix and Glucose tablets; heating pads, oral thermometers, and sphygmomanometers.

Special Factors: Satisfaction guaranteed; returns accepted within 30 days; shipping included; min. order $15 on credit cards.

SUNBURST BIORGANICS; 838 Merrick Rd.; Baldwin, NY 11510 (800) 645-8448/ Cat.: free/ Save: 25–70%/ Pay: C, MO, MC, V **Sells:** nutritional supplements and toiletries/ Mail order only

$$$/

Comment: Sunburst, established in 1972, offers a complete line of vitamins, minerals, and other supplements marketed under the Sunburst label. Toiletries and many other health products shown in the 48-page catalog.

Sample Goods: Formula equivalents of standard name-brand vitamin/mineral supplements; Sunburst's exclusive formulations; pet vitamins, stress and geriatric formulas, etc. Products contain no sugar, starch, salt, or preservatives. Diet aids, creams and lotions, shampoo, loofahs, electric juice extractors, teas, candies, and other products available.

Special Factors: Satisfaction guaranteed; returns accepted within 30 days for refund or exchange; shipping included; min. order $15 on credit cards.

TULI-LATUS PERFUMES, LTD.; 146-36 13th Ave.; P.O. Box 422; Whitestone, NY 11357-0422 (718) 746-9337/ Broch.: free (2, 4, 7, 10)/ **Save:** to 86%/ **Pay:** C, MO, AE, MC, V **Sells:** ''copycat'' fragrances/ **Shop:** 136–56 39th Ave., Flushing, NY; M–F 9:30–4:30

$$$ ✉ / ☎

Comment: Tuli-Latus makes "exquisite renditions" of some of the world's finest, most expensive women's perfumes and men's colognes at up to 86% less than the cost of the original. Est. in 1971.

Sample Goods: 33 women's scents, including copies of Joy, Shalimar, L'Air du Temps, Chloé, Opium, Lauren, Ivoire, and Patou's "1,000." Men's scents, sold in perfume form, include versions of Russian Leather, Gucci For Men, and Guerlain's Le Mouchoir de Monsieur. Perfumes offered in a choice of bottles, including French glass and lead crystal with glass stoppers; refillable purse atomizers with funnel and pouch are $8. Biocare facial cream, lotion cleanser, and body lotion also available.

Special Factors: Perfumes boxed on request; returns of unused perfume accepted within 15 days for refund or credit; min. order $15 on credit cards.

VALRAY INTERNATIONAL, INC.; 739 N.E. 40th Ct.; Ft. Lauderdale, FL 33334-3037 (305) 563-8411/ Broch.: free/

Save: 20–70%/ Pay: C, MO, MC, V Sells: beauty products/
Mail order only

$$/

Comment: Valray markets "Rejuvenation" skin treatments
and cosmetics under its house label, Maximilian. The brochure
lists key ingredients in each product and recommendations for
use. Est. in 1975.

Sample Goods: Lotions, creams, and cleansers for mature
skin; some fortified with collagen and jojoba oil ($8–$13); "Scrub
Plus" cleanser for oily skin, facial masks for older skins, eye and
throat cream, wrinkle smoother, and bleaching cream; founda-
tion, powder, blush, lipstick, cover stick, mascara, and eyebrow
pencil. Priced 20–70% below comparable products.

Special Factors: Satisfaction guaranteed; returns accepted
within 30 days for refund or credit.

VITAMIN SPECIALTIES CO.; 8200 Ogontz Ave.; Wyncote,
PA 19095 (215) 885-3800/ Cat.: free/ Save: 40–60%/ Pay:
C, MO, MC, V Sells: nutritional supplements/ Shop: 19 other
locations in PA, NY, NJ

$$$/ /

Comment: Vitamin Specialties sells its own brand of vitamins,
minerals, dietary supplements, and nonprescription drugs for
40% to 60% less than the comparable name-brand products.
Good-quality products; 92-page catalog. Est. in 1948.

Sample Goods: Mega, multi, single, and "natural" vitamin
and mineral formulations in tabs, caps, syrups, sublingual tablets, and powder; special formulas for adolescents, senior citi-

zens, pregnant women, children, vegetarians, etc.; formula
equivalents of name brands; amino acids, RNA/DNA, natural
whole glandular products, and enzymes also offered. OTC remedies, including formula equivalents of name-brand products, featured at large savings; books on nutrition and health, pet vitamins, herbal tea, diet aids, toiletries, etc.

Special Factors: Returns of goods with unbroken seals accepted within 30 days; shipping included; min. order $15.

**WESTERN NATURAL PRODUCTS; 511 Mission St.; P.O.
Box 284; South Pasadena, CA 91030** (818) 441-3447/ Cat.:
free/ Save: 30–50%/ Pay: C, MO, MC, V Sells: nutritional
supplements/ Mail order only
$$$$/ 🖂 / ☎

Comment: Western Natural sells formula equivalents of
name-brand products for up to 50% less, and uses natural
sources for the ingredients. Est. in 1971.

Sample Goods: Formula equivalents of Theragran, Myadec,
Z-bec, Stress Tabs, One-A-Day, etc.; other vitamins, minerals,
enzymes, and dietary supplements; Nature's Gate products for
skin and hair; kelp, ginseng, pet vitamins, and more. Western's
"Plan 1" ($4.25 per 100) compares to Theragran ($11 or more
per 100); similar savings on other formula equivalents.

Special Factors: Satisfaction guaranteed; returns accepted;
shipping included on orders over $12.

SEE ALSO:

Dairy Association Co., Inc. . . . Bag Balm liniment . . .
   ANIMAL
Erewhon Mail Order . . . natural cosmetics and toiletries . . .
   FOOD
The Finals . . . small selection hair- and body-care products,
   vitamins . . . CLOTHING
Whole Earth Access . . . massagers, Fuchs brushes . . .
   GENERAL

HOME

Decor
Floorcoverings, wall and window treatments, lighting, upholstery materials, tools, and services.

Furnishings
Household furnishings of all types, including outdoor furniture; office furnishings, and services.

Kitchen
Cookware, bakeware, restaurant equipment, and food storage.

Linen
Bed, bath, and table textiles, accessories, and services.

Maintenance
Hardware, tools, equipment, supplies, and materials.

Table Settings
China, crystal, glass, flatware, woodenware, related goods and services.

Decor

Floorcoverings, wall and window treatments,
lighting, upholstery materials,
tools, and services.

**AMERICAN DISCOUNT WALLCOVERINGS; 1411 Fifth
Ave.; Pittsburgh, PA 15219** (800) 245-1768/ Info: PQ/
Save: 10–40%/ Pay: C, MO, MC, V Sells: wallcoverings, win-
dow treatments/ Shop: same address; M-F 9-5, Sa 9-1

$$/ / ☎

Comment: American Discount, est. in 1905, offers savings of
up to 40% on the best in decorator wall and window treatments
and upholstery fabrics. Samples of grass cloth, sold at to 50%
below list, are available upon request.

Sample Goods: Wallcoverings (discounted 15% to 20%) and
upholstery and decorator fabrics (discounted 10% to 20%) by
Advent, Artex, Birge, Comark, Decorator's Walk, Eisenhart,
Greeff, Imperial, Judscott, Laura Ashley, Marimekko, Quad-
rille, Sanitas, Scalamandre, Schumacher, United, Walltex, York,
Zumsteg, etc.; custom window treatments (discounted 25% to
40%) by Levolor, Del Mark, Joanna, Kirsch, Verosol, Nanik,
Flexalum, and Bali. Grasscloth and "string" wallpaper also
available.

Special Factors: PQ by phone or letter with SASE; all goods first quality; returns accepted within 20 days; request order form when obtaining price quote.

THE FABRIC CENTER; 519 Electric Ave.; Fitchburg, MA 01420 (617) 343-4402/ PL: free/ Save: 25–50%/ Pay: C, MO, MC, V Sells: decorator fabrics/ Shop: same address

$$$/ ✉ / ☎

Comment: The Fabric Center has been in business since 1933, selling fine fabrics to home decorators at savings of up to 50% on suggested list prices.

Sample Goods: Decorator fabrics for upholstery and window treatments by Covington, Schumacher (including Waverly Fabrics), John Wolf, Robert Allen, George Harrington, Andrea Dutton, Fabricade, Emmess, Paul Barrow, American Textile, etc.; price list includes roster of fabrics by selected manufacturers but represents a sample of what is stocked.

Special Factors: PQ by phone or letter with SASE.

GURIAN FABRICS INC.; 276 Fifth Ave.; New York, NY 10001 (800) 221-3477/ Broch.: $1/ Save: 40%/ Pay: C, MO, MC, V Sells: crewel fabric, accessories/ Shop: same address; M–F 9–5

$$$/ ✉ / ☎

Comment: Gurian stocks crewel fabric that is "handmade at the foot of the Himalayas in fabled Kashmir," as well as a selection of home accessories made from the embroidered cloth. Brochure includes decorating suggestions.

Sample Goods: Crewel fabrics worked in the stylized flower-and-vine designs of traditional patterns; multicolored, white-on-white, green/blue, brown/gold, red, and rust/gold color combinations. Embroidered on hand-loomed Indian cotton, 52″ wide; the fabric can be washed by hand or dry cleaned. Chair seats, pillow covers, tote bags, bedspreads, and tablecloths also available; samples of the fabric available for $1 each.

Special Factors: Quantity discounts on purchases of full bolts of fabric; satisfaction guaranteed; returns accepted within 15 days; min. order $25 on credit cards.

KING'S CHANDELIER COMPANY; P.O. Box 667; Eden, NC 27288 (919) 623-6188/ Cat: $2/ Save: to 50%/ Pay: C, MO, MC, V Sells: house-brand and Strass chandeliers/ Shop: same address, M–Sa 10–4:30

$$$/ ✉ / ☎

Comment: The Kings have been designing and producing chandeliers since 1935 and offer much of their stock in the 96-page catalog. There are designs to suit every taste and prices for all budgets.

Sample Goods: Chandeliers, candelabras, and wall sconces in a range of styles: Victorian, "Colonial," contemporary, and many variations on the classic lighting fixture dripping with prisms, pendalogues, faceted balls, and ropes of crystal buttons. Austere styles with brass arms and plain glass shades also available. Magnificent designs made of Strass crystal are offered as well. Options include different finishes on the metal parts, hurricane or candelabra tapers, candelabra or standard sockets, and candle or bulb bases. Individual and replacement parts stocked as well.

Special Factors: Satisfaction guaranteed; returns accepted within 5 days for refund or credit; min. order $15 on chandelier parts, $100 on credit cards.

LAMP WAREHOUSE/NEW YORK CEILING FAN CENTER; 1073 39th St.; Brooklyn, NY 11219 (718) 436-8500/ Info: PQ/ **Save:** 10–30%+/ **Pay:** C, MO, AE, MC, V **Sells:** lamps, ceiling fans/ **Shop:** same address; M, T, F 9–5:30, Th 9–5, Sa & Su 10–5

$$$/ /

Comment: The Lamp Warehouse was established in 1954 and is noted for its comprehensive inventory of lamps and lighting fixtures. A related concern, New York Ceiling Fan Center, offers name-brand ceiling fans at a discount.

Sample Goods: Lamps, lighting fixtures, and track lighting by Stiffel, Quoizel, American Lantern, and many other firms; ceiling fans by Casablanca and Hunter.

Special Factors: PQ by phone or letter with SASE; store closed Wednesdays.

N. PINTCHIK, INC.; 478 Bergen St.; Brooklyn, NY 11217 (718) 783-3333/ Info: PQ/ **Save:** to 40%/ **Pay:** C, MO, DC,

MC, V **Sells:** wall and floor finishes, treatments/ **Shop:** same address; also New York, NY

$$$/ ✉ / ☎

Comment: This firm was founded over 70 years ago by Nathan Pintchik and has become one of New York City's favorite sources for home-improvement items. City agencies, decorators, and countless do-it-yourselfers are all customers. Noted for special finishes and colors not available elsewhere.

Sample Goods: Over 2,000 wallpaper patterns; window treatments by Levolor, Louverdrape, and other firms; paint by Pratt & Lambert, Benjamin Moore, Pittsburgh Paints, Luminall, Emalj, Red Devil, etc.; flooring by Armstrong, Hartco, Kentile, Lees, etc. Paint color chips available upon request; custom wallpaper designs available, including logos; vertical shades can be laminated in fabrics or wallpaper.

Special Factors: PQ by phone or letter with SASE; returns accepted within 3 weeks; 20% restocking fee; institutional and commercial accounts welcomed.

ROBINSON'S WALLCOVERINGS; Dept. W-U; 225 W. Spring St.; Titusville, PA 16354 (814) 827-1893/ Cat. & Samples: 50¢/ Save: to 50%/ Pay: C, MO, AE, MC, V Sells: wallpaper, decorator fabrics/ **Shop:** same address

$$$/ ✉ / ☎

Comment: Robinson's went into business in 1919, and its catalog prices look as if they haven't risen much in the intervening years. Matching fabrics and home accessories have been added in the past few catalogs.

Sample Goods: Paper, scrubbable vinyl, and flocked wallcoverings; in patterns suitable for bathrooms, dining rooms, dens, bedrooms, nurseries, kitchens, etc.; all papers are pretrimmed, and most prepasted. Tools and supplies for hanging also offered. Complementary fabrics available for many wallpaper patterns; cabinets, lighting fixtures, and window treatments are also featured in the catalog.

Special Factors: Satisfaction guaranteed; returns accepted within 30 days; min. order $10 on credit cards.

SANZ INTERNATIONAL, INC.; P.O. Box 1794; High Point, NC 27261 (919) 883-4622/ Flyers: free/ Save: 30–90%/ Pay: C, MO, cert. check Sells: wallpaper, decorator fabrics/ Shop: other locations in NC

$$$/ ✉ / ☎

Comment: This firm, est. in 1977, is associated with The Hang It Now stores, Greensboro Wallcoverings, Wallpaper Now, and Interiors by Sanz. Decorator discounts of up to 90% are offered on a fine selection of wallcoverings and fabric.

Sample Goods: Wallcoverings and decorator fabrics by Greeff, Schumacher (including Waverly Fabrics), Brunschwig & Fils, Scalamandré, York Imperial, Color House, United, and 500 other firms; imported grasscloth available (request information and samples); furniture, lamps, carpeting, and other home furnishings also available through Sanz (inquire for information).

Special Factors: PQ by phone or letter with SASE; shipping included.

SHAMA IMPORTS, INC.; P.O. Box 2900; Farmington Hills, MI 48018 (313) 553-0261/ Broch.: free/ Save: 50%/ Pay: C, MO, MC, V Sells: crewel fabrics, home accessories/ Mail order only

$$$/ ✉ / ☎

Comment: Shama offers excellent prices on Indian crewel fabrics and home accessories, featured in the 8-page brochure, which also includes decorating suggestions.

Sample Goods: Crewel fabrics, hand-embroidered on hand-loomed cotton, in traditional serpentine flower-and-vine motifs; a range of colors and some distinctive designs are shown in the brochure. Background (unembroidered) fabric available by the yard, as well as crewel chair and cushion covers, tote bags, bedspreads, and tablecloths; all fabric is 52″ wide and can be washed by hand or dry cleaned. Samples available for $1 each; those showing ¼ of the complete pattern are $5 (ref.).

Special Factors: Satisfaction guaranteed; uncut, undamaged returns accepted within 30 days for refund or credit; quantity discounts on purchases of full bolts.

SHIBUI WALLCOVERINGS; P.O. Box 1638; Rohnert Park, CA 94928 (800) 824-3030/ Broch. & Samples: $2, ref./ Save: 50–60%/ Pay: C, MO, MC, V Sells: grasscloth, "natural" wallcoverings/ Mail order only

$$$/ ✉ / ☎

Comment: Shibui, which has been doing business by mail for over 20 years, sells fine wallcoverings made of natural materials

—jute, grasses, cork, leaves, etc. Cost of brochure and samples can be redeemed with order.

Sample Goods: Jute-fiber grasscloth, rush cloth, cork "foliage" papers, textured weaves, and linen wallcoverings; the cork papers feature boiled, bleached leaves applied to colored papers and create a dramatic effect. The textured weaves include several that look like linen, at a fraction of the price. All the papers are sold in triple-roll bolts (3′ × 36′); paperhanging tool kits and adhesives available as well.

Special Factors: Single and double rolls can be cut from regular bolts (not returnable); larger samples available upon request; satisfaction guaranteed; returns accepted within 30 days; shipping included.

WELLS INTERIORS INC.; 7171 Amador Plaza Rd.; Dublin, CA 94568 (800) 547-8982/ Cat., Color Card, PL: $4/ Save: to 60%/ Pay: C, MO, MC, V Sells: window treatments, accessories/ Shop: same address; 9 other locations in CA and OR

$$$$/ /☎

Comment: Wells Interiors guarantees "the lowest prices" on its goods and will beat any other dealer's price down to cost on a wide range of top brands. Prices run to 60% below retail, and the literature package includes the Kirsch "Window Shopping" book—128 pages of products and decorating ideas.

Sample Goods: Levolor's Riviera, Thrifty Custom, and vertical lines (in all fabrics, materials, colors, and options offered by Levolor); Louverdrape vertical blinds; Roc-Lon "sew-it-yourself" Roman insulated shades; Del Mar woven woods, Softlight shades, and metal blinds and verticals at 50% off; Kirsch drapery rods and hardware, woven woods, pleated shades, decorator roller shades, verticals, and mini-blinds all available, and new lines by the same firms.

Special Factors: PQ by phone or letter with SASE; shipping included on blinds up to 84″ long; written confirmation required on phone orders.

SEE ALSO:

S & C Huber, Accoutrements . . . floor cloths . . . GENERAL

Stuckey Brothers Furniture Co., Inc. . . . name-brand lamps, mirrors, clocks . . . HOME—Furnishings

Thai Silks . . . upholstery-weight silks . . . CRAFTS

Furnishings

Household furnishings of all types, including
outdoor furniture.

**BARNES & BLACKWELDER, INC.; 1804 Pembroke Rd.;
Greensboro, NC 27408** (800) 334-0234/ Broch.: free/ Save:
30–43%/ **Pay:** C, MO, cert. check **Sells:** furniture, wallcoverings, carpets/ **Shop:** same address; M–F 9–5, Sa by appt.
$$$/ ✉

Comment: John Barnes (of John Barnes Interiors) and Wayne
Blackwelder joined forces in 1972, bringing together many years
of experience in the furniture industry with marketing know-how. Inquiries taken over 800 line; brochure states the price-quote and payment terms. Interior designers on staff.

Sample Goods: Furniture, carpeting, rugs, and accessories
by Henredon, Drexel, Sligh, Hickory, American Drew, Ficks
Reed, Heritage, White of Mebane, Madison Square, Baker, Sherrill, Serta, Wildwood Lamps, Lee Woodard, Young Hinkle,
Thomasville, Century, Barcalounger, Herschede Clocks, Gulistan, Pande Cameron, Karastan, etc., at 40% to 43% off list;
fabrics and wallcoverings by Greeff, Brunschwig & Fils, Payne,
David & Dash, Clarence House, Lee/Jofa, Scalamandre, Schumacher, etc., at 30% below list; partial brands listing in brochure.

Special Factors: PQ by phone or letter with SASE; 30% deposit required; shipment by van or common carrier; file damages claims with hauler; B & B "will always accept final responsibility to insure that you will be another satisfied customer."

THE BEDPOST, INC.; 795 Bethel Rd.; Columbus, OH 43214 (614) 459-0088/ Cat.: $2.50/ Save: 20–50%/ Pay: C, MO, MC, V Sells: waterbed sets, bedroom furniture/ **Shop:** same address; M–F 10:30–9, Sa 10:30–6, Su 12–5

$$$/

Comment: You can save up to 50% on furnishings and accessories for bed and bath at The Bedpost, including a comprehensive selection of waterbed sets and equipment. Est. in 1979.

Sample Goods: Waterbeds and frames, liners, heaters, etc.; hot tubs, saunas, spas, bath equipment, bedroom furnishings, etc. Manufacturers include Bassett, Stanley, Burlington, America the Elegant, Broyhill, Trendwest, Pacific Frames, Avery, etc. Prices up to 50% below comparable retail or list; additional discounts on selected items.

Special Factors: PQ by letter.

BLACKWELDER'S INDUSTRIES, INC.; RR 12-390; Statesville, NC 28677 (800) 438-0201/ Cat. & Broch.: $5/ Save: 30–50%/ Pay: C, MO, MC, V Sells: home and office furniture, accessories/ **Shop:** Hwy. 21, Statesville; M–Sa 9–6

$$$$/

Comment: This firm, founded in 1938 to give the consumer access to fine furniture at fair prices, delivers value, selection, and service. Well-regarded; has a "club" discount program detailed in brochure; 10 catalogs available in addition to "master" catalog (ordering information in brochure).

Sample Goods: Home and office furnishings, grandfather clocks, pianos, Oriental rugs and carpeting, lamps, etc., by American of Martinsville, Bassett, Brown Jordan, Kittinger, Lane, Sligh, Thayer-Coggin, Dresher, Swann, Brass Bed of America, Chickering, Masson Hamil, Bösendorfer, Myrtle, Herman Miller, Pande Cameron, Karastan, Bigelow, Milliken, and many others; discounts of up to 50% and further savings through the "Share the Secret" plan. Well-priced house line of classic and contemporary leather-upholstered furniture.

Special Factors: PQ by phone or letter with SASE; shipment by van or common carrier; satisfaction guaranteed; returns accepted within 30 days; 20% restocking fee charged, applicable to subsequent purchase made within 90 days.

A BRASS BED SHOPPE; 12421 Cedar Rd.; Cleveland Heights, OH 44106 (216) 371-0400/ Cat.: free/ Save: 50%/ Pay: C, MO, AE, MC, V, Sells: brass and white-iron beds, waterbeds/ Shop: same address; Tu & Th 12–8, W, F, Sa 12–6, Su 1–5

$$$/ /

Comment: The black-and-white catalog from this firm showcases 20 bed styles, but the Shoppe stocks many more. Real savings of 50% on list prices; inexpensive waterbed systems and accessories also available. Est. in 1977.

Sample Goods: Brass and white-iron beds (headboard and footboard) in classic and contemporary designs; prices from $120 for a twin headboard ($232 for complete bed); all brass finished in baked epoxy. Catalog gives post diameters and headboard and footboard heights. "Flotation systems" (waterbed sets) with mattress, foundation, fill kit, water conditioner, and instructions offered; 15-year warranty. Waterbed frames free with purchase of headboard and footboard.

Special Factors: PQ by phone or letter with SASE; layaway plan available; parts and workmanship "guaranteed to meet with your satisfaction"; returns accepted.

CANNONDALE'S; Rte. 113 S., Drawer 1107; Berlin, MD 21811 (800) 522-1776/ Broch.: (1 & 6)/ Save: to 50%/ Pay: C, MO, MC, V **Sells:** brass and white-iron beds/ **Shop:** same address

$$$/ /

Comment: Cannondale's offers savings of up to 50% on brass and white-iron beds in traditional styles. Specify "brass" or "white iron" brochure when writing.

Sample Goods: Over 20 different bed designs in brass and white iron; all brass beds constructed of .032 gauge solid brass (no plate); most finished in baked epoxy, though some polished models are available. Prices from under $275 for complete brass beds; headboards available separately.

Special Factors: Satisfaction guaranteed; authorized returns accepted within 30 days; layaway plan available.

CHERRY HILL FURNITURE, CARPET & INTERIORS; P.O. Box 7045, Furnitureland Station; High Point, NC 27264 (800) 328-0933/ Cat.: $3, ref./Save: 40–50%/ Pay: C, MO, cert. check Sells: home and office furniture, accessories/ Mail order only

$$$$/ / ☎

Comment: A wide range of home and office furnishings, accessories, and rugs and carpeting is available here at prices that average 45% off list. The "Contract Division" serves the needs of developers, purchasing directors, architects, and others furnishing residential or commercial complexes. Est. in 1933.

Sample Goods: Office furnishings by Alma, Baker Contract, Condi, Cartwright, Hardwood House, Steelcase, Knoll, Vecta, etc.; floor coverings by Karastan, Lees, Pande Cameron, Bigelow, etc.; over 500 manufacturers of home furnishings and accessories represented as well. Request "Living with Drexel Heritage" catalog of decorating ideas or "Portfolio of Catalogs" showcase of lines by different manufacturers; $3 each, refundable. Listing of brands and ordering information free upon request.

Special Factors: PQ by phone or letter with SASE; inquiries accepted over 800 line; delivery by common carrier or van line.

EDGAR B. FURNITURE PLANTATION; P.O. Box 849; Clemmons, NC 27012 (800) 334-2010/ Cat.: $12/ Save: 35–40%/ Pay: C, MO, MC, V Sells: furniture and accessories/ Shop: Hwy. 158, Clemmons; M–F 9–6, Sa 9–2

$$$/ / ☎

Comment: The "B" here stands for Broyhill, the family of furniture fame that founded this company in 1979. It sells the Broyhill brand plus lines of furnishings by other manufacturers. A free brochure lists the brands.

Sample Goods: Furniture, accessories, wallcoverings, and decorator fabrics by 50 firms, including Thomasville, Henredon, Century, Davis, Hickory, Drexel, and others. Complete decorating services available.

Special Factors: PQ by phone or letter with SASE; delivery by common carrier or van line.

THE FURNITURE BARN OF FOREST CITY, INC.; P.O. Box 609, Bypass 74; Forest City, NC 28043 (704) 287-7106/ Brands List: free/ Save: 40–50%/ Pay: C, MO, MC, V, CHOICE Sells: home furnishings, bedding, accessories/ Shop: same address; M–Sa 10–6

$$$$/ ✉ / ☎

Comment: The Furniture Barn has been shipping fine furnishings nationwide since 1979 and is known for its prompt handling of orders and excellent delivery service.

Sample Goods: Furniture, bedding, and decorative accents by Lane, American Drew, Bassett, Bernhardt, Broyhill, Caro-Craft, Casa Bique, Clark Casual, D & F Wicker, Freeman & Co., National of Mt. Airy, Hickory Mfg. Co., Keller, Maddox, Park Place, Thomasville, Sligh, Stanley, Thayer Coggin, Young Hinkle, Tropitone, White of Mebane, etc. Brands list includes complete roster of manufacturers represented and terms of purchase.

Special Factors: PQ by phone or letter with SASE; shipment by van or common carrier; 33% deposit required.

MURROW FURNITURE GALLERIES, INC.; P.O. Box 4337; Wilmington, NC 28406 (800) 334-1614/ Broch.: free/ Save: 30–50%/ **Pay:** C, MO, MC, V **Sells:** home furnishings, bedding, accessories/ **Shop:** 3514 S. College Rd., Wilmington, NC

$$$$/ ✉ / ☎

Comment: Murrow was founded in 1979 and represents over 500 manufacturers (listed in the brochure). The extensive selection of brands and consistently good discounts make this one of the best furniture discounters around.

Sample Goods: Furnishings, bedding, and accessories by Thomasville, Drexel, White of Mebane, Baker, Henredon, Sligh, Hickory, Broyhill, Casa Bique, Dixie, Ficks Reed, National of Mt. Airy, Barcalounger, American Drew, LaBarge, John Widdicomb, Madison Square, Harden, Gilliam, Thayer Coggin, Wildwood Lamps, Stiffel, Link Taylor, Century, Stanley, Young Hinkle, Emerson Leather, Knob Creek, Tropitone, Greeff, Mobel, Stanton Cooper, etc. Delivery options and terms of sale detailed in brochure.

Special Factors: PQ by phone or letter; deposit required.

PLEXI-CRAFT QUALITY PRODUCTS CORP.; 514 W. 24th St.; New York, NY 10011 (212) 924-3244/ Cat.: $2/ Save: to 75%/ **Pay:** C, MO, MC, V **Sells:** acrylic furnishings, accessories/ **Shop:** same address; M–F 9:30–5, Sa 11–4

$$$/ ✉ / ☎

Comment: Plexi-Craft manufactures its own line of Lucite™ and Plexiglas™ goods, and its prices are up to 75% less than those charged in department and specialty stores for comparable products. New items are added constantly, and the firm handles custom work.

Sample Goods: Acrylic furnishings and accessories, including pedestals, cubes, telephone and computer stands, shelving, etageres, wine racks, bathroom fixtures, desk accessories, magazine racks, towel holders, albums, chairs, and occasional, coffee, and dining tables.

Special Factors: PQ by phone or letter with SASE on custom work.

QUALITY FURNITURE MARKET OF LENOIR, INC.; 2034 Hickory Blvd. S.W.; Lenoir, NC 28645 (704) 728-2946/ Brands List: free with SASE/ Save: to 50%/ Pay: C, MO, cert. check Sells: furnishings, bedding, accessories/ Shop: same address; M–Sa 8:30–5
$$$$/ 📧

Comment: Quality Furniture Market has been in business since 1954 and takes its name seriously; the brochure will invite you to check the firm's ratings with Dun and Bradstreet, the Lyons listing, and the Lenoir Chamber of Commerce. Excellent selection; prices are 15% to 20% over cost, compared to the usual 110% to 125%.

Sample Goods: Indoor and outdoor furniture, bedding, and home accessories by American Drew, Art Flo, Artisan Brass Beds, Barcalounger, Bassett, Brandt Cabinet Works, Broyhill, Burlington House, Emerson Leather, Flair, Gilliam, Grand Manor, Habersham Plantation, Henredon, Hekman, Drexel, Dresher, Miller Desk, Molla, Morris Greenspan Lamps, Sealy, Serta, Selig, Shoal Creek, Stanley, Swan Brass Beds, Tropitone,

Venture, Waverly Fabrics, Young Hinkle, and hundreds of other firms. Terms and other conditions are stated clearly in the brochure.

Special Factors: PQ by phone or letter with SASE; all orders prepaid before shipment; shipment by common carrier.

ROBERTS BRASS COMPANY; 24 Park Lane Rd.; New Milford, CT 06776 (203) 354-6142/ Cat: $1/ Save: to 40%/ Pay: C, MO, MC, V Sells: brass beds/ Shop: same address; M–Sa 10–5:30, Su 12–5

$$$$/ /

Comment: "We do not cover our products with artificial coatings!" proclaims the brochure from Roberts, which sells handsome traditional brass beds at prices up to 40% below those of comparable goods.

Sample Goods: The 6-page color catalog shows traditional brass beds, embellished with curving brass and ball finials, as well as some more restrained styles. All are made of solid brass and available in 4 standard sizes. Decorative options (different types of finials) available without cost on certain models. Complete beds sold with headboard, footboard, and steel side rails; headboards available separately as well.

Special Factors: Satisfaction guaranteed; returns accepted within 30 days if packed in original carton; layaway and installment purchase plans available.

JAMES ROY FURNITURE CO., INC.; 15 E. 32nd St.; New York, NY 10016 (212) 679-2565/ Brands List: free (quarterly)/ **Save:** 33% + / **Pay:** C, MO, MC, V **Sells:** home and office furnishings, bedding, carpeting/ **Shop:** same address; M–Sa 9:30–5:15

$$$$/ ✉ / ☎

Comment: James Roy offers you discounts of *at least* 33% on the suggested list prices of furnishings, bedding, and carpeting from over 200 manufacturers. Roy has been in business for over 25 years; professional service.

Sample Goods: Furnishings, accessories, bedding, and carpeting by Drexel, Henredon, Thayer Coggin, Broyhill, Lane, Stiffel, Heritage, Sealy, Thomasville, Simmons, Pennsylvania House, Stanley, and scores more; brochure includes a complete roster of brands represented, and terms and conditions of purchase.

Special Factors: PQ by phone or letter with SASE; credit cards accepted for payment of deposit only; final payments must be paid by C, MO, or cert. check.

SHAW FURNITURE GALLERIES; P.O. Box 576; Randleman, NC 27317 (800) 334-6799/ Broch.: free/ Save: 40% + / Pay: C, MO, MC, V Sells: furnishings/ Mail order only

$$$/ ✉ / ☎

Comment: The Shaw family has been selling furniture at a discount since 1940 and offers over 300 brands from which to choose. The brochure lists about half the manufacturers represented; inquire if you're pricing an item by a firm not mentioned, since it may be carried.

Sample Goods: Furnishings by American Drew, Bassett, Baker, Binswanger Mirrors, Brass Beds of America, Broyhill, Burlington, Butler, Carsons, Chaircraft, Council Craftsmen, Davis Cabinet, Directional, Dresher, Ficks Reed, Flexsteel, Gilliam, Hekman, Habersham Plantation, Henredon, Henry Link, Hickory, Hitchcock Chair, Link-Taylor, Madison Square, Pulaski, Ross, Selig, Sealy, Serta, Seth Thomas, Schoonbeck, Sherrill, Stanley, Stuart, Stiffel, Tropitone, White of Mebane, etc.

Special Factors: PQ by phone or letter with SASE; shipment by van or common carrier; min. order $100.

STUCKEY BROTHERS FURNITURE CO., INC.; Rte. 1, P.O. Box 527; Stuckey, SC 29554 (803) 558-2591/ Info: PQ/ Save: 30–40%/ Pay: C, MO, V Sells: indoor and outdoor furnishings, accessories/ Shop: same address

$$$/ ✉ / ☎

Comment: Stuckey is South Carolina's answer to High Point —it sells a full line of furniture and accessories at North Carolina prices, represents over 300 manufacturers, and has been doing business by mail since 1948.

Sample Goods: Furnishings and accessories by Hickory, Thomasville, Broyhill, Dixie, Stanley, Hekman, Ficks Reed, Fairfield, Drake Smith, Craftique, Madison Square, Nichols & Stone, Ridgeway Clocks, Singer, Stiffel, Thayer Coggin, Westwood Lamps, La-Z-Boy, Bassett, Serta, Sealy, American Drew, Lane, Samsonite, etc.; patio furniture by Finkel, Lyon-Shaw, Meadowcraft, Molla, Plantation Patterns, Tropitone, Winston, and Woodard is also featured. Nursery furnishings, clocks, lamps, mirrors, and bedding available.

Special Factors: PQ by phone or letter with SASE.

RICHARD P. ZARBIN AND ASSOCIATES; 225 W. Hubbard St.; Chicago, IL 60610 (312) 527-1570/ Info: PQ/ Save: 40%/ Pay: C, MO, cert. check **Sells:** furniture, bedding, carpeting/ **Shop:** same address; M–F 9–5, Sa 9–3

$$$/

Comment: The Zarbin family has been selling top furniture, bedding, and carpeting since 1969, and its reliable mail-order department offers you a hassle-free way to save 40% on the best in home decor.

Sample Goods: Full lines from Drexel, Directional, Baker, Century, Broyhill, Dixie, La Barge, Hickory, Gilliam, Thomasville, Lane, Harden, Stiffel, Flexsteel, Selig, American of Martinsville, Barcalounger, Henredon, Heritage, Henry Link, Link-Taylor, Karpen, Sealy, Salem, Lees, Galaxy, Monticello, Masland, and many others. Most goods shipped from manufacturers' warehouses to the trucker; deliveries within the Chicago area include uncrating and setup.

Special Factors: PQ by phone or letter with SASE; include manufacturer's name, item stock number, and fabric and grade numbers, if applicable.

SEE ALSO:

Business & Institutional Furniture Company . . . office, institutional furniture . . . OFFICE

Buy Direct, Inc. . . . computer furniture . . . OFFICE

Frank Eastern Co. . . . office furniture . . . OFFICE

The Gailin Collection . . . English solid cast-brass beds . . . HOME—Table Settings

Grayarc . . . small selection office chairs, work stations . . . OFFICE

Sanz International, Inc. . . . name-brand furnishings . . . HOME—Decor

Sierra Fitness Distributors . . . posture chairs . . . SPORTS

Irv Wolfson Company . . . small selection name-brand bedding, recliners, dinette sets . . . APPLIANCES

Kitchen

Cookware, bakeware, restaurant
equipment, and food storage.

**A COOK'S WARES; 3270 37th St. Ext.; Beaver Falls, PA
15010-1263** (412) 846-9490/ Cat.: $1 / Save: 20–50%/ Pay:
C, MO, cert. check, AE, MC, V Sells: cookware, kitchen uten-
sils/ Mail order only

$$$/

Comment: A Cook's Wares is run by two devoted cooks who
choose the best in cookware and food-preparation equipment
and sell it at savings of up to 50%. Informative catalog; many
hard-to-find items. Est. in 1981.

Sample Goods: Cookware lines by All-Clad, Le Creuset,
Leyse, Polarware, Spring Copper, Cuisinart, and Vollrath;
Mauviel hotel-weight copper pots and pans; bakeware by Pil-
livuyt, Isabelle Marique Blue Steel, and Chicago Metallic (Vil-
lage Baker and Bakalon). Cutlery and food-preparation equip-
ment featured, including Melitta coffee roasters, Peacock copper
and brass pot racks, Bron mandolines, Chambord infusion coffee
makers, Braun grinders and coffeemakers, J.K. Adams wooden
knife blocks, Taylor Woodcraft work tables and cutting boards,
Cuisinart food processors, and goods by Atlas, Mouli, Henckels,
Wusthof-Trident, F. Dick, Victorinox, DMT, Le Prix, William
Bounds, B. Waldow, Sparta, Cogebi, Mouli, and other firms.

Special Factors: Competitors' prices met; satisfaction guaranteed; returns accepted within 30 days.

FIVESON FOOD EQUIPMENT, INC.; 324 S. Union St.; Traverse City, MI 49684-2586 (800) 632-7342/ Cat.: free with 2-stamp SASE/ Save: 40%/ Pay: cert. check, MC, V Sells: commercial restaurant equipment/ Shop: same address; M–F 8–5:30

$$$/

Comment: Fiveson has been selling restaurant equipment to the food-service industry since 1937 and offers consumers the same products at an average of 40% below list prices.

Sample Goods: Pizza ovens, popcorn machines, commercial refrigerators and Garland ranges, Hobart (commercial) equipment, ice machines, Hamilton Beach bar mixers, Univex deli slicers and mixers, steam tables, griddles, Belgian waffle irons, coffee brewers, Libbey glassware, Pyrex and Corning china, food-storage units, and restaurant furnishings featured in past catalogs.

Special Factors: PQ by phone or letter with SASE.

KAPLAN BROS. BLUE FLAME CORP.; 523 W. 125th St.; New York, NY 10027-3498 (212) 662-6990/ Broch.: free with SASE/ Save: 50%/ Pay: C, MO, cert. check Sells: commercial restaurant equipment/ Shop: same address; M–F 8–5

$$$/

Comment: Kaplan Bros., est. in 1945, sells commercial restaurant equipment at 50% below list prices. The Garland brochure is sent on request; inquire for Kaplan's prices. Prompt service.

Sample Goods: Garland commercial stoves, including the popular 6-burner model (over $1,400 list, 50% off here); Garland fryers, ovens, griddles, salamanders, and other equipment. Used equipment available in the store.

Special Factors: PQ by phone or letter with SASE; have kitchen flooring, wall insulation, and exhaust system evaluated before ordering and upgrade before installation if necessary.

M.A. KNUTSEN INC.; P.O. Box 65095; West Des Moines, IA 50265 (515) 279-9075/ Broch. & PL: $2, ref./ Save: 30%/ Pay: C, MO, MC, V Sells: cookware, cutlery/ Shop: 504 Maple St., West Des Moines

$$$/ /

Comment: M.A. Knutsen offers savings of 30% on several lines of popular cookware and utensils. Many items seldom available at "sale" or discount prices. Est. in 1972.

Sample Goods: Complete lines of Cuisinart Stainless Cookware and Calphalon, including the Cuisinart food-preparation machines, attachments, and cookbooks; Wustof Trident knives, Baker's Advantage black steel bakeware, and other lines. Only first-quality goods offered.

Special Factors: Satisfaction guaranteed; returns accepted within 30 days for exchange, refund, or credit; min. order $20.

**PARIS INTERNATIONAL INC.; PARIS BREAD PANS; 500
Independence Ave. S.E.; Washington, DC 20003** (202)
544-6858/ **PL:** free/ **Save:** to 50%/ **Pay:** C, MO, cert. check
Sells: bakeware/ Mail order only

$$$$/ ✉ / ☎

Comment: Paris International sells bread pans designed by
owner Clyde Brooks; the pans compare to others sold for twice
as much and have been recommended in *The Cook's Catalogue*.
Other useful, well-priced baking equipment also available. Est.
in 1966.

Sample Goods: French bread pans of non-stick quilted aluminum (2 18″ double-loaf pans, $9.95); 18″ double-trough pans
($8) for Italian loaves, French bâtards, or San Francisco sour-
dough bread (comprehensive sourdough recipe and instruction
booklet included). "Whole Oven Baking Sheet" in 2 sizes for
standard and wall ovens, useful for large batches of cookies, etc.

Special Factors: Shipping, insurance included.

WORLD'S FARE; P.O. Box 5678; Smithtown, NY 11787
(800) 621-5199/ **Cat.:** free (1, 3, 9)/ **Save:** to 20%/ **Pay:** C,
MO, MC, V **Sells:** cookware, gifts/ Mail order only

$$/ ✉ / ☎

Comment: World's Fare, est. in 1968, publishes a 28-page
catalog of cookware and gourmet gifts. Reasonable prices; sale
items featured in each catalog.

Sample Goods: Copper kitchen accents and serving pieces,
aluminum stockpots, stainless fish poachers, mixing bowls, clay

bakers, wok sets, Atlas pasta machines, cappucino machines, mugs, molds, wine racks, and similar gourmet gifts and cookware shown in past catalogs.

Special Factors: Satisfaction guaranteed; returns accepted within 30 days; min. order $15 on credit cards.

SEE ALSO:

Bondy Export Corp. . . . . Farberware cookware . . .
   APPLIANCES
Chanute Iron & Supply Co., Inc. . . . . Insinkerator garbage
   disposers . . . HOME—Maintenance
Clothcrafters, Inc. . . . . dish towels, potholders, coffee filters,
   etc. . . . GENERAL
Erewhon Trading Co. . . . . cookware . . . FOOD
Landis House . . . Pfaltzgraff bakeware . . . HOME—Table
   Settings
The Mexican Kitchen . . . Mexican cookware . . . FOOD
Mr. Spiceman . . . cookware and kitchen gadgets . . . FOOD
Regal Greetings & Gifts, Inc. . . . . kitchen helpers . . .
   GENERAL
Robin Importers, Inc. . . . . name-brand kitchen cutlery, knife
   blocks, pepper mills, etc. . . . HOME—Table Settings
Simpson & Vail . . . tea-brewing utensils, teapots . . . FOOD
Spiegel, Inc. . . . . name-brand cookware . . . GENERAL
Sultan's Delight Inc. . . . . utensils for Mid-East cooking . . .
   FOOD
Whole Earth Access . . . name-brand cookware, kitchen
   appliances . . . GENERAL
Zabar's . . . name-brand counter appliances, cookware . . .
   FOOD

Linen

Bed, bath, and table textiles,
accessories, and services.

EZRA COHEN CORP.; 307 Grand St.; New York, NY 10002
(212) 925-7800/ Cat.: free/ Save: 25–60%/ Pay: C, MO, AE,
MC, V Sells: bed, bath linens/ **Shop:** same address; Su–F
8:30–5:30

$$$$/ ✉ / ☎

Comment: Cohen has been selling bed and bath linens for over
50 years. A catalog showing part of the inventory is published
for mail-order customers, but the full range of products may be
seen in the store.

Sample Goods: Bed linens by Wamsutta, Stevens, Martex,
Cannon, Burlington, and Springmaid; designer lines by Dior,
Katja, Laura Ashley, Bill Blass, etc.; towels by Fieldcrest, Martex, and Cannon; Northern Feather pillows, Dyne comforters,
Dakotah bedspreads, bath carpeting, and closet organizers also
available. Custom services offered: shams, bed ruffles, and sheets
for nonstandard mattresses.

Special Factors: PQ by phone or letter with SASE.

**THE COMPANY STORE INC.; 1205 S. 7th St.; La Crosse,
WI 54601** (800) 356-9367/ Cat.: free (1, 3, 8)/ Save: to 50%/
Pay: C, MO, AE, MC, V Sells: down-filled pillows, comforters/
Shop: same address; also Village of Plover, Oshkosh, Eau
Claire; and Red Wing, MN

$$$/ ✉/ ☎

Comment: The Company Store, factory outlet of Gillett In-
dustries, publishes a 20-page catalog of well-priced down bed-
ding and a range of linen. Top quality, excellent selection,
prompt service. Parent firm est. in 1911.

Sample Goods: Box, channel, and ring-stitched down com-
forters; crib-sized and spring-weight comforters; down-filled
mattress pads, etc. High loft power, down-proof materials, and
hand-guided quilting among the product features. Complement-
ing pillows in baby/boudoir, butterfly, neckroll, Continental,
standard, queen, and king sizes and shapes also available; vinyl
storage bags, duvets, shams, bed ruffles, and related items of-
fered. Down-filled robes, jackets, and coats by Gloria Vanderbilt
and Bill Blass shown as well.

Special Factors: PQ by phone or letter with SASE; custom
services available; satisfaction guaranteed; returns accepted.

**THE DOWN OUTLET; Pine St. Extension; P.O. Box 451;
Nashua, NJ 03060** (603) 883-9024/ Broch.: free/ Save: 25–
35%/ Pay: C, MO, MC, V Sells: down-filled comforters, outer-
wear/ Shop: same address; also 156 Ridge St., Freeland, PA;
638 Quekuechan St., Fall River, MA

$$$/ ✉/ ☎

Comment: The Down Outlet manufactures its high-quality comforters (under the "Nimbus" label) and down-filled outerwear at savings of to 35% of the retail prices.

Sample Goods: Down-filled comforters in twin, full/queen, and king sizes; 2 fills for normal and chilly sleeping environments; channel construction, down-proof cotton covers, hardwearing piped edges featured. Zippered poly/cotton duvets available, also at savings. Down-filled vests, Taslan pullovers, heavy-duty parkas stocked in several colors and sizes.

Special Factors: Comforters guaranteed for 10 years against defects in construction and workmanship; satisfaction guaranteed; returns accepted within 30 days for exchange, refund, or credit.

DREAMY DOWN FASHIONS, INC.; 287 W. Butterfield Rd., Suite 175; Elmhurst, IL 60126 (312) 941-3840/ Broch.: free/ Save: 45–55%/ Pay: C, MO, AE, MC, V Sells: down-filled bedding/ Mail order only

$$/ ✉ / ☎

Comment: Dreamy Down sells luxury-grade comforters, pillows, and bed linens at an average of 45% below prices charged for name-brand goods of comparable quality. Handsome 12-page color catalog; several unique lines.

Sample Goods: "Elan" comforter filled with white goose down, 550-plus fill power, all-cotton down-proof cover, corded edges ($249 compared to $390); "Aristocrat," filled with duck down, 450-plus fill power, box-stitched; several other styles in different fills, fill powers, colors, etc. Feather beds, lambswool mattress covers, pillows, shams, and a wide range of duvets offered. Dramatic hand-painted duvet covers a notable offering. Tips on comforter use and care given in catalog.

Special Factors: All comforters warrantied 3–10 years; satisfaction guaranteed; returns accepted within 30 days.

ELDRIDGE TEXTILE CO.; 277 Grand St.; New York, NY 10002 (212) 925-1523/ Info: PQ/ Save: 30–40%/ Pay: C, MO, MC, V Sells: bed, bath, table linens/ Shop: same address; Su–F 9–5:30

$$$/ / ☎

Comment: Eldridge has been selling soft goods and housewares since 1939, and offers savings of 30% to 40% on top brands. Other home decor lines are sold in the store.

Sample Goods: Bed, bath, and table linens by Cannon, Fieldcrest, Martex, Dakotah, Jabara, Utica, Sunweave, Springmaid, Croscill, Dan River, Crowncrafts, Wamsutta, Curtron, Burlington, Howard, Jackson, Saturday Knight, etc. Wallpaper and window treatments also available at the store.

Special Factors: PQ by phone or letter with SASE; returns accepted on unused goods for refund or credit.

HARRIS LEVY; 278 Grand St.; New York, NY 10002 (800) 221-7750/ Info: PQ/ Save: 25–40% Pay: C, MO, MC, V Sells: bed, bath, table linens/ Shop: same address; Su–Th 9–5:30, F 9–4:30

$$$/ / ☎

Comment: Levy is one of the plums of New York City's Lower East Side—a firm that sells the creme de la creme of bed, bath, and table linens at savings to 40%. One-of-a-kind and imported items available in the store.

Sample Goods: Egyptian percale and linen sheets; Belgian crash towels; Irish damask tablecloths; bed coverings from Switzerland, England, France, and Italy. Goods for bed and bath by major mills: Springmaid, Dan River, Martex, Wamsutta, Fieldcrest, Burlington, Stevens, etc. Levy's is known for its custom services: monogramming, special sheet sizes and shapes, tablecloths, dust ruffles, curtains, pillow cases, etc., in sheeting or your own fabric.

Special Factors: PQ by phone or letter with SASE; min. order $15 on credit cards.

RUBIN & GREEN INC.; 290 Grand St.; New York, NY 10002 (212) 226-0313/ Info: PQ/ Save: 30–40%/ Pay: C or MO Sells: bed, bath, table linens/ Shop: same address; Su–F 8:30–5:15

$$$/

Comment: Rubin & Green discounts a wide selection of bed, bath, and table linens by major mills 30% to 40% off list prices. Discontinued lines offered at special savings in the store.

Sample Goods: Bed, bath, and table linens by Wamsutta, Burlington, Martex, Springmaid, Bates, etc.; bath carpeting by Carter; shower curtains by Bloomcraft and Ames; Faribo blankets; comforters, napkins, tablecloths, and other goods.

Special Factors: PQ by phone or letter with SASE; min. order $5.

J. SCHACHTER CORP.; 115 Allen St.; New York, NY 10002
(212) 533-1150/ Cat.: $1, ref./ Save: 20–50%/ Pay: C, MO,
MC, V **Sells:** down-filled bedding, linens/ **Shop:** same address; Su–F 9–4:30

$$$/ ✉ / 🎀

Comment: Schachter has been making comforters and pillows
for the bedding industry and recovering old comforters for pri-
vate customers since 1919. Custom work is featured in the 16-
page catalog, but finished goods also available.

Sample Goods: Custom-made comforters, coverlets, bed
ruffles, pillow shams, duvets, and shower curtains. Filling
choices for comforters include lambswool, polyester, white goose
down, and a nonallergenic synthetic down alternative. Sheets
from Wamsutta, Cannon and Martex bath linens, Carter cotton
bath rugs, Northern Feather pillows, Dyne comforters, Hudson
Bay blankets, goods by Dan River, Schachter's own stock com-
forters and accessories, and related goods also available.

Special Factors: PQ by phone or letter with SASE. Min.
order $35 on credit cards.

**SHORLAND TEXTILE CO.; 274 Grand St.; New York, NY
10002** (212) 226-0228/ Info: PQ/ Save: 25–40%/ Pay: C,
MO, MC, V **Sells:** bed, bath, table linens/ **Shop:** same ad-
dress; Su–F 9–5

$$$/ ✉

Comment: Shorland has been selling linens for 63 years and offers a wide range of products by the major mills at savings to 40%. Specials and discontinued lines featured in the store.

Sample Goods: Bed, bath, and table linens by Fieldcrest, Springmaid, Martex, Wamsutta, Dan River, and other major manufacturers.

Special Factors: PQ by phone or letter with SASE; returns accepted on unused goods for refund or credit.

SEE ALSO:

Clothcrafters, Inc. . . . cotton placemats and napkins, flannel sheets, towels, shower curtains . . . GENERAL

Gohn Bros. . . . sheets, blankets, towels . . . CLOTHING

Gurian Fabrics Inc. . . . crewel bedspreads, tablecloths, etc. . . . HOME—Decor

Quilts Unlimited . . . antique, old, custom-made quilts . . . ART, ANTIQUES

Robin Importers . . . Carefree table linens . . . HOME—Table Settings

Rubens Babywear Factory . . . bassinet, crib sheets . . . CLOTHING

Shama Imports, Inc. . . . crewel bedspreads, tablecloths, etc. . . . HOME—Decor

Thai Silks . . . embroidered Chinese table linens . . . CRAFTS

Whole Earth Access . . . wool blankets, down comforters . . . GENERAL

Irv Wolfson Company . . . foreign-current electric blankets . . . APPLIANCES

Workmen's Garment Co. . . . small selection Cannon, generic bath and dish towels . . . CLOTHING

Maintenance

Hardware, tools, equipment, supplies, and materials.

ARCTIC GLASS SUPPLY, INC.; Rte. 1-N, Box 157; Spring Valley, WI 54767 (715) 639-3762/ Cat.: $2, ref./ Save: 40–60%/ Pay: MO, cert. check, MC, V Sells: insulated glass panels/ Shop: outlets in WI and MN; hours in Spring Valley by appt.

$$$$/

Comment: When Joseph Bacon found that second-quality patio door panels doubled perfectly as passive solar panels in the greenhouse he was building, and were over 60% less expensive, he turned the solution into a business venture. Specs and detailed information in literature. Est. in 1979.

Sample Goods: Martin and Anderson patio door panels; double and triple panes with ¼" air spaces; panels with ½" air spaces sometimes available; glass is ³⁄₁₆" thick and panes are double-sealed. Flaws do not affect performance of panes. Suitable applications listed in brochure.

Special Factors: All panels guaranteed against leakage or failure for 10 years; installation instructions, including retrofitting, included in literature; quantity discounts available.

CHANUTE IRON & SUPPLY CO., INC.; 402 N. Malcolm; Chanute, KS 66720 (316) 431-9290/ Info: PQ/ Save: 25–50%/ Pay: C, MO, cert. check **Sells:** plumbing supplies, fixtures/ **Shop:** same address

$$$/ ✉

Comment: Chanute stocks a full range of fixtures and equipment for plumbing, heating, and air conditioning. A portion of the inventory is available by mail, at savings that should inspire do-it-yourself remodeling efforts. Est. in 1941.

Sample Goods: Plumbing supplies, fixtures, and tools, including Delta faucets, Insinkerator garbage disposers, Wayne pumps, Miami Carey medicine chests and accessories, Aqua Glass whirlpools and Owens Corning fiberglass tubs and showers, Crane fixtures, swimming pool supplies and chemicals, tools by Rigid and Kline, and the professional line of tools by Black & Decker. Replacement parts for all types of faucets also stocked.

Special Factors: PQ by phone or letter with SASE.

PLASTIC BAGMART; 400 Maple Ave.; Westbury, NY 11590 (516) 997-3355/ PL: free/ Save: 40–60%/ Pay: C, MO, cert. check **Sells:** plastic bags/ **Shop:** same address

$$$/ ✉

Comment: The BagMart offers plastic bags in sizes most frequently used in homes, offices, and industry. Savings run up to 60% on the prices charged for smaller lots in supermarkets and variety stores. Est. in 1980.

Sample Goods: Plastic bags in sizes from 2″ × 3″ to 43″ × 46″, ¼ mil thick; garbage and trash cleanup bags, kitchen and office wastecan bags, food-storage bags, large industrial-type bags, zip-top styles, plastic shopping bags, etc. Case lots only (100–1,000 bags per case).

Special Factors: PQ by letter with SASE; satisfaction guaranteed; returns accepted within 15 days.

PROTECTO-PAK; P.O. Box 5096; Longview, TX 75608
(214) 297-3985/ PL & Samples: $2, ref. (6 & 12)/ Save: 35%/ Pay: C or MO Sells: zip-top plastic bags/ Mail order only

$$$/

Comment: Protecto-Pak, est. in 1983, offers plastic zip-top bags at savings that average 35% below comparable retail. Their uses are almost endless, and they're great space-savers if storage is limited.

Sample Goods: Zip-top, heavy-duty plastic bags from 2″ × 3″ to 13″ × 15″; seal makes them relatively watertight. Suggested uses: storing crafts supplies, spare parts from kits, polished silverware (wrapped in cloth), buttons and surplus trim for different garments, tobacco, daily doses of medications and dietary supplements, office supplies, photographs, hosiery and clothing in luggage and drawers, hardware, jewelry, etc. Special sizes, thicknesses available; printing services (minimum 10,000). All bags approved for food storage.

Special Factors: PQ by letter with SASE; quantity discounts available; min. order $10.

THE RENOVATOR'S SUPPLY, INC.; 5503 Renovator's Old Mill; Millers Falls, MA 01349 (413) 659-3773/ Cat: $2; $5, 3 yrs. (1, 5, 7, 9, 11)/ Save: to 70%/ Pay: C, MO, MC, V Sells: reproduction hardware, fixtures/ Shop: same address; also Danvers, Brookline, Sturbridge, Plymouth, MA; Darien, CT; Albany, Utica, NY; Flemington, Cherry Hill, NJ; Providence, RI

$$$/ ✉ / ☎

Comment: Your $2 (or $5 for a full three years of issues) will bring you "America's most irresistible home decorator discount catalog," 48 color pages of hardware, fixtures, and accessories for period homes. Excellent selection of hard-to-find reproduction items; est. in 1978.

Sample Goods: Iron, brass, and porcelain bath hardware and plumbing fixtures; oak bathroom accessories; drawer, window, and door hardware of every era; brass, porcelain, and iron; lighting fixtures of every sort; glass lamp shades; wall plates; copper lanterns and weathervanes; wrought-iron door knockers and latches, hinges, screws, sash hardware, bolts, fireplace tools, grills, candle holders, etc.; tin and copper matchboxes, pierced tin lampshades, brass candlesticks, replacement leather chair seats, etc.

Special Factors: Shipping included on orders over $20; quantity discounts available; satisfaction guaranteed; returns accepted within 30 days.

SOUTHEASTERN INSULATED GLASS; 6477 Peachtree Ind. Blvd.; Atlanta, GA 30360 (404) 455-8838/ Cat: $1, ref./ Save: 50%/ Pay: C, MO, MC, V Sells: insulated glass panels/ Shop: same address; M–F 7–5

$$$/ ✉ / ☎

Comment: Southeastern manufactures insulated (thermopane) glass panels and skylights and can sell them to you at factory-direct prices of 50% below list. Complete specs are given in the literature. Est. in 1975.

Sample Goods: Insulated glass panels, to 46″ × 90″, in ⅛″ tempered glass with ⅓″ air spaces; sold sealed and unframed. Applications include greenhouses, grow frames, porch enclosures, storm windows, etc. Skylights sold completely assembled in aluminum frames. Plain and bronze-tinted glass available; butyl flashing tape, glazing tape, butyl caulking compound, and setting blocks stocked.

Special Factors: Installation details for specific applications included in literature; terms of warranty stated as well.

SEE ALSO:

AAA All Factory, Inc. . . . vacuum cleaners, floor machines, rug shampooers, ceiling fans . . . APPLIANCES

ABC Vacuum Cleaner Warehouse . . . vacuum cleaners . . . APPLIANCES

Alfax Mfg. . . . trash-can liners . . . OFFICE

American Vacuum & Sewing Machine Corp. . . . vacuum cleaners, supplies . . . APPLIANCES

The Bedpost, Inc. . . . hot tubs . . . HOME—Furnishings

Bondy Export Corp. . . . vacuum cleaners . . . APPLIANCES

Clothcrafters, Inc. . . . mosquito netting, flannel polishing cloths . . . GENERAL

Grayarc . . . trash bags, wipes, door mats, etc. . . . OFFICE

Greater New York Trading Co. . . . vacuum cleaners . . . HOME—Table Settings

Great Tracers . . . custom-made name stencils . . . CRAFTS

Mid America Vacuum Cleaner Supply Co. . . . vacuum cleaners, floor machines, parts, attachments; small appliance parts . . . APPLIANCES

Table Settings

China, crystal, glass, flatware, woodenware, and related goods.

**A. BENJAMIN & CO., INC.; 80-82 Bowery; New York, NY
10013** (212) 226-6013/ Info: PQ/ Save: 25–75%/ Pay: C,
MO, cert. check **Sells:** tableware, giftware/ **Shop:** same address; M–Sa 8–4 (closed Sa July & Aug.)
$$$/

Comment: A. Benjamin has been selling top brands in china, stemware, flatware, and giftware since 1944. Diamonds and jewelry are sold in the store, but not by mail. Savings of up to 75% are available.

Sample Goods: China, stemware, flatware, and giftware by Noritake, Mikasa, Franciscan, Coalport, Gorham, Reed & Barton, Wallace, Lunt, International, Oneida, Towle, Supreme, etc. Stock includes current lines and discontinued patterns and styles.

Special Factors: PQ by phone or letter with SASE; mention this book when calling or writing; min. order $50 on some types of goods.

EMERALD; 184 High St.; Boston, MA 02110 (617) 423-7645/ Cat: free/ Save: to 50%/ Pay: C, MO, AE, MC, V Sells: Irish collectibles, handcrafts/ Mail order only

$$$/ ✉

Comment: This well-known Irish firm, actually located in Ballingeary, County Cork, has order-processing arrangements with an agent in the U.S. Prices are up to 50% less than those charged by U.S. firms. Est. in 1963.

Sample Goods: Waterford crystal stemware and giftware; extensive selection Belleek tableware and giftware; Wedgwood and Royal Doulton tableware and gifts, including Beatrix Potter figurines, Bunnykins, and Peter Rabbit lamps and table settings; Aynsley's Teddleybears nurseryware; figurines by Goebel, Border Fine Arts, Royal Doulton, Irish Dresden, Lladro, Belleek, and Hummel; walking sticks and other authentic Irish handcrafts. Membership in the "Collectors' Club" includes newsletters with special offers, advance catalog mailings, and discount coupons ($10 fee).

Special Factors: Orders sent from Ireland; dutiable goods charged duty upon delivery; satisfaction guaranteed, authorized returns accepted; min. order $20 on credit cards.

FORTUNOFF; DIRECT SALES DIVISION; P.O. Box 1550; Westbury, NY 11590 (800) 344-3449/ Cat.: $1/ Save: to 50%/ Pay: C, MO, AE, DC, MC, V Sells: jewelry, table settings/ Shops: M–W 10–6, Th 10–8, F & Sa 10–6; Su 12–5; also New York, NY; Paramus, Wayne, NJ

$$$/ ✉/ ☎

Comment: Fortunoff, while known for its stupendous selection of estate and contemporary jewelry, features fine tableware at sale prices year 'round. Great prices on sterling flatware.

Sample Goods: Flatware, from stainless to sterling, by C. J. Vander, Oneida, Towle, Reed & Barton, Kirl-Stieff, Lunt, International, etc.; china, crystal, and giftware by top manufacturers also stocked. Stores carry wide selection of other goods, including patio furniture, leather goods, decorative accents for the home, linens for bed and bath, organizers, and similar items.

Special Factors: PQ by phone or letter with SASE.

THE GAILIN COLLECTION; P.O. Box 53921; Fayetteville, NC 28305 (800) 334-5698/ Cat.: free/ Save: 35–55%/ Pay: C, MO, MC, V **Sells:** table settings, brass beds/ Mail order only

$$/ ✉ / ☎

Comment: "Nobody in the country can match our prices" on English and French china and crystal and Strass chandeliers from Germany, says Gailin. This purchasing agent places orders with European suppliers, who ship goods directly to consumers. Est. in 1982.

Sample Goods: China by Coalport, Aynsley, Crown Staffordshire, Royal Crown Derby, Minton, Spode, Royal Worcester, Wedgwood, and Limoges (Haviland, Raynaud, Bernardaud, and Parlon); crystal by Baccarat, St. Louis, Waterford, Edinburgh, and Stuart. Strass crystal chandeliers and reproduction antique English brass beds (lacquered finish) are also offered.

Special Factors: Bridal registry, locator (for items not normally listed by Gailin), and replacement (for discontinued patterns and suites) services available; duty charged; customs-clearing service available; min. order varies on different services and lines of items ($200 on credit cards).

GREATER NEW YORK TRADING CO.; 81 Canal St.; New York, NY 10002 (212) 226-2809/ Brands List: free with SASE/ **Save:** 20–60%/ **Pay:** C, MO, cert. check **Sells:** tableware, giftware, appliances/ **Shop:** same address; M–F 10–6, Su 10–5

$$$/

Comment: Greater New York Trading has flourished on the trade of shrewd New Yorkers, who know a discount when they see one. In business for over 50 years, it's known for great buys on fine tableware.

Sample Goods: China by Aynsley, Bernardaud Limoges, Franciscan, Ginori, Lenox, Hutschenreuther, Mikasa, Minton, Portmeiron, Rosenthal, Spode, Royal Copenhagen, Royal Doulton, Royal Worcester, Wedgwood, etc.; crystal stemware and gifts by Avitra, Baccarat, Val St. Lambert, Galway, Kosta Boda, Stuart, Orrefors, etc.; flatware (stainless, plate, and sterling) by Christofle, Kirk-Stieff, Lunt, Oneida, Towle, Gorham, Tuttle, Wallace, Reed & Barton, Georg Jensen, International, Rogers, etc.; figurines and collectibles by Royal Doulton and Lladro also featured. Large and small appliances, TVs, typewriters, and vacuum cleaners by Hotpoint, G.E., Frigidaire, Amana, Tappan, KitchenAid, Panasonic, RCA, Toshiba, Sylvania, SCM, Olivetti, Adler, Hermes, Hoover, Eureka, and other manufacturers also available.

Special Factors: PQ by phone or letter with SASE; min. order on certain items.

LANDIS HOUSE; 132 E. Main St.; Palmyra, PA 17078 (717) 838-6134/ Broch.: $1, ref./ **Save:** 20–39%/ **Pay:** C, MO, MC, V **Sells:** Pfaltzgraff tableware and giftware/ **Shop:** same address

$$/ / ☎

Comment: You'll find Pfaltzgraff's complete line of tableware and gifts here at a flat 20% off list prices, year 'round (up to 39% off dinnerware bought in sets, compared to prices on individual pieces). The $1 fee brings you an assortment of manufacturer's brochures and information.

Sample Goods: Pfaltzgraff stoneware dinnerware, glassware, serving pieces, bakeware, and accessories and decorative pieces. A range of patterns inspired by Americana (yelloware, quilt motifs, salt-glaze crocks, etc.), plus the handsome all-white "Heritage." Hand-applied designs and glazes; all stoneware is chip-resistant and safe in dishwasher, microwave oven, and conventional oven. All pieces warranted by Pfaltzgraff against defects in workmanship or materials for 1 year.

Special Factors: Satisfaction guaranteed; min. order $15 on credit cards.

ROBIN IMPORTERS, INC.; 510 Madison Ave.; New York, NY 10022 (800) 223-3373/ Broch.: free with SASE/ **Save:** 20–60%/ **Pay:** C, MO, AE, DC, MC, V **Sells:** tableware, giftware, kitchenware/ **Shop:** same address; M–F 9:30–5:45, Sa 10–5

$$$$/ / ☎

Comment: Robin carries an exhaustive stock of tableware, kitchenware, and table and kitchen linens at prices to 60% below list—even lower if an item or line is being discontinued. Color brochures show examples of the inventory, but no prices are listed.

Sample Goods: China by Adams, Arabia, Arita, Arzberg, Bernardaud Limoges, Block, Coalport, Denby, Fitz and Floyd, Franciscan, Heinrich, Mikasa, Rauchart, Rosenthal, Spode, Villeroy & Boch, etc.; crystal from Sasaki, Orrefors, Kosta Boda, Daum, Lalique, Baccarat, Iittala, Waterford, Galway, Atlantis, Val St. Lambert, etc.; flatware by Yamazaki, Dalia, Georgian House, Gorham, Henckels, International, Lauffer, Lunt, Oneida, Stanley Roberts, Towle, Supreme Cutlery, Wallace, W.M.F. Fraser, etc. Lladro figurines, Sadek bakeware, cutlery by Sabatier, Henckels, Wustof Trident, etc., and Carefree table linens also available.

Special Factors: PQ by letter with SASE; 800 line for orders only.

ROGERS & ROSENTHAL, INC.; 105 Canal St.; New York, NY 10013 (212) 925-7557/ PL: free with SASE/ Save: to 65%/ Pay: C or MO Sells: tableware/ Shop: same address $$$/

Comment: Rogers and Rosenthal are two old names in silverware and china and represent the business of this firm: the best in table settings, at to 65% below list prices.

Sample Goods: China, crystal, glassware, and flatware (stainless, plate, and sterling) by top manufacturers, including International, Gorham, Towle, Reed & Barton, Wallace, and Lunt.

Special Factors: PQ by phone or letter with SASE.

RUDI'S POTTERY, SILVER & CHINA; 178A Rte. 17 N.; Paramus, NJ 07652 (800) 631-2526/ Broch.: free (5 & 9)/ Save: 20–60%/ Pay: C, MO, MC, V Sells: tableware/ Shop: same address

$$$/

Comment: Rudi's has been in business for 20 years and in that time has built its inventory to include some of the finest goods available, at savings of up to 60% on list prices.

Sample Goods: China, stemware, and flatware by Gorham, Lunt, Towle, Wallace, International, Kirk-Stieff, Waterford, Bucellati, Lenox, Royal Doulton, Spode, Baccarat, Tiffin, Val St. Lambert, Christofle, Galway, Mikasa, Orrefors, Kosta Boda, Lalique, Daum, Sevres, Minton, Rosenthal, Georg Jensen, Royal Copenhagen, Bernardaud and Ceralene Limoges, Royal Worcester, Coalport, Belleek, Noritake, Stuart, Arzberg, Fitz and Floyd, Reed & Barton, Wedgwood, Tuttle, Ginori, etc.

Special Factors: PQ by phone or letter with SASE.

NAT SCHWARTZ & CO., INC.; 549 Broadway; Bayonne, NJ 07002 (800) 526-1440/ Cat.: free/ Save: to 65%/ Pay: C, MO, MC, V Sells: tableware, giftware, jewelry/ Shop: same address; M, Th, F 11–8, Tu & Sa 11–5

$$/

Comment: Schwartz, est. in 1959, publishes a 48-page color catalog filled with fine china, crystal, flatware, jewelry, and gifts that represents just a fraction of the firm's inventory. Excellent customer-service department.

Sample Goods: China and giftware by Lenox, Wedgwood, Minton, Royal Doulton, Royal Crown Derby, Coalport, Royal Worcester, Aynsley, Spode, Pickard, Gorham, Belleek, Boehm, Lladro, etc.; crystal stemware and giftware by Stuart, Galway, Val St. Lambert, Waterford, Wedgwood, Gorham, Lenox, Queen Lace, and Mikasa; flatware and holloware by Towle, Gorham, Wallace, Tuttle, Reed & Barton, International, Lunt, Kirk-Stieff, Oneida, Georgian House, Lauffer, etc. Jewelry and watches also featured in catalog.

Special Factors: PQ by phone or letter with SASE (inquiries accepted over 800 line); gift-forwarding service, bridal and gift registries maintained; satisfaction guaranteed; special orders accepted with nonrefundable 20% deposit; returns accepted.

ALBERT S. SMYTH CO., INC.; 25 Aylesbury Rd.; Timonium, MD 21093 (800) 638-3333/ Cat.: $1/ Save: to 50%/ Pay: C, MO, AE, CHOICE, DC, MC, V Sells: tableware, giftware, jewelry/ Shop: same address

$$/ /

Comment: All that gleams and glitters can be found at Smyth, at savings of up to 50% on comparable retail and list prices. Excellent customer-service department.

Sample Goods: Wide range of jewelry, including gold-filled pieces, strands of semiprecious beads, gem solitaires and pearls, etc.; excellent group of pierced earrings with jackets; watches by

Citizen, Seiko, and Pulsar. Home decorative accents and tableware include clocks by Seiko, Citizen, and Howard Miller; pewter candlesticks, coffee sets, punch bowls, and tableware by Lenox, Wedgwood, Noritake, Wallace, Royal Doulton, Spode, Waterford, Reed & Barton, Towle, and Gorham. The $1 fee brings a year of catalogs, which show a fraction of the inventory.

Special Factors: PQ by phone or letter with SASE; bridal registry, gift consultations, and gift-forwarding services; satisfaction guaranteed; returns accepted (except personalized or custom-ordered items) within 30 days.

SEE ALSO:

A Cook's Wares . . . Pillivuyt porcelain serving pieces, pepper mills . . . HOME—Kitchen

JEWELRY, GEMS, AND WATCHES

Fine, fashion, and costume jewelry; loose stones, watches, and services.

This book gives you access to firms that offer everything from flea-market neck chains for pennies to diamond and emerald collars costing close to $200,000. Before you buy in the "high end," you must know and understand terms and industry standards to determine what offer represents the best value. We could use this space to tell you the difference between rolled and filled gold, what "GIA-certified" signifies, and the meanings of "chatoyant," "rutile," "dichroic," and other interesting words used in gemology. Instead, we're citing references and urge you to read all the publications mentioned here. They'll help you become an educated consumer.

But becoming a wise consumer takes a different kind of knowledge. Before you purchase a piece of jewelry, you should know *why* you're buying it. You're in the clear if all you want is a bit of color to enhance an outfit, since you're not going to insist on the perfect Burmese ruby. You're probably still on safe ground if you're buying for the sake of having a specimen—a strand of semiprecious beads or a small diamond (and we mean small)— since you're likely to look for the lowest price around. You enter the danger zone when you approach gems and jewelry with large amounts of money, ignorance, and wishful thinking. Wishful thinking is what leads uninformed consumers to believe they can better dealers who've been in the business for 20 years and know exactly what they're selling. It leads people to buy as "investors" on the basis of undocumented appreciation figures, expect similar rates of return on their stones or jewelry, and experience disappointment. (Buying an "investment-grade" piece does not an investor make.)

Wishful thinking is believing that an appraisal value equals a resale value. Don't mistake an appraisal value for the amount of money you could get for your gems or jewelry; it's a measure of the market value of the stones, which may be as high as three to four times the resale value. Since inflated appraisals may also cost you extra insurance premium dollars, make sure your valuations are realistic. Protect yourself by getting at least two, preferably by GIA-trained jewelers or dealers.

There are many worthwhile publications on gems and jewelry; one we found quite useful is *All About Jewelry: The One Indispensable Guide for Buyers, Wearers, Lovers, Investors* by Rose Leiman Goldenberg. The book covers precious and semiprecious stones, pearls, metals, and other materials used in jewelry and includes color plates (Arbor House Publishing Co., 1983). It may be available in your local library.

The Better Business Bureau publishes a pamphlet called "Jewelry," which is available from local offices or by mail. See the introduction to the "Appliances" chapter for the address and information.

The FTC has established guidelines for the jewelry trade and publishes pamphlets for consumers that discuss the meanings of terms, stamps and quality marks, etc. Request "Gold Jewelry," "Bargain Jewelry," and "Guidelines for the Jewelry Industry" from the Federal Trade Commission; Public Reference Office; Washington, DC 20580.

The GIA can tell you what should appear on a GIA report and confirm whether an appraiser has been trained by the organization. For more information, write to the Gemological Institute of America, Inc.; 1180 Ave. of the Americas; New York, NY 10036. There is also a GIA office in Santa Monica, CA.

And the Jeweler's Vigilance Committee can tell you whether your dealer is among the good, the bad, or the ugly. This trade association monitors the industry and promotes ethical business practices. For more information, write to the Jeweler's Vigilance Committee; 1180 Ave. of the Americas, 8th Fl.; New York, NY 10036.

DEL-MAR CO.; 705 Frisco; Houston, TX 77022-9990 (713) 695-0158/ Cat.: $3, ref./ Save: to 50%/ Pay: C, MO, cert. check Sells: "pounded gold" jewelry/ Mail order only

$$/ ✉

Comment: Del-Mar sells its unusual gold jewelry through a 16-page color catalog; most of the selection is western-style belt buckles and cabochons. Very low prices.

Sample Goods: "Pounded gold" jewelry formed of melted, purified gold nuggets pounded into sheets, combined with flakes of gold, set in resin. Turquoise, copper, abalone, and silver also used in the settings. Pendants, pierced and drop earrings, and undrilled "stones" offered; a wide range of pounded-gold cabochons set in a choice of western belt buckles, bolo ties, and money clips featured. Many of the cabochons are embedded with gold or cloisonné figures or emblems; cowboy boots, saddles, logos for the Knights of Columbus and Shriners, bears, ducks, Mercury dimes, eagles, bowling pins, dice, trout, etc. Prices begin at under $2 for undrilled "stones."

Special Factors: Quantity discounts available.

DIAMONDS BY RENNIE ELLEN; 15 W. 47th St., Rm. 401; New York, NY 10036 (212) 896-5525/ Cat.: $2/ Save: 50–75%/ Pay: C, MO, cert. check Sells: diamond jewelry/ Shop: same address; by appt. only

$$$$/ ✉

Comment: It's hard to believe that you can buy diamond engagement rings wholesale, but that's Rennie Ellen's business.

Save up to 75% on the price of similar jewelry sold elsewhere. Rennie Ellen is honest, reputable, and personable.

Sample Goods: Custom-cut diamonds of any shape, size, and quality, set to order in platinum or gold. The color catalog shows samples of Ms. Ellen's design work, including rings, pendants, and earrings set with diamonds, rubies, sapphires, emeralds, amethysts, tourmalines, pearls, and opals.

Special Factors: Returns accepted within 5 working days; shop open to customers by appointment only; detailed bill of sale included with each purchase.

GOLD N' STONES; Box 636; Sterling, AK 99672 (907) 262-9713/ Cat.: $1, ref./ Save: 10–40%/ Pay: C, MO, cert. check
Sells: Alaskan, semiprecious stone jewelry/ Mail order only
$$$/

Comment: Jade jewelry is the strong suit at this firm, which was founded in 1972. Prices begin at just $1; many items suitable for craftspeople or retailers.

Sample Goods: Pendants of all types, including bezels filled with polished jade chips, jade bead necklaces and bracelets, earrings, rings, stickpins, etc. Other jewelry and accessories available in tumbled Alaskan garnets, hematite, and walrus ivory; gold nuggets sold unmounted or in bezels on pendants and earrings. Bulk jade, soapstone, jasper, and agate available; jewelry findings, bolo cord, and gift boxes also offered.

Special Factors: Jewelry guaranteed against damage for 5 years; returns accepted for repairs or replacement.

GOOD 'N' LUCKY PROMOTIONS; P.O. Box 370; Henderson, NV 89015 (702) 564-3895/ PL: $1, ref. (quarterly)/ Save: 40–70%/ Pay: C, MO, MC, V Sells: job-lot items, jewelry/ Mail order only

$$$/ ✉/ ☎

Comment: You never know what you'll find at Good 'N' Lucky—the catalog is geared for the flea-market operator and features "quick sale" items of every sort. Many available in lots under a dozen. Est. in 1971.

Sample Goods: Enameled butterfly pins, birthstone rings, olivewood cross pendants, jade necklaces, cubic zirconia rings, strands of tumbled amethyst, copper bracelets, tie tacks, children's jewelry, men's rings, and similar goods shown in past catalogs; Chinese fans, sunglasses, porcelain knickknacks, steak knives, whoopee cushions, Elvis posters, X-ray glasses, rain bonnets, sealing tape, fish hooks, bandannas, arrowheads, clock motors, and similar goods also offered at job-lot prices.

Special Factors: Separate catalogs of adult novelties ($1) and jewelry ($2) available through the general catalog; quantity discounts available; min. order $30.

HONG KONG LAPIDARIES, INC.; c/o Zarlene; 31 W. 47th St., 2nd Fl.; New York, NY 10036 (800) 223-7814/ Cat.: $1 (1 & 7)/ Save: 10–35%/ Pay: C, MO, MC, V Sells: jewelry supplies, finished jewelry/ Mail order only

$$/ ✉/ ☎

Comment: This New York City firm sells a wide range of precious and semiprecious stones in a variety of forms. The 32-page catalog shows items of interest to hobbyists as well; prices to 35% below comparable retail. Est. in 1977.

Sample Goods: Cabochons, beads, loose faceted and cut stones, strung chips, etc.; pearls, garnets, amethyst, onyx, abalone, and many other types of semiprecious stones and materials; Egyptian clay scarabs, coral, cameos, cubic zirconia, yellow jade, and cloisonné jewelry and objets d'art. Square and disc inlays in intaglios suitable for decorating jewelry boxes or game boards; tiger's eye and onyx belt buckles, stone buttons, etc.

Special Factors: Quantity discounts available; satisfaction guaranteed; returns accepted within 12 days; min. order $12.

HOUSE OF ONYX; 120 Main St.; Greenville, KY 42345
(800) 626-8352/ Cat.: free/ Save: 40–60%/ Pay: C, MO, MC, V Sells: investment-grade stones, jewelry, gifts/ Shop: same address; M–F 9–4

$$$$/ ✉ / ☎

Comment: The House of Onyx publishes a 56-page tabloid catalog filled with reports on the gem industry and listings of diamonds and other precious stones, as well as specials on gifts and jewelry. Over 50,000 clients worldwide; fair prices.

Sample Goods: Aztec onyx chess sets, ashtrays, bookends, vases, statuettes, candlesticks, jewelry, etc.; ivory necklaces, bracelets, netsuke, and gift items; cloisonné beads, jewelry, and artware; soapstone, rose quartz, tiger's eye, lapis lazuli, turquoise, and agate carvings. The jewelry includes semiprecious bead necklaces, freshwater and cultured pearls, diamond rings, earrings, and pendants, etc. Wide range of investment stones; discounts of 50% and 60% offered on *parcels* of $2,000 to $12,-500.

Special Factors: Satisfaction guaranteed; returns accepted within 5 days; references listed in catalog; min. order $25.

INTERNATIONAL IMPORT CO.; P.O. Box 747; Stone Mountain, GA 30086-0747 (404) 938-0173/ Cat.: free/ Save: see text/ Pay: C, MO, cert. check Sells: cut and polished stones/ Shop: by appt. only

$$$/ ✉ / ☎

Comment: International lists about 3,000 different cut precious and semiprecious stones in its 56-page catalog, a fraction of the firm's inventory of over 100,000 stones. Highly respected in the gem trade. Est. in 1950.

Sample Goods: Cut gems, from actinolite to zircon, listed in the catalog with weight, size, shape, and color specifications. Prices run from a few dollars to several thousand; many invest-ment-grade stones listed.

Special Factors: All purchases made on approval basis; de-posit of 50% required; returns accepted within 5 days; prices about a third less than retail on comparable stones; min. order $10.

J B JEWELRY; P.O. Box 04458; Milwaukee, WI 53204 (414) 242-4822/ Cat.: $1/ Save: 40%/ Pay: C, MO, cert.

check, MC, V **Sells:** fine and costume jewelry/ Mail order only

$$$/

Comment: J B Jewelry markets Hallmark jewelry, which is sold nationwide in jewelry shops for twice as much. The 18-page catalog shows suggested list prices; J B discounts these by 40%.

Sample Goods: Diamond solitaires, wedding bands, diamond slides and studs, and other fine jewelry set with rubies, sapphires, emeralds, and pearls. Men's rings, including onyx and diamond classics; birthstone jewelry; very affordable rings, bracelets, and pendants set with opals, cubic zirconia, aquamarines, garnets, amethysts, and smoky topaz quartz also available.

Special Factors: All jewelry gift-boxed; satisfaction guaranteed; returns accepted within 30 days except worn, personalized, or special-order items.

LOVE'S, INC.; LOVE'S PLAZA; P.O. Box 3086; Rock Hill, SC 29731-3086 (800) 845-6151/ Cat.: $1, ref. (3 & 9)/ Save: 25–50%/ Pay: C, MO, AE, MC, V **Sells:** fine and fashion jewelry/ **Shop:** same address

$$$/

Comment: The 16-page catalog from Love's shows some real buys on jewelry for every taste and budget. Fashion jewelry featured; savings to 50% and more. Est. in 1967.

Sample Goods: Pierced earrings from under $10; classic diamond solitaires, anniversary bands, gold ropes and chains, shell earrings, shrimp rings, and signet rings; tricolored gold and silver jewelry; ropes of gold balls and semiprecious stone beads; diamond-studded men's rings; Mikimoto cultured pearl necklaces and bracelets; cubic zirconia earrings, rings, and pendants; Seiko, Pulsar, and Concord watches; many other lines and items.

Special Factors: PQ by phone or letter with SASE; watches not shown in catalog; diamond solitaires sold with lifetime trade-in privilege; satisfaction guaranteed; returns accepted within 14 days.

P & J COMPANY; 740 N. Plankinton Ave., Suite 824; Milwaukee, WI 53203 (414) 271-5396/ Cat.: $1, ref./ Save: 30–60%/ Pay: C, MO, MC, V Sells: fashion jewelry/ Mail order only

$$/ ✉ / ☎

Comment: P & J, founded in 1983, manufactures 400 gold and silver products and wholesales them to jewelers. The same goods are offered to consumers at savings of 30% or more below comparable retail.

Sample Goods: Classic grape-cluster ring, horseshoe tie tack/ pin, and a brooch with the figure of a duck in flight offered in a choice of sterling silver or 14K gold. Many other pieces available.

Special Factors: Satisfaction guaranteed; returns accepted within 30 days.

PIZAZZ, INC.; 337 W. Concord Pl.; Chicago, IL 60614 (312) 266-7776/ Broch.: $2 and SASE, ref. (1 & 9)/ Save: 40–75%/

Pay: C, MO, cert. check **Sells:** costume and fashion jewelry
Mail order only

$$$/

Comment: Pizazz sells just that: a little zip and fanfare for your waist, ears, and throat at prices that will leave you light-hearted. Both consumer and retailer should check this source for its values—savings of up to 75% on comparable retail prices.

Sample Goods: Dozens of cloisonné belt buckles in striking motifs, from butterflies to modern geometrics, sold with leather belts (about $10 each); brilliantly colored kiln-fired enamel drop and post earrings ($4–$6); lengths of synthetic pearls, coral, and turquoise; stands of genuine agate, rose quartz, amethyst, jasper, and other semiprecious stones also offered; decorative clasps available.

Special Factors: PQ by phone or letter with SASE; quantity discounts available.

R/E KANE ENTERPRISES; DIVISION OF RENNIE ELLEN;
P.O. Box 1745; Rockefeller Plaza; New York, NY 10185
(212) 869-5525/ **Cat.:** see text/ **Save:** 50%+/ **Pay:** C, MO,
cert. check **Sells:** stock, custom-made cubic zirconia jewelry/
Shop: 15 W. 47th St.; by appt. only

$$$$/

Comment: If you have diamond tastes but a rhinestone budget, consider the best alternative to the natural stone: cubic zirconia. This division of "Diamonds by Rennie Ellen" sells stock and custom-made C.Z. jewelry at just $10 a carat.

Sample Goods: Cubic zirconia jewelry, including rings, earrings, bracelets, necklaces, etc.; custom designs executed. C.Z., a synthetic stone, is harder than glass or zircons and the best impostor on the market. C.Z. weighs 80% more than diamonds; a 1.8-carat C.Z. stone (or an even 2 carats) is about the same size as a 1-carat diamond.

Special Factors: See catalog from "Diamonds by Rennie Ellen" for more information.

GINGER SCHLOTE; Box 19523-M; Denver, CO 80219-0253 (303) 934-1168/ Cat.: free/ Save: to 60%/ Pay: C, MO, cert. check **Sells:** economy jewelry findings/ Mail order only
$$/ / ☎

Comment: Ginger Schlote's firm is just 5 years old, but she's had many years of experience working with her father in his jewelry/mounting-parts business. Many bargains here for the craftsperson on a budget.

Sample Goods: Economy chains, findings, and some finished jewelry; some items gold-filled or sterling silver, but most made of base metal with a white or yellow (golden) "lifetime" finish. Over 3 dozen chain styles starting at 52¢ each; novel pendants, rings, keyrings, bolas, cord tips, tack pins, etc. Jewelry and lapidary supplies include earring wires and clips, pendant mountings, bell caps, jump rings, clutchbacks, pushnuts, cement, presentation boxes, etc.

Special Factors: Bonus offers listed in catalog; satisfaction guaranteed; returns accepted within 10 days.

SEE ALSO:

Antique Imports Unlimited . . . antique jewelry . . . ART, ANTIQUES

Beautiful Beginnings . . . small selection costume jewelry . . . HEALTH

Beautiful Visions, Inc. . . . small selection costume jewelry . . . HEALTH

Beauty Buy Book . . . small selection costume jewelry . . . HEALTH

Berry Scuba Co. . . . name-brand diving watches . . . SPORTS

The Best Choice . . . chronograph sports watches . . . SPORTS

Bondy Export Corp. . . . Seiko and Casio watches . . . APPLIANCES

Central Skindivers of Nassau, Inc. . . . name-brand diving watches . . . SPORTS

The Finals . . . sports watches . . . CLOTHING

Fortunoff . . . fine, fashion, costume jewelry . . . HOME—Table Settings

Hunter Audio-Photo, Inc. . . . Timex, Seiko, Bulova watches . . . APPLIANCES

Jems Sounds, Ltd. . . . name-brand watches . . . APPLIANCES

Royal Silk, Ltd. . . . small group fashion jewelry . . . CLOTHING

RSP Distributing . . . closeout jewelry . . . GENERAL

Sales Citi, Inc. . . . name-brand watches . . . APPLIANCES

Nat Schwartz & Co., Inc. . . . small selection fine jewelry . . . HOME—Table Settings

Albert S. Smyth Co., Inc. . . . fine and costume jewelry, watches . . . HOME—Table Settings

LEATHER GOODS

Small leather goods, briefcases, handbags, attaché cases, luggage, trunks, and services.

While researching the first edition of this book several years ago, we were asked to keep mum about the brands these firms carried. We asked why, and were told that if the major department stores, stocking the same products and usually selling at full retail, saw a discounter getting publicity—and sales—they'd threaten to pull their accounts with the manufacturers unless *they* promised to cut off supplies to the discounter. But in the past few years there's been a tremendous boom in off-price shopping, and manufacturers know that positive brand identification doesn't depend on association with a flashy retailer. So it's the discounters who have the clout now, and it's because *you've* insisted on bargains. Strike one blow against vertical price fixing!

The firms listed here stock everything you should need to tote your effects around town, to the office, and around the world. In addition to handbags, briefcases, suitcases, steamer and camp trunks, and small leather goods, some companies also stock cases for musical instruments and portfolios for models and artists.

If you're buying luggage, consider the number of different materials available and the pros and cons of each before making your purchase. Molded plastic is almost indestructible, but it's heavy and scuffs easily. Rip-stop nylon is the lightest material widely available, but it's easily punctured and affords the contents little protection against hard knocks or even rain. Soft-sided vinyl and reinforced fabric luggage can be punctured and torn, but isn't as heavy as the molded type. Leather is luxurious and can be quite durable, but usually shows scuffs and makes a great target for thieves working baggage areas at airports. You can add to this list on your own: consider your own needs and buy accordingly.

One last tip: don't buy luggage with attached wheels. Baggage handlers say the wheels often jam in conveyor systems and are usually ripped off by the time you've taken a few trips. Collapsible luggage carriers, which can be taken with you as hand baggage, solve the problem of getting bags around in huge, porter-less terminals.

Additional listings of firms selling small leather goods and handbags can be found in "Clothing."

ACE LEATHER PRODUCTS, INC.; 2211 Ave. U; Brooklyn, NY 11229 (800) 342-5223/ Cat.: free with SASE (6 & 10)/ Save: 20–40%/ Pay: C, MO, MC, V **Sells:** luggage, leather goods/ **Shop:** same address

$$$/ ✉/ ☎

Comment: Top brands in luggage and leather goods are available here, at to 40% below manufacturers' suggested retail prices. The Oct. catalog is published for the holiday season, and the June catalog may not be available, so a price quote is recommended. In business for over 60 years.

Sample Goods: Luggage by American Tourister, Ventura, Boyt, Lark, French, Samsonite, and Andiamo (30% to 40% off list); briefcases and attaché cases by Schlesinger, Lion, Yale, Grace, Atlas, Michael Scott, and Scully (20% off list); handbags and small leather goods by Meyers, Etienne Aigner, Liz Claiborne, Stone Mountain, Dooney & Bourke, and 33 East; travel alarms by Bulova, Seiko, and Linden; small leather goods by a range of manufacturers.

Special Factors: PQ by phone or letter with SASE.

ALTMAN LUGGAGE; 135 Orchard St.; New York, NY 10002 (212) 254-7275/ Info: PQ/ Save: 20–50%/ Pay: C, MO, AE, DC, MC, V **Sells:** luggage, leather goods/ **Shop:** same address; Su–F 9–6

$$$/ ✉/ ☎

Comment: Altman's has been a fixture on the Lower East Side for years and remains true to the spirit of the area by discounting top brands of leather goods and luggage up to 50%. Store shoppers will find a selection of imported briefcases and leather goods worth noting.

Sample Goods: Briefcases and attaché cases, luggage, and other leather goods by Bally, Ventura, Hartmann, Atlas, Schlesinger, Lark, Samsonite, Michael Scott, and other firms; artists' portfolios also stocked.

Special Factors: PQ by phone or letter with SASE.

A TO Z LUGGAGE; 4627 New Utrecht Ave.; Brooklyn, NY 11219 (718) 435-2423/ Cat.: free/ Save: 20–60%/ Pay: C, MO, AE, DC, MC, V Sells: luggage, leather goods/ Shop: same address; 3 other locations in New York City
$$$/

Comment: A to Z has been in business for nearly half a century, supplying New Yorkers with luggage and leather goods at to 60% below list prices. The catalog is published for the holiday season; price quotes are recommended.

Sample Goods: Luggage, briefcases and attaché cases, and other leather goods by Samsonite, American Tourister, Hartmann, Amelia Earhart, Lark, Ventura, and many other manufacturers. Artists' portfolios, steamer trunks, and related goods also available. The service department handles repairs.

Special Factors: PQ by phone or letter with SASE.

BETTINGER'S LUGGAGE SHOP; 80 Rivington St.; New York, NY 10002 (212) 475-1690/ Info: PQ/ Save: 30–50%/

Pay: C, MO, AE, DC, MC, V **Sells:** luggage, leather goods/ **Shop:** same address; Su–F 9:30–6

$$$/ ✉ / ☎

Comment: The Bettingers have been helping New Yorkers pack up and go since 1914, and they know their stock. Comprehensive selection; the store is crammed and usually busy, but worth a visit for such items as steamer trunks and nonbranded goods.

Sample Goods: Luggage and leather goods by Oleg Cassini, Skyway, Atlas, Andiamo, Boyt, Ventura, Lark, Wings, Fulton, American Tourister, Samsonite, etc.; attaché cases, briefcases, artists' portfolios, instrument cases, sample cases, steamer trunks, and other goods available. Irregular goods available at large discounts in the store.

Special Factors: PQ by phone or letter with SASE.

CARRY-ON LUGGAGE, INC.; 97 Orchard St.; New York, NY 10002 (212) 226-4980/ **Info:** PQ/ **Save:** 30–50%/ **Pay:** C, MO, MC, V **Sells:** luggage, leather goods/ **Shop:** same address; Su–F 9:45–5:45

$$$/ ✉ / ☎

Comment: This is one of the better bets for consistently low prices on a full range of leather goods—bags of every sort, by virtually every manufacturer. Even much-requested designer goods are knocked down at least 30%.

Sample Goods: Luggage, briefcases and attaché cases, leather goods, artists' portfolios, steamer trunks, and related goods by a full range of firms and designers, including Samsonite, Tumi,

Wings, Amelia Earhart, St. Thomas, Anne Klein, Ralph Lauren, Christian Dior, Bill Blass, Pierre Cardin, Invicta, Verde, Harrison, Schlesinger, Rolfs, Diane Von Furstenberg, Michael Scott, etc.

Special Factors: PQ by phone or letter with SASE.

INNOVATION LUGGAGE; 487 Hackensack Ave.; River Edge, NJ 07661 (800) 631-0742/ Broch.: free/ Save: 20–50%/ Pay: C, MO, AE, DC, MC, V Sells: leather goods, luggage/ Shop: 14 other locations in NY and NJ

**$$$/ / **

Comment: Innovation is the largest independent Samsonite dealer in the U.S. and has an excellent selection of luggage, briefcases, and other leather goods by a range of manufacturers. The 10-page brochure is available during the holiday season; at other times, inquire for a PQ.

Sample Goods: Luggage, portfolios, briefcases and attaché cases, handbags, and small leather goods by Amelia Earhart, Tumi, Lark, American Tourister, Ventura, Hartmann, Skyway, Invicta, Land, Samsonite, etc.; excellent savings on one-of-a-kind items and closeouts (Bally briefcases have appeared in the stores at 50% off list); the brochure includes a selection of gift items as well as stock leather goods.

Special Factors: PQ by phone or letter with SASE; min. order $15.

SEE ALSO:

Bondy Export Corp. . . . . Samsonite luggage . . .
   APPLIANCES

Custom Coat Co. . . . gloves, moccasins, bags, small leather goods . . . CLOTHING

Dairy Association Co., Inc. . . . Tackmaster leather conditioner . . . ANIMAL

The Deerskin Place . . . leather wallets, shoulder bags . . . CLOTHING

The Finals . . . nylon getaway, duffle bags . . . CLOTHING

Holabird Sports Discounters . . . racquet bags . . . SPORTS

International Solgo, Inc. . . . name-brand luggage . . . APPLIANCES

Pagano Gloves . . . deerskin and cowhide wallets, keycases, handbags . . . CLOTHING

The Renovator's Supply, Inc. . . . trunk hardware . . . HOME —Maintenance

Sales Citi, Inc. . . . Samsonite attaché cases . . . APPLIANCES

Sunco Products Corp. . . . suede and cowhide work gloves . . . CLOTHING

MEDICAL
AND SCIENTIFIC

Prescription drugs, hearing aids, contact lenses and eyeglasses, and post-surgery supplies and equipment.

Buying your medications by mail is both convenient and often much less expensive than having prescriptions filled at the local drugstore. Even the prices of generic drugs are lower by mail, affording you savings of up to 60% on some commonly prescribed remedies. You can also save up to half the cost of hearing aids, contact lenses, eyeglasses, breast forms, and products for the ostomate and convalescent patient by ordering them from the firms listed here.

Wonder what to do with your old eyeglasses? Help others who can't afford them, even at a discount, see more clearly. Send them to New Eyes for the Needy; P.O. Box 332; Short Hills, NJ 07078.

Want to keep up with government news on medicine and regulatory matters? Subscribe to *FDA Consumer*, published ten times yearly. Rate information and order forms are included in the "U.S. Government Books" catalog, available free upon request from the Superintendent of Documents; U.S. Government Printing Office; Washington, DC 20402; Attn: Books Catalog.

For related products, see the listings in "Health and Beauty."

BRUCE MEDICAL SUPPLY; 411 Waverly Oaks Rd.; P.O. Box 9166; Waltham, MA 02254 (800) 225-8446/ Cat.: free (quarterly)/ Save: 20–60%/ Pay: C, MO, MC, V **Sells:** ostomate, general medical products/ Mail order only

$$$$/ 🖂 / ☎

Comment: The Bruce Medical Supply catalog is a valuable aid to anyone involved in the ongoing care of ostomates—those who've had tracheostomies, colostomies, ileostomies, and urostomies—as well as those with needs for general medical supplies and equipment (nonprescription). Prices discounted up to 60%.

Sample Goods: Ostomy supplies, including collection pouches, dressings, adhesives and removers, disks and seal rings, irrigators, lubricants, cleansing products, disinfectants, etc.; bathtub safety benches, tub grips, decubitus (bed sore) protection, wheelchairs, canes, crutches, magnifying glasses, sphygmomanometers, stethoscopes, compresses, etc., also stocked. Fitness equipment, books on related topics, and sundry medical-care supplies available as well.

Special Factors: Goods shipped in unmarked boxes; satisfaction guaranteed.

RIC CLARK COMPANY; 9530 Langdon Ave.; Sepulveda, CA 91343 (818) 892-6636/ Cat.: free/ Save: 50%+/ Pay: C or MO **Sells:** hearing aids/ Mail order only

$$$$/ 🖂

Comment: Mr. Clark publishes a catalog featuring 6 hearing-aid models, designed for varying degrees of hearing loss. Note that Mr. Clark recommends that you see a physician before buying an aid; you must sign a waiver if you don't provide a physician's note stating that you need an aid.

Sample Goods: Aids for losses from mild to severe, including in-the-ear models, "compression" aids said to "cushion" sudden loud noises, and standard models. Prices half those charged by hearing-aid dealers. A $10 deposit entitles you to a month's free trial, after which you may return the aid for a complete refund or keep it. Batteries and repairs available.

Special Factors: Satisfaction guaranteed; all aids warrantied; budget plan available ($20 a month, 10% finance charge).

FEDERAL/GETZ PHARMACY SERVICE; Second and Main Sts.; Madrid, IA 50156 (800) 247-1236/ Cat.: free/ Save: to 60%/ Pay: C, MO, MC, V Sells: OTC, prescription drugs, supplements/ Shop: same address

 $$$/ ✉ / ☎

Comment: Federal/Getz Pharmacy offers a valuable service to people receiving ongoing drug treatments: prescriptions filled by mail, at up to 60% less (on generic equivalents of name-brand drugs) than suggested list prices.

Sample Goods: Vitamins and dietary supplements, OTC remedies, generic prescription drugs, beauty aids, etc.; generic dietary supplements and prescription drugs, formula equivalents of name-brand products, are sold at up to 60% less than their counterparts. Drugs are listed with trade names, list prices, chemical names, and the lower generic prices; service is prompt.

Special Factors: Satisfaction guaranteed; returns accepted within 30 days; shipping and insurance included; min. order $5.

LINGERIE FOR LESS; 11075 Erhard; Dallas, TX 75228 (214) 341-9575/ Info: PQ/ Save: to 75%/ Pay: C, MO, cert. check Sells: mastectomy forms/ Shop: Dallas, Plauo, and Austin, TX

$$$$/ ✉

Comment: This firm sells a mastectomy form that's won praise from many women for its comfort as well as its price. The shop also offers discounted lingerie and underwear.

Sample Goods: The "Soft Touch Breast Form," a molded gel breast form that has been compared to others selling for more than 3 times as much; available in 7 sizes; designed to fit all types of brassieres.

Special Factors: PQ by phone or letter with SASE; include size; form is unconditionally guaranteed for 1 year.

NATIONAL CONTACT LENS CENTER; 1188 Montgomery Dr.; Santa Rosa, CA 95405 (707) 542-3404/ Cat.: 25¢/ Save: to 50%/ Pay: C, MO, MC, V Sells: contact lenses/ Shop: same address; M–F 8:30–5

$$$/ ✉

Comment: The Santa Rosa Optometry Center runs this lens-by-mail service, which can save you up to 50% on your next pair.

Best suited for the person accustomed to wearing lenses, since additional costs of being fitted and monitored while learning to wear them may offset savings completely.

Sample Goods: All hard and soft lenses, including lines by Hydrocurve, Bausch & Lomb, Flexlens, Aquaflex, etc.; colored lenses and extended-wear models also stocked.

Special Factors: PQ by phone or letter with SASE; prescription required for filling order.

PHARMACEUTICAL SERVICES; 126 W. Markey Rd.; Belton, MO 64012-1792 (816) 331-0700/ PL: free/ Save: 20–60%/ Pay: C or MO Sells: OTC, prescription drugs, supplements/ Shop: same address; M–F 9–6, Sa 9–2

$$$/ ✉ / ☎

Comment: You can save up to 60% on your next prescription if your doctor approves filling with the generic equivalent of the name-brand drug or product. Excellent stock, prompt service, and a year-end printout of all your prescriptions make this a good alternative to the local drugstore.

Sample Goods: Vitamins and dietary supplements, OTC remedies, medical devices, and generic pharmaceuticals; save an additional 10% on all purchases by paying a $12 yearly fee; prescription must be supplied with order.

Special Factors: Satisfaction guaranteed; shipping and insurance included on prescription drugs.

PRESCRIPTION DELIVERY SYSTEMS; 136 S. York Rd.; Hatboro, PA 19040 (800) 441-8976/ Broch.: free; Save: to 40%/ Pay: C, MO, MC, V Sells: OTC remedies, prescription drugs, supplements/ Shop: same address

$$$/ ✉ / ☎

Comment: Prescription Delivery Systems offers over 50,000 generic and name-brand drugs, at prices to 40% below list or comparable retail. Inquiries are accepted over the 800 line; prescriptions are filled after orders are received, and billed to you later. Known for its prompt service.

Sample Goods: Generic and name-brand drugs and pharmaceutical items; OTC remedies, dietary supplements, and related goods.

Special Factors: Orders over $100 must be prepaid; satisfaction guaranteed.

RITEWAY HAC; P.O. Box 59451; Chicago, IL 60659 (312) 539-6620/ Broch.: free/ Save: to 50%+/ Pay: C or MO Sells: hearing aids/ Mail order only

$$$/ ✉

Comment: The brochure features 8 hearing aids for a range of hearing losses; flexible terms and trial policy. Up to 50% less than dealer prices.

Sample Goods: Royaltone and Dynavex aids, including in-the-ear, over-the-ear, power (body), and other models; brochure includes specs on frequency, range, and battery type and life for each aid. A $20 nonrefundable deposit buys you a 30-day trial period, after which the aid can be returned or you can purchase it for a third down, and the rest in monthly installments of $10 (no finance charges).

Special Factors: Satisfaction guaranteed.

SEE ALSO:

Ad-Lib Astronomics . . . name-brand telescopes . . . CAMERAS

Allyn Air Seat Co. . . . air-filled wheelchair seat liners . . . SPORTS

Animal Veterinary Products, Inc. . . . animal biologicals, medications . . . ANIMAL

Bailey's, Inc. . . . first-aid kits, ImmunIvy, ImmunOak . . . TOOLS

Comp-U-Card . . . prescription drugs . . . GENERAL

Danley's . . . name-brand telescopes . . . CAMERAS

Executive Photo & Supply Corp. . . . Celestron telescopes . . . CAMERAS

47st Photo, Inc. . . . Celestron, Cometron telescopes . . . CAMERAS

Harvest of Values . . . nutritional supplements . . . HEALTH

Kansas City Vaccine Company . . . livestock and pet biologicals, medications . . . ANIMAL

Mardiron Optics . . . name-brand telescopes . . . CAMERAS

Omaha Vaccine Co., Inc. . . . biologicals, pharmaceuticals for livestock . . . ANIMAL

Orion Telescope Center . . . name-brand telescopes . . . CAMERAS

PBS Livestock Drugs . . . livestock biologicals, instruments . . . ANIMAL

Plastic BagMart . . . zip-top plastic bags . . . HOME— Maintenance

Puritan's Pride, Inc. . . . nutritional supplements, thermometers, heating pads, sphygmomanometers . . . HEALTH

Star Pharmaceutical, Inc. . . . nutritional supplements, OTC remedies, sphygmomanometers . . . HEALTH

Sunburst Biorganics . . . nutritional supplements . . . HEALTH

United Pharmacal Company, Inc. . . . biologicals, instruments for animal care and treatment . . . ANIMAL

Vitamin Specialties Co. . . . nutritional supplements, OTC remedies . . . HEALTH

Wear-Guard Work Clothes . . . lab coats . . . CLOTHING

Western Natural Products . . . nutritional supplements . . . HEALTH

Wholesale Veterinary Supply, Inc. . . . biologicals, veterinary surgical supplies . . . ANIMAL

MUSIC

Instruments, supplies,
and services.

Based in New York City as we are, we know that professional musicians don't pay full price for their fine instruments. Odds are they bought them from one of the sources we've included here. Our listees sell top-quality music products. While these outlets usually serve the knowledgable, they're perfectly happy to work with you even if you're a rank neophyte. You can save hundreds of dollars on top-rate equipment, and if you're equipping a band, you might save enough money to buy the van and pay the roadies. When buying instruments, go for quality—they can last a lifetime or even several, and the resale market for quality pieces is good. Buy wisely today, and you may be selling your "vintage" ax to Guitar Trader 20 years down the road for several times what you paid!

A.L.A.S. ACCORDION-O-RAMA; 16 W. 19th St.; New York, NY 10011 (212) 675-9089/ Cat.: free/ Save: 20–40%/ Pay: C, MO, MC, V **Sells:** accordions, accessories/ **Shop:** same address; M–F 9–4:30, Sa 10:30–3:30

$$$/ ✉/ ☎

Comment: A.L.A.S. has been in business for over 35 years and boasts an extensive inventory of new and used accordions, all sold at a discount. Authorized dealer and factory-service center for several leading brands.

Sample Goods: Instruments by Dellare, Hohner, Polytone, Excelsior, Arpeggio, Avanti, Cordovox, Paolo Soprani, Iorio, Elka, Cintioli, Nunzio, Sano, Serenelli, Crumar, and Scandalli; catalog features color photos of individual models with specs. Accordion synthesizers, speakers, organ-accordions, stands, and the invisible strap by Bandoleer also available.

Special Factors: Trade-ins accepted.

SAM ASH MUSIC CORP.; 124 Fulton Ave.; Hempstead, NY 11550 (800) 645-3518/ Cat.: free/ Save: 30–50%/ Pay: C, MO, AE, MC, V **Sells:** musical instruments, electronics/ **Shop:** same address; also Forest Hills, Huntington, Hempstead, White Plains, Brooklyn, and New York, NY; and Paramus, NJ

$$$/ ✉/ ☎

Comment: In 1924, a violinist and bandleader named Sam Ash opened a musical-instruments shop in Brooklyn. It's still family-run, but now boasts 8 stores and patronage by superstars, schools and institutions, and the military, in addition to ordinary individuals. Regular 50%-off specials a feature.

Sample Goods: Musical instruments, electronics, sound systems, recording equipment, specialized lighting, and accessories by hundreds of manufacturers, including Acoustic Research, Alembic, Ashly, Bach, Biamp, Bose, Buffet, Bundy, Casio, Cerwin-Vega, Deagan, Delta Lab, Electro-Voice, Ensonia, Fender, King, Getzen, Gibson, Gretsch, Guild, Hohner, Ibanex, JBL, LeBlanc, Ludwig, Marshall, Martin, Moog, Multivox, Ovation, Paiste, Pearl, Peavey, Roland, Siel, Tangent, Tapco, Wurlitzer, Yamaha, Zildjian, etc.; sheet music offered; repairs and service; trade-ins accepted.

Special Factors: PQ by phone or letter with SASE; catalog represents a fraction of the inventory; min. order $15.

CARVIN; 1155 Industrial Ave.; Escondido, CA 92025-2477
(619) 747-1710/ Cat.: free/ Save: to 40%/ Pay: C, MO, cert. check Sells: Carvin-brand musical instruments, accessories/ Mail order only
$$$/ ✉/ ☎

Comment: Carvin manufactures its own line of instruments and equipment, made to exacting specifications. Color catalog lists specs, features, and individual guarantees of each instrument; prices to 40% below comparable models.

Sample Goods: Mixers, amps, mikes, monitor systems, and electric guitars; guitars are styled after old Les Pauls, but designed for contemporary music needs. All products sold under a 10-day free trial arrangement; servicing and performance testing performed under the warranty is free of charge; warranties range from 1 to 5 years, depending on the item.

Special Factors: Satisfaction guaranteed; returns accepted for refund; min. order $10.

FRED'S STRING WAREHOUSE; 212 W. Lancaster; Shillington, PA 19607 (215) 777-3733/ Cat.: $1 (1, 4, 9)/ **Save:** 40%/ **Pay:** C, MO, CHOICE, MC, V **Sells:** replacement strings for fretted instruments/ **Shop:** same address

$$$/

Comment: Fred's offers strings for almost every sort of fretted instrument at savings of 40% off list or comparable retail; electronics are also stocked.

Sample Goods: Steel, brass, and bright and phosphor bronze strings for all guitars; pedal steel, mandolin, bass, banjo, violin, sitar, autoharp, bouzouki, and other strings; brands include Martin, Vega, Darco, D'Addario, Savarez, Ernie Ball, GHS, Guild, John Pearse, Dr. Thomastik-Infeld, Gibson, Aranjuez, Fender, and Black Diamond, among others. Picks, cables, harmonicas, DiMarzio pickups, Ibanex effects boxes, the Crybaby, mikes, and capos also available at a discount.

Special Factors: Authorized returns accepted within 14 days.

FREEPORT MUSIC; 41 Shore Dr.; Huntington Bay, NY 11743 (516) 549-4108/ Broch.: $1, ref./ **Save:** 20–60%/ **Pay:**

C, MO, MC, V **Sells:** musical instruments, electronics, accessories/ Mail Order only

$$$$/ ✉ / ☎

Comment: Freeport is determined to make itself irresistible to the musician, with a "we-will-not-be-undersold" discount policy, excellent selection, and good service. Est. in 1921; professional staff.

Sample Goods: Ludwig drums (40% off); drums and sets by Pearl, SlingerLand, and Tama; guitars by Dobro, Guild, Martin, Yamaha, and Gibson; Kawai pianos and organs, Morley, Roland Boss, Ampeg, Marshall, and Fender amps and electronics; DiMarzio pickups, Shure mikes, Franz metronomes, etc.; woodwind instruments by Selmer, King, LeBland, and Buffet; Selmer brasses; Leigh woodwind accessories; Armstrong flutes; Moog electronics; Hohner harmonicas; strings, reeds, valve oil, cases, disco lighting, FM wireless transmitters, etc.

Special Factors: PQ by phone or letter with SASE; used instruments available; trade-ins accepted; min. order $10, $25 on credit cards.

GUITAR TRADER; 12 Broad St.; Red Bank, NJ 07701; Attn: Bugs (201) 741-0771/ **Cat.:** see text/ **Save:** 40%/ **Pay:** C, MO, MC, V **Sells:** vintage, new musical instruments, electronics/ **Shop:** same address

$$$/ ✉ / ☎

Comment: The catalog from Guitar Trader, *Vintage Guitar Bulletin,* is $20 for a year's subscription (12 issues; 2 years, $25). The price is refundable with purchase, and it's a great investment for the serious collector. New instruments are sold on a price-quote basis, and want lists for vintage instruments are accepted. This firm is run by experts, and can handle any question you might have about the vintage instruments listed in the *Bulletin*.

Sample Goods: Used and vintage guitars, violins, banjos, mandolins, ukeleles, amps, and other electronics; new acoustic and electric guitars and some electronics by Ovation, Martin, Guild, Washburn, Gibson, Honda, Dean, Kramer, Hofner, BC Rich, Rickenbacker, Fender, and DiMarzio.

Special Factors: PQ by phone or letter with SASE; subscriptions to the *Bulletin* can be charged to credit cards; back issues available.

INTERSTATE MUSIC SUPPLY; P.O. Box 315; New Berlin, WI 53151 (414) 786-6210/ Cat.: free/ Save: 20–50%/ Pay: C, MO, MC, V **Sells:** musical instruments, electronics, accessories/ Mail order only

$$$/ / ☎

Comment: The Cascios have been in business for over 40 years, selling instruments and accessories at discount prices. Their own line of equipment, Interstate Music Supply, is marketed with nationally distributed brands in the 96-page catalog.

Sample Goods: Instruments, electronics, recording equipment, and accessories by such manufacturers as King, Conn, Ludwig, Fender, Gibson, Martin, Selmer, Gemeinhardt, Armstrong, Leblanc, Getzen, and Besson. Savings of up to 50%; catalog shows a fraction of the extensive inventory.

Special Factors: PQ by phone or letter with SASE; min. order $25.

**KENNELLY KEYS MUSIC AND DANCE, INC.; 5030 208th
St. S.W.; Lynnwood, WA 98036** (800) 426-6409/ Cat.: free/
Save: 30–40%/ Pay: C, MO, AE, MC, V Sells: musical in-
struments/ Shop: same address; also Seattle, Bellevue, Ever-
ett, Monroe, and Redwood, WA

$$$/ /

Comment: Marching bands, student musicians, guitarists—
take note: Kennelly has an excellent selection of instruments and
equipment for all of you, at savings of up to 40% on suggested
list prices. The repair department offers its services to mail-order
customers.

Sample Goods: Woodwind, brass, and percussion instru-
ments; guitars, speakers, amps, tuners, effects boxes, autoharps,
mikes, stage lighting, mike cords, snakes, etc., by Armstrong,
Artley, Bach, Benge, Buffet, Bundy, Deagon, Fender, Gemein-
hardt, Getzen, Gibson, Electro-Voice, Korg, Larilee, LeBlanc,
Ludwig, Ovation, Pearl, Polytone, Rico, Roland, Selmer, Vito,
and many others.

Special Factors: PQ by phone or letter with SASE; author-
ized returns accepted.

**MANDOLIN BROTHERS LTD.; 629 Forest Ave.; Staten
Island, NY 10310-2576** (718) 981-3226/ Cat.: free/ Save:
37½%/ Pay: C, MO, AE, MC, V Sells: vintage fretted in-
struments/ Shop: same address; M–Sa 10–5

$$$/ /

Comment: Mandolin sells vintage fretted instruments at good market prices, and offers select new instruments at an average of 37½% below list prices.

Sample Goods: Vintage guitars, mandolins, banjos, and other instruments; new mandolins, guitars, banjos, and electronics by Martin, Ovation, and Guild.

Special Factors: PQ by phone or letter with SASE.

MANNY'S MUSICAL INSTRUMENTS & ACCESSORIES, INC.; 156 W. 48th St.; New York, NY 10036 (212) 819-0756/ Info: PQ/ Save: 30–50%/ Pay: C, MO, MC, V Sells: musical instruments, electronics, accessories/ Shop: same address; M–Sa 9–6

$$$/ ✉ / ☎

Comment: Manny's has been selling musical instruments for over 50 years, and it's rare to go into the store on New York City's "Music Row" without seeing a famous face from the world of rock and roll. Sales are run regularly, bringing prices down even farther than the standard 30% to 50% below list.

Sample Goods: Musical instruments, electronics, and accessories of every type, from amps and mixers to fine woodwinds and brass instruments. The roster of brands is comparable to those offered by Sam Ash.

Special Factors: PQ by phone or letter with SASE.

MOGISH STRING CO.; P.O. Box 493-WU; Chesterland, OH 44026 (216) 729-3470/ Cat.: free/ Save: 51%/ Pay: C, MO, cert. check **Sells:** strings, musical instruments, electronics/ Mail order only

$$$/ ✉

Comment: Jim Moogish began his business selling guitar strings and accessories 8 years ago, and today publishes a 20-page catalog of "fretted instruments and accessories for the discriminating musician."

Sample Goods: Strings by Martin, D'Addario, Vega, GHS, Guild, Gibson, Fender, S.I.T., Ernie Ball, Savarez, La Bella, Dr. Thomastik, Prim, Piastro, etc.; picks, capos, straps, and other accessories also stocked. Shure mikes, DiMarzio pickups, and guitars by Guild, Yamaha, Gibson, and Fender are sold as well.

Special Factors: PQ by phone or letter with SASE.

NATIONAL EDUCATIONAL MUSIC COMPANY, LTD.; 1181 Rte. 22; Box 1130-WMU; Mountainside, NJ 07092 (800) 526-4593/ Cat.: free (3 & 8)/ Save: to 50%/ Pay: C, MO, AE, MC, V **Sells:** musical instruments/ Mail order only

$$$$/ ✉ / ☎

Comment: NEMC has been supplying school bands with instruments since 1959 and offers you the same equipment at savings of up to 50% on list prices.

Sample Goods: Brass, woodwind, and percussion instruments by Armstrong, Signet, LeBlanc, Selmer, Bundy, Vito,

King, Gemeinhardt, Yamaha, Artley, Conn, Schreiber, Holton, Gill, Benge, Musser, Bach, Ludwig, SlingerLand, Mirafone, Sabian, Roth, DEG, and many other firms listed in the catalog.

Special Factors: PQ by phone or letter with SASE.

RAINBOW MUSIC; Poughkeepsie Plaza Mall, Rte. 9; Poughkeepsie, NY 12601-5326 (914) 255-5552/ Cat.: free (quarterly)/ Save: 40%/ Pay: C, MO, AE, MC, V Sells: new, vintage musical instruments, electronics/ Shop: same address; M & T 11–6, W, Th, F 11–9, Sa 10–6

$$$/ ✉/ ☎

Comment: Rainbow's choice group of vintage instruments and electronics is featured in the catalog; these collectors' items are priced as low as business sense permits, and sell quickly. A good selection of new equipment is offered as well.

Sample Goods: Vintage instruments and electronics; new equipment by Fender, Gibson, Hamer, Alembic, Rickenbacker, Steinberger Sound, Kramer, Ovation, Yamaha, Martin, Alvarez-Yairi, and Adamas; amps from Legend, Roland, Marshall, Fender, and Music Man; effects boxes, pickups, strings, keyboards, speakers, equipment cases, mixers, tape decks, and other equipment stocked at savings of up to 40%.

Special Factors: PQ by phone or letter with SASE; used guitars and amps purchased; trade-ins accepted.

SILVER & HORLAND, INC.; 170 W. 48th St.; New York, NY 10036 (212) 869-3870/ Info: PQ/ Save: 30–50%/ Pay: C,

MO, cert. check **Sells:** new, used, vintage instruments, electronics/ **Shop:** same address; M–Sa 9:30–6

$$$$/ ✉

Comment: Silver & Horland offers a complete range of musical instruments, electronics, and accessories. The firm has been selling by mail since 1935, and discounts new equipment up to 50%.

Sample Goods: New, used, and vintage instruments; new equipment by Seiko, Yamaha, Takamine, Givson, Fender, Guild, Martin, Selmer, Armstrong, etc.; no percussion instruments or harps; Moog, guitars, brass instruments, and supplies —reeds, valve oil, picks, mouthpieces, strings, etc.

Special Factors: PQ by phone or letter with SASE; repair service available; trade-ins accepted; min. order $15.

SUPERSAVE MUSIC; P.O. Box 944; Morganton, NC 28655
Cat.: $1/ Save: 30% +/ Pay: C, MO, cert. check **Sells:** instruments, supplies, accessories/ Mail order only

$$/ ✉

Comment: SuperSave publishes a 33-page catalog of instruments, accessories, and musical-instrument supplies, all priced 30% or more below comparable retail or list price.

Sample Goods: Instrument stands, picks, drum heads, bongos, cowbells, harmonicas, violin bridges, effects boxes, cleaning equipment and supplies, drum keys, amp corners, and glides, and related goods; brands include Schaller, Yamaha, Shure, Vega, Darco, Gibson, LaBella, D'Addario, Fender, Guild, etc.

Special Factors: Excellent selection of maintenance and repair equipment.

TERMINAL MUSICAL SUPPLY, INC.; 166 W. 48th St.; New York, NY 10036 (212) 869-5270/ Info: PQ/ Save: to 40%/ Pay: C, MO, MC, V Sells: musical instruments, accessories/ Shop: same address

$$$/ ✉ / ☎

Comment: Terminal Music began its life as a pawnshop and is now a fixture on "Music Row," or West 48th Street in New York City. Large collection of used instruments; new equipment discounted up to 40% off list prices.

Sample Goods: Classical, band, fretted, string, keyboard, percussion, and Latin instruments; new equipment by all the major manufacturers, and such hard-to-find brands as Madiera and Suzuki guitars. Instruction manuals, metronomes, and other accessories also available.

Special Factors: PQ by phone or letter with SASE; used instruments sold in the store only; trade-ins accepted.

SEE ALSO:

Bettinger's Luggage Shop . . . instrument cases . . .
   LEATHER
Blackwelder's Industries, Inc. . . . name-brand pianos . . .
   HOME—Furnishings
Executive Photo & Supply Corp. . . . Casio musical keyboards
   . . . CAMERA

Focus Electronics, Inc. . . . Casio musical keyboards . . .
   APPLIANCES
47st Photo, Inc. . . . Casio musical keyboards . . . CAMERA
Sultan's Delight Inc. . . . esoteric musical instruments . . .
   FOOD

OFFICE
AND COMPUTING

Office machines, furniture, and supplies;
computers, peripherals, and software; and
printing and related services.

Want to score points with the company or move your own venture into *Fortune*'s golden circle? Get hard-headed about office expenses. Chances are good that you're not getting the best possible prices on supplies, printing, furnishings, and the countless items needed to keep the workplace running. You should shop as dilligently for correction film and daisy wheels as you do for computer systems and word processors. In the process, you have to look that nonsense about being "loyal" to a supplier squarely in the face.

An important link in the budgetary chain is the office manager, who's delegated the task of ordering supplies. You should know what that person's up against—if your company doesn't place regular orders, it's common practice for the supplier to send a sales rep around to apply a little charm to the hapless manager. The pressure tactics are usually effective, since it's difficult to turn down a person who only wants to help restock the storeroom. You can begin a cost-control program by having the person you delegate as purchaser send for the catalogs listed here, so you build up a file of discount sources for all your needs.

On computers: if you're a first-time buyer or seeking to upgrade your system, the best advice we can give you is to read, read, and read some more. Attend demonstrations of new products. Watch colleagues at work with different hardware or programs, and ask questions—don't assume that anything does what it's claimed to do, as quickly, as easily, or as neatly as the ads would have you believe. Develop a vigorous skepticism for the term "compatible," and make sure you understand the limitations of such hardware and software before you buy. At some point, the industry will have to standardize, but until then it's "caveat emptor," in spades. The reading material we recommend includes everything Peter A. McWilliams has written (especially for those just learning about computers); *The Whole Earth Software Catalog* and its quarterly update, *Whole Earth Software*

Review; and *How to Buy Software,* by Alfred Glossbrenner. The books are available in most bookstores and are updated regularly; the quarterly is $18 per year (four issues) from Whole Earth Software Review; P.O. Box 27956; San Diego, CA 92128. There are thousands of books on the market to guide you through the purchase of hardware and software and the use of specific systems, and many of them merit your attention. Don't limit yourself to what we've listed; they're cited because we found them accessible and their authors honest. Further, their reviews of products we'd used coincided with our own evaluations. In addition to books, there are scores of magazines and newsletters that cover every facet and name in computing. Once you're beyond the neophyte stage of computer literacy, you may find some of these helpful in getting the most use from your system. The books mentioned previously include reviews of a number of prominent and obscure periodicals and can serve as a guide to what you may find worthwhile.

The firms listed here can save you thousands of dollars on computer costs, and there's one that offers discounts of up to 50% on the tool you'll need when the circuits blow from hardware overload: a pen.

ALFAX MFG.; 431 Canal St.; New York, NY 10013 (800) 221-5710/ Cat.: free/ Save: 25–50%/ Pay: C, MO, AE, MC, V Sells: office and institutional furnishings, accessories/ Mail order only

$$$/ ✉ / ☎

Comment: Alfax has been in business since 1946 and does most of its business with commercial buyers. The best discounts are given on quantity purchases, but even individual items are reasonably priced.

Sample Goods: Office, nursery, cafeteria, library, conference-room, and other furnishings; stackable chairs in several styles; a range of files and literature-storage systems; P.A. systems, trophy cases, carpet mats, lockers, hat racks, park benches, heavy steel shelving, prefabricated offices, computer stations and work centers, etc. Many products have home applications, and all the furnishings and files are designed for years of heavy use.

Special Factors: Satisfaction guaranteed; commercial and institutional accounts welcomed; free layout service for those designing offices.

AMITY HALLMARK, LTD.; 149-44 41st Ave.; Flushing, NY 11355 (718) 939-2323/ Broch.: free/ Save: to 60%/ Pay: C, MO, cert. check Sells: offset printing/ Mail order only

$$/ ✉

Comment: Amity has been in the printing business for 35 years, has upgraded its equipment, and can now offer an extensive range of faces, point sizes, and special effects. Certain types of services and runs are priced well below the competition—don't miss this firm when you're pricing your next job.

Sample Goods: Offset printing of letter, legal, and 11″ × 17″ sheets; index cards, envelopes, carbonless sets, etc.; colored, heavy, and card stock, gummed labels, cutting, colored inks, reductions and enlargements, halftones, folding, punching, padding, collating, numbering, and other special services and papers available as well.

Special Factors: PQ by phone or letter with SASE; shipping included on orders to 15 states; min. order $20.

BUSINESS & INSTITUTIONAL FURNITURE COMPANY;
611 N. Broadway; Milwaukee, WI 53202 (800) 558-8662/
Cat.: free (1 & 7)/ Save: 30–40%/ Pay: C, MO, AE, MC, V
Sells: office and institutional furnishings/ Mail order only

$$$/ /

Comment: Although the best prices at B&I are found on quantity purchases, even individual pieces are competitively priced. Geared for those furnishing offices and institutions; many items appropriate to home use as well.

Sample Goods: Office furniture and machines, including desks, chairs, files, bookcases, credenzas, etc.; lockers, storage cabinets, handtrucks, carts, stools, folding tables, data and literature storage units, computer work stations, waste cans, mats, announcement boards, outdoor furniture, prefabricated offices, energy-saving devices, etc.; the office machines include 3M desktop copiers, check writers, coin sorters, collators, paper folders, duplicators, addressers, phones, dictating machines, calculators, etc.

Special Factors: PQ by phone or letter with SASE; "three-year, no-risk guarantee."

BUY DIRECT, INC.; 216 W. 18th St.; New York, NY 10011-4594 (212) 255-4424/ Cat.: $2, ref./ Save: 15-40%/ Pay: C, MO, cert. check **Sells:** computer supplies, office machines/ **Shop:** same address; M–F 9–5

$$$/ ✉

Comment: Buy Direct, once known for its great deals on stationery, typewriter ribbons, and other materials for the world of "paper," has developed a complete computer-supplies department. Save up to 40% on quantity purchases.

Sample Goods: Products for computers, word processors, copiers, and microfiche systems; disks, ribbons, daisy wheels, typing elements, correction film, disk storage units, copier supplies, cleaning kits, labels, envelopes, forms, and many other types of goods are offered. Brands include IBM, Qume, Diablo, Burroughs, Wang, NEC, GP Technologies, Camwil, Ko-Rec-Type, Verbatim, 3M, Maxell, Nashua, Wilson Jones, etc. Office furniture, including computer stands and work stations, files, and ergonomic seating, offered. Name-brand office machines stocked as well.

Special Factors: PQ by phone or letter with SASE; authorized returns accepted; restocking fee may be charged; min. order $50 to open business account.

CALIFORNIA DIGITAL; 17700 Figueroa St.; Carson, CA 90248 (800) 421-5041/ Info: PQ/ Save: to 50%/ Pay: C, MO,

MC, V Sells: computer software, hardware/ Shop: same address

$$$/ ✉/ ☎

Comment: Hardware, software, and technical advice are the stock in trade at California Digital, the last given freely. Excellent prices on peripherals, programs, and miscellany for business and personal computers.

Sample Goods: Computers, modems, terminals, printers, monitors, diskettes, and other computer-related goods by Teac, Tandon, Juki, Remex, Apple, Okidata, NEC, Epson, Amdek, Princeton Graphics, Wyse, Silver-Reed, Diablo, Sanyo, IBM, Eagle, Ampro, Dysan, Maxell, Memorex, Scotch, Verbatim, and other firms.

Special Factors: PQ by phone or letter with SASE; returns accepted on defective goods; repair and service department.

COMPUTER CONNECTION; 12841 S. Hawthorne Blvd.; Hawthorne, CA 90250 (800) 732-0304/ Info: PQ/ Save: to 50%/ Pay: C, MO, MC, V Sells: computers, peripherals, software/ Mail order only

$$$/ ✉/ ☎

Comment: The Computer Connection offers the latest in hardware and software at savings of up to 50% on list prices and will try to beat any lower advertised price for the same item.

Sample Goods: Printers, modems, computers, monitors, disk drives, and software by and for IBM, Apple, Kaypro, Sanyo, Okidata, Riteman, Qume, Star Micronics, Tava, Sanyo, NEC,

Compaq, Tandon, Panasonic, Epson, C-Itoh, Brother, Dynax, Juki, Toshiba, AST Research, Quadram, Hayes, Princeton Graphics, etc.

Special Factors: PQ by phone or letter with SASE.

COMPUTER HUT OF NEW ENGLAND, INC.; 101 Elm St.; Nashua, NJ 03060 (800) 525-5012/ PL: free/ Save: 15–50%/ Pay: C, MO, cert. check, MC, V Sells: computers, peripherals, software/ Shop: same address; M–F 9–6, Sa 9–5; also 524 S. Hunter; Witchita, KS

$$/ / ☎

Comment: Computer Hut stocks the latest programs, peripherals, and computer systems by top manufacturers, at savings of up to 50% on list prices.

Sample Goods: Disk drives by Tandon, Panasonic, Shugart, Teac, Maynard Electronics, Quadram, AST Research, Tecmar, Hercules, Amdek, Microlog, and Paradise; hard-disk systems from Maynard and Tallgrass; printers by Epson, Brother, Dynax, C-Itoh, NEC, Okidata, Toshiba, IDS, and Daisywriter; modems by Hayes and Novation; computers by IBM, Compag, and NEC.

Special Factors: PQ by phone or letter with SASE; authorized returns accepted.

CONROY-LAPOINTE, INC.; 12060 S.W. Garden Pl.; Portland, OR 97223 (800) 547-1289/ Info: PQ/ Save: 20–80%/

Pay: C, MO, cert. check, AE, MC, V **Sells:** computers, peripherals, software/ Shop: same address

$$$$/ ✉/ ☎

Comment: Conroy-LaPointe, which has been selling computers and electronics since 1958, lays claim to the title of "world's largest computer mail-order firm." Good business references, enthusiastic recommendations from consumer publications; little "support" or advice.

Sample Goods: Computers, peripherals, software, diskettes, and accessories by IBM, Apple, Amdek, Alloy, Control Data, Concorde, Teac, Rana, Princeton Graphic, Quadram, Zenith, Hayes, Novation, Epson, Juki, Tally, Okidata, Maxell, CDC, Maynard, Microsoft, Magnum, Tecmar, Titan, Dysan, Fuji, Generik, Verbatim, etc.; most prices 30% to 50% below list; specials, closeouts, and overstocked models to 80% off.

Special Factors: PQ by phone or letter with SASE; monthly ads in *Byte* and *PC World;* all sales final, returns accepted on defective goods or firm's error only.

FRANK EASTERN; 599 Broadway; New York, NY 10012
(800) 221-4914/ Cat.: free (1 & 5)/ Save: 30–50%/ Pay: C, MO, MC, V **Sells:** office supplies, equipment/ Shop: same address

$$$$/ ✉/ ☎

Comment: Frank Eastern, in business for over 45 years, offers equipment and supplies for business and home offices at discounts of 30% to 50% below list and comparable retail. Specials are run in every catalog.

Sample Goods: Products by 3M-Scotch, Swingline, BIC, Rubbermaid, etc., including pens, markers, tape, files, envelopes, typing aids, word-processing accessories, stands, etc. Eastern's "Tidi-Files" for publications storage are a regular best buy. Furnishings include filing cabinets (lateral, conventional, transfer, etc.); executive and clerical seating, wood and steel desks, wood bookcases, fireproof Sentry safes, literature and magazine racks, computer work stations, data-reference storage equipment, folding chairs, etc.

Special Factors: PQ by letter with SASE; quantity discounts available; satisfaction guaranteed; returns accepted; min. order $75 on credit cards.

ECONOMY SOFTWARE; 2040 Polk St.; San Francisco, CA 94109 (800) 227-4780/ PL: free/ Save: 30–50%/ Pay: C, MO, AE, MC, V **Sells:** computer, word-processor software/ Mail order only

$$$/ /

Comment: Economy is "dedicated to providing the finest software and hardware for the IBM-PC and compatibles at the lowest possible price." The firm boasts a large inventory, and sells at up to 50% below list prices.

Sample Goods: Programs and hardware by a range of manufacturers, including Advanced Logic Systems, Alpha, Anderson Bell, Ashton-Tate, ASI, CDEX, Central Point Software, Continental, Digital Research, Fox & Geller, Hayes, IMSI, IUS, Lifetree Systems, Lotus, Micropro, Microsoft, Peachtree, Perfect Software, Pickles Trout, Quadram, Software Publishers, Sorcim, Vertex Systems, Videx, Visicorp, Wang, Maxell, Memorex, and many others.

Special Factors: PQ by phone or letter with SASE on items not listed in brochure; products guaranteed against manufacturing defects; quantity discounts available; corporate accounts welcomed.

800-SOFTWARE INC.; 940 Dwight Way, Suite 14; Berkely, CA 94710 (800) 227-4587/ Cat.: free/ Save: 30–50%/ Pay: C, MO, AE, MC, V Sells: computer software/ Mail order only $$$$/ ✉ / ☎

Comment: 800-Software has won recommendations from computer buffs who have access to discount sources in New York City but prefer 800's prices, selection, and technical support. The 48-page catalog includes brief descriptions of each program; specials are run on a frequent basis.

Sample Goods: Programs for the IBM-PC and compatibles, including those made by ALS, Alpha, Amdke, Ashton-Tate, AST, ATI, CDEX, Central Point Software, Continental, Digital Research, Fox & Geller, Frederick Electronics, Funk Software, Hayes, IMSI, IUS, Lifeboat, Micropro, Microsoft, Oasis, Peachtree, Perfect Software, Professional Software, Quadram, Software Publishers, Sorcim, Vertex Systems, Visicorp, Wang, and many others.

Special Factors: PQ by phone or letter with SASE on items not listed in catalog; products guaranteed against manufacturing defects; quantity discounts available; corporate accounts welcomed.

ENVELOPE SALES COMPANY; Normandy, TN 37360
(615) 857-3333/ Broch.: free/ Save: to 60%/ Pay: C or MO
Sells: business stationery/ Mail order only

$$$$/ ✉

Comment: This firm offers mailers in a broad range of sizes, paper weights, styles, and colors, at prices up to 60% less than those charged by other discount suppliers. Popular examples are shown in the color brochure.

Sample Goods: Windowed and plain envelopes, size 6 ¾ to 12, in 7 colors; privacy-tinted bill-payers; business-reply and return envelopes; brown kraft mailers, with and without clasps, are available printed and unprinted in 9 sizes; business letterhead and matching envelopes in 10 type styles, available in water-marked bond (20 and 35 lb.). Logos and colored inks offered at an additional fee; brochure prices include printing (up to 4 or 6 lines, depending on the item).

Special Factors: Most items sold in minimum lots of 1,000.

47ST. COMPUTING; 36 E. 19th St.; New York, NY 10003
(800) 221-7774/ Info: PQ/ Save: to 50%/ Pay: C, MO, AE, MC, V Sells: computers, peripherals, software/ Shop: same address; other NYC locations

$$$/ ✉ / ☎

Comment: This is the computer division of 47st. Photo, one of New York City's largest camera and electronics discounters. Like the parent company, it carries a huge range of products at savings of up to 50%, including the latest technology.

Sample Goods: Computers, peripherals, and software by IBM, Apple, Kaypro, Compac, Hyperion, Datamac, AT&T, NEC, Epson, Sharp, Hewlett-Packard, Panasonic, Sanyo, Olivetti, Texas Instruments, Hayes, Teac, Taxan, Princeton Graphic, Notation, Comrex, Okidata, Silver-Reed, Juki, Qume, Brother, Toshiba, Atari, and other firms; diskettes from Fuji, Nashua, IBM, Maxwell, 3M, and Verbatim also available.

Special Factors: PQ by phone or letter with SASE; min. order $35.

GRAYARC; Greenwoods Industrial Park; P.O. Box 2944; Hartford, CT 06104-2944 (800) 243-5250/ Cat.: free (see text)/ **Save:** 15–50%/ **Pay:** C, MO, MC, V Sells: office supplies, equipment/ Mail order only

$$$/ 🖂 / ☎

Comment: Grayarc's business forms, machines, and office supplies are priced to save your company money and designed to expedite all kinds of business procedures. The 60-page catalog is packed with good values; save up to 50% on some items.

Sample Goods: Reply messages, purchase orders, work proposals, invoices, statements, sales slips, insurance memos, bills of lading, receiving reports, and credit memos in carbon and carbonless sets; plain and windowed envelopes in several sizes and colors; interoffice envelopes; Tyvek, brown kraft, and white paper mailers; business letterhead, cards, and memos; etc. Custom design and printing services offered. Equipment includes printing calculators from Royal, Seiko, and Unitrex; Brother electronic typewriters; 3M compact copiers; cash registers, time clocks, literature racks, shelving, office chairs, etc.

Special Factors: Specify "general supplies" or "computer forms" catalog; include make and model of computer or word processor with computer catalog request; satisfaction guaranteed; returns accepted within 30 days.

HABER'S; 33 Essex St.; New York, NY 10002 (212) 473-7007/ Info: PQ/ Save: 33–50%/ Pay: C, MO, MC, V Sells: sporting goods, pens/ **Shop:** same address; M–Th 8:30–6:30, F & Su 9–6

$$$$/ ✉ / ☎

Comment: Haber's offers a curious mix of products—sporting goods and office supplies—at solid savings of up to 50%. Toys and games are also stocked.

Sample Goods: Mont Blanc, Dupont, Aurora, Waterman, Cross, Parker, Sheaffer, Lamy, and Elysèe writing instruments are available by mail; sporting equipment and apparel by Head, Dunlop, Prince, Tretorn, Wilson, Davis, Adidas, Converse, Nike, ProKeds, and Puma, and name-brand toys and office equipment are offered in the store.

Special Factors: PQ by phone or letter with SASE.

ROBERT JAMES CO., INC.; P.O. Box 2726; Birmingham, AL 35202 (800) 633-8296/ Cat.: free/ Save: to 70%/ Pay: C, MO, cert. check Sells: office supplies/ Mail order only

$$$$/ ✉ / ☎

Comment: Robert James, in business for almost 50 years, offers first-quality office supplies at job-lot prices through its 40-page catalog. Excellent source for daily and special office needs.

Sample Goods: Printed and plain business envelopes, kraft envelopes, mailers; copier paper and labels; files and filing cabinets of every type; paper trimmers, clips, scissors, punches, staplers, tape, etc.; typing and word-processing ribbons, tapes, wheels, and elements; binders and binding machines; accounting supplies; phones and phone machines; desk organizers, literature racks, pens and markers, shipping supplies, memos and receipt books, word-processing and computer forms, labels, binders, work stations, etc.; paper shredders, time clocks, chairs (executive, clerical, folding) and desks, and other goods offered.

Special Factors: PQ by phone or letter with SASE; quantity discounts available; satisfaction guaranteed; returns accepted within 30 days; corporate accounts welcomed.

JILOR DISCOUNT OFFICE MACHINES, INC.; 1020 Broadway; Woodmere, NY 11598 (516) 374-5806/ Info: PQ/ Save: 20–50%/ Pay: C, MO, cert. check, C.O.D. Sells: electronics, office machines/ Shop: same address; M–F 10–5:30, Sa 10–4

$$/ / ☎

Comment: Jilor has been selling by mail for 10 years and offers service and repairs of office machines as well as savings of up to 50% on new equipment.

Sample Goods: Typewriters by Smith-Corona, Olympia, Brother, Olivetti, and Silver-Reed; calculators by Sanyo, Sharp,

Canon, and Texas Instruments; dictation equipment by Sony, Sanyo, Olympus, and Panasonic; phones and phone machines by Uniden, Webcor, Teleconcepts, Panasonic, ITT, Comdial, and Telequest.

Special Factors: PQ by phone or letter with SASE; orders shipped on C.O.D. basis if goods in stock when ordered; goods not in stock ordered from manufacturer after payment received; authorized returns accepted on defective goods; insure all returns and send return-receipt requested; store closed Saturdays in July and Aug.

LINCOLN TYPEWRITERS AND MICRO MACHINES; 100 W. 67th St.; New York, NY 10023 (212) 787-9397/ Info: PQ/ Save: to 40%/ Pay: C, MO, C.O.D. Sells: office machines/ Shop: same address

$$$/

Comment: Lincoln specializes in typewriters and calculators, runs a busy repair and service department, and accepts corporate accounts. Savings run to 40% on many items; identify yourself as a reader of this book when requesting a price quote.

Sample Goods: Typewriters and calculators by IBM, SCM, Olivetti, Royal, Olympia, Hermes, Silver-Reed, Adler, Juki, Brother, and other manufacturers. Ribbons, cartridges, and other supplies available in the store.

Special Factors: PQ by phone or letter with SASE; manufacturers' warranties on some items extended by Lincoln; printers and computer-related peripherals may be added to inventory in the future.

LYBEN COMPUTER SYSTEMS; 1250 Rankin Dr.; Troy, MI 48084 (313) 589-3440/ Cat.: free/ Save: to 50%/ Pay: C, MO, MC, V Sells: computer software/ Mail order only

$$$/ ✉ / ☎

Comment: Lyben offers a full range of computer supplies but has especially good prices on disks and diskettes—up to 50% off suggested list.

Sample Goods: Disks, diskettes, printer paper, and other supplies by Memorex, Dysan, Verbatim, and other firms. All goods sold by the box or carton.

Special Factors: PQ by phone or letter with SASE.

MICRO MART, INC.; Technology Corporate Campus; 3159 Campus Dr.; Norcross, GA 30071 (800) 241-8149/ Info: PQ/ Save: to 60%/ Pay: C, MO, MC, V Sells: computers, peripherals, software/ Shop: also Atlanta, GA; New Orleans, LA; Miami, Tampa, Orlando, Ft. Lauderdale, FL; Louisville, KY; Tyson's Corner, Rockville, MD; Pittsburgh, PA

$$$$/ ☎

Comment: Micro Mart can offer savings of up to 60% on an excellent selection of computers, peripherals, and software for business applications. Newest corporate networking and protocol conversion equipment a feature.

Sample Goods: Disk drives, diskettes, hard disks, multifunction boards, modems, monitors, printers, plotters, chips, CRTs, programs, keyboards, diskettes, mice, etc., by IBM, Apple, Epson, Smith-Corona, Orchid, Toshiba, Star Micronics, Tandon, Peachtree, Lotus, Fox & Geller, Norton, ATI, Borland, Lattice, Microsoft, Hercules, Quadram, Amdek, Wyse, Dysan, Maynard, C-Itoh, Qume, Diablo, and Digital Research.

Special Factors: PQ by phone or letter with SASE; advice given over the phone; call for location of nearest store or order over WATS line.

NATIONAL BUSINESS FURNITURE, INC.; 222 E. Michigan St.; Milwaukee, WI 53202 (800) 558-1010/ Cat.: free (5 & 11)/ Save: 35–40%/ Pay: C, MO, MC, V Sells: office furnishings, supplies/ Mail order only

$$$/ ✉ / ☎

Comment: Furnish your office for less through the 48-page NBF catalog, which offers everything from announcement boards to portable offices. Savings run up to 40%. Est. in 1975.

Sample Goods: Office systems, seating (executive and clerical, luxury and economy, ergonomic, conference, folding, stacking, reception, etc.); desks and tables for every purpose; filing cabinets (including contemporary and traditional wooden cabinets); credenzas, bookcases, shelving, computer work stations, desk organizers, literature racks, service carts, lockers, floor mats, coffee centers, etc. Manufacturers include Jansko, High Point, PFI, Indiana Desk, Miller, Lakeshore, Sidex, Lifeline, Cole, Global, La-Z-Boy, Jefsteel, Raynor, Royal, Fire King, Paymaster, West Bend, O'Sullivan, Samsonite, Lee Metal, Atlantic Cabinet, AVM, Virco, Akro, Fairfield, etc.

Special Factors: PQ by phone or letter with SASE; quantity discounts available.

PACIFIC EXCHANGES; 100 Foothill Blvd.; San Luis Obispo, CA 93401 (800) 235-4137/ PL: free with SASE/ Save: 33–45%/ Pay: C, MO, MC, V Sells: computer disks, storage units/ Mail order only

$$$/ ✉ / ☎

Comment: Pacific Exchanges offers great buys on computer software and disk-storage units and runs specials periodically.

Sample Goods: Disks and diskettes by Dysan, Memorex, BASF, 3M-Scotch, TDK, Nashua, Wabash, and Verbatim; floppy-disk saver kits; head-cleaning diskettes; file boxes for floppy-disk storage; etc.

Special Factors: PQ by phone or letter with SASE; shipping included; min. order box of 10 disks.

PEARL BROTHERS OFFICE MACHINERY & EQUIPMENT; 476 Smith St.; Brooklyn, NY 11231 (718) 875-3024/ Broch.: free with SASE/ Save: 25–40%/ Pay: C, MO, cert. check Sells: office machines/ Shop: same address

$$$$/ ✉

Comment: Pearl combines 37 years of top customer service with discounts of 25% to 40% on a good selection of office machines.

Sample Goods: Typewriters, check writers, calculators, word processors, and cash registers by IBM, Royal-Adler, Max, Casio, TEAL, Sharp, Paymaster, Olympia, Towa, and Hèrmes. Repair and service department.

Special Factors: PQ by phone or letter with SASE.

QUILL CORPORATION; 100 S. Schelter Rd.; P.O. Box 4700; Lincolnshire, IL 60197-4700 (312) 634-4850/ Cat.: free/ Save: 15–50%/ Pay: C or MO **Sells:** office supplies, equipment/ Mail order only

$$$$/ ✉ / ☎

Comment: Quill, founded in 1956, offers businesses, institutions, and professionals savings of up to 50% on a wide range of office supplies and equipment. Real buys on Quill's house brand of typing and computer supplies.

Sample Goods: Files, envelopes, mailers, film and tapes for typewriters, word processors, and printers; phone message and receipt books, rubber stamps, labels, scissors, paper trimmers, pens and pencils, copiers and supplies, binders, dictating machines, accounting supplies, chairs, etc.

Special Factors: Request catalog on business letterhead; satisfaction guaranteed; returns accepted; corporate accounts welcomed.

RAPIDFORMS, INC.; 501 Benigno Blvd.; Bellmawr, NJ 08031-2554 (800) 257-8354/ Cat.: free (see text)/ Save: to 40%/ Pay: C or MO **Sells:** business forms, stationery/ Mail order only

$$/ ✉ / ☎

Comment: Rapidforms provides a full range of business forms designed for every commercial purpose, which are formatted to expedite transactions. Quick shipment is featured. Est. in 1940.

Sample Goods: General business forms catalog: statements, invoices, order forms, work orders, estimate and price-quote forms, sales slips, blanks, phone records, memos, checks, personnel notices, continuous computer forms, business cards and stationery, mailers and mailing-room supplies, etc. Retail/service catalog: similar line of forms, and shopping bags, gift boxes, wrapping paper, ribbon and bows, label guns, etc. Computer forms catalog: complete stock of continuous forms and stationery.

Special Factors: Specify catalog requested by title, shipping included on prepaid orders; quantity discounts available; min. order $10.

TRIPLE A SCALE & MFG. CO.; 2945 Southwide Dr.; Memphis, TN 38118 (901) 363-7040/ Flyer: free (1 & 6)/ Save: 30% (see text)/ Pay: C or MO **Sells:** pocket scale/ **Shop:** same address

$$$$/

Comment: This firm manufactures and sells a pocket precision scale that has a multitude of uses. Identify yourself as a reader of this book when you order and you may deduct 30% from the price of the scale.

Sample Goods: A precision scale that measures up to 4 oz., packed in a pocket-sized case with current postal rate charts. Suggested uses: postage determination, food measurement, lab use, craft and hobby needs, and weighing herbs. A finger ring allows the scale to hang while measurements are taken.

Special Factors: Scale guaranteed to perform "accurately and properly" for 5 years; replacements or repairs made during warranty period; shipping included.

TURNBAUGH PRINTERS SUPPLY CO.; 104 S. Sporting Hill Rd.; Mechanicsburg, PA 17055-3057 (717) 737-5637/ Cat.: 50¢/ **Save:** see text/ **Pay:** C or MO **Sells:** printing supplies, new and used equipment/ **Shop:** same address; M–F 8:30–4:30

$$$/

Comment: Turnbaugh offers the printer working in the manner of Gutenberg new and used presses, type, and related equipment and supplies. Savings on used equipment are as much as 70% compared to the price of new goods; stock is listed in *Printer's Bargain News,* a broadside published every two years. Est. in 1931.

Sample Goods: Printing presses (hand, antique, treadle, power); offset machines, paper trimmers, stapling machines, folders, booklet stitchers, punching machines, numbering machines, etc. Brands often available include Chandler & Price, Kelsey, Baltimore, and Gordon. Descriptions include general condition, bed dimensions, and general equipment. Type, leads, rules, leaders, quoins, keys, spacers, gauge pins, printer's saws, composing sticks, cold padding cement, ink, type cleaner, rollers, type cabinets and cases, engraving tools, bone paper folders, embossing powder, paper stock, shipping tags, etc. also offered.

Special Factors: PQ by letter with SASE; *no printing services available;* min. order $15.

TYPEX BUSINESS MACHINES, INC.; 23 W. 23rd St.; New York, NY 10010 (800) 221-9332/ PL: free with SASE/ Save: 30% +/ Pay: C, MO, MC, V Sells: office machines/ Shop: same address; M–Th 9:30–6, F 9:30–2, Su 10–6

$$$/

Comment: Typex has been in business since 1935, but offers the latest in office machines and supplies. Service and repairs are available in the store and to local customers. Specialty typewriters a feature. Savings run from 30% to 50%.

Sample Goods: Typewriters, calculators, disk drives, copiers, cash registers, and supplies by and for SCM, Silver-Reed, Royal, Olympia, Juki, Sierra, Hèrmes, Olivetti, Brother, Nikkam, IBM, Sharp, Canon, Casio, Panasonic, and Texas Instruments. Foreign-language typewriters available.

Special Factors: PQ by phone or letter with SASE; SASE required with all correspondence if reply desired.

WOLFF OFFICE EQUIPMENT CORP.; 1841 Broadway; New York, NY 10023 (212) 581-9080/ Info: PQ/ Save: 5–40%/ Pay: C, MO, MC, V Sells: office machines, computers, furnishings/ Shop: same address; M–F 8:15–5

$$$/

Comment: Wolff has an extensive inventory of office machines and furniture, as well as a full range of computers and supplies. It's known to local businesses for its well-staffed service and repair department. Savings run up to 40%.

Sample Goods: Typewriters, calculators, check writers, dictation machines, and phone machines by SCM, Olivetti, IBM, Sharp, Sanyo, Olympia, Kaypro, Hewlett-Packard, Texas Instruments, Smith-Victor, etc. Computers and peripherals, word processors, and software by a range of firms, including IBM, Wang, and Hewlett Packard.

Special Factors: PQ by phone or letter with SASE; authorized returns accepted; 15% restocking fee; min. order $100.

SEE ALSO:

The American Stationery Co., Inc. . . . custom-printed
   stationery, note pads, envelopes . . . BOOKS
Annex Outlet, Ltd. . . . name-brand phones, phone machines
   . . . APPLIANCES
Bernie's Discount Center, Inc. . . . name-brand phones, phone
   machines . . . APPLIANCES
Blackwelder's Industries, Inc. . . . leather and name-brand
   office furniture . . . HOME—Furnishings
Bondy Export Corp. . . . name-brand typewriters, phones,
   phone machines, Parker pens . . . APPLIANCES
Cherry Hill Furniture, Carpet & Interiors . . . name-brand
   office furniture . . . HOME—Furnishings
Crutchfield . . . name-brand phones, phone equipment . . .
   APPLIANCES
Executive Photo & Supply Corp. . . . name-brand computers,
   peripherals, calculators, phone machines, typewriters,
   Canon copiers . . . CAMERAS
Focus Electronics, Inc. . . . name-brand computers,
   peripherals, software; phones, phone machines; Parker
   pens; Canon copiers . . . APPLIANCES
47st Photo, Inc. . . . name-brand phones, phone machines,
   typewriters; Canon copiers . . . CAMERAS
Garden Camera . . . name-brand phones, phone machines,
   typewriters . . . CAMERAS

Greater New York Trading Co. . . . name-brand typewriters
. . . HOME—Table Settings

Great Tracers . . . custom-made name stencils . . . CRAFTS

Hunter Audio-Photo, Inc. . . . name-brand calculators, pens
. . . APPLIANCES

International Solgo, Inc. . . . name-brand pens, calculators,
typewriters . . . APPLIANCES

Jems Sounds, Ltd. . . . name-brand calculators, phones, phone
machines . . . APPLIANCES

L & D Press . . . imprinted business cards, stationery, lateral
files; Sentry safes . . . BOOKS

LVT Price Quote Hotline, Inc. . . . name-brand computers,
peripherals, calculators, typewriters, phones, phone
machines . . . APPLIANCES

Olden Camera & Lens Co., Inc. . . . name-brand phones,
phone machines . . . CAMERAS

Plastic BagMart . . . plastic trash-can liners . . . HOME—
Maintenance

James Roy Furniture Co., Inc. . . . name-brand office
furniture . . . HOME—Furnishings

S & S Sound City . . . name-brand calculators, phones, phone
machines . . . APPLIANCES

Sales Citi, Inc. . . . name-brand phones, phone machines . . .
APPLIANCES

Sharp Photo . . . name-brand calculators, Pearlcorder
microcassettes . . . CAMERA

The Videotime Corp. . . . Franklin computers, software . . .
APPLIANCES

Whole Earth Access . . . name-brand office electronics . . .
GENERAL

SPORTS
AND RECREATION

Equipment, clothing, supplies,
and services for all kinds of
sports and recreational
activities.

If the high price of recreation equipment seems unsporting to you, you've turned to the right place. Discounts of 30% are standard among many of the suppliers listed here, who sell clothing and equipment for cycling, running, golfing, skiing, aerobics, tennis and other racquet sports, skin and scuba diving, camping, hunting, hiking, basketball, triathaloning, soccer, and other pleasures. Racquet stringing, club repair, and other services are usually priced competively as well. Buying your gear by mail may be the only sport that repays a nominal expenditure of energy with such an enhanced sense of well-being.

We'd like to thank the Printing House Racquetball & Squash Club of New York City for assistance in obtaining material for this chapter.

ALLYN AIR SEAT CO.; Dept. WBMC; 18 Millstream Rd.; Woodstock, NY 12498-1524 (914) 679-2051/ Flyers: free/ Save: to 20%/ Pay: C, MO, cert. check **Sells:** air-filled vehicle seats/ **Shop:** same address; hours by appt.

$$$/ ✉/ ☎

Comment: Allyn Air sells an air-filled cushion that should help you go the distance, whether you're traveling by bike, car, plane, truck, or wheelchair. Other products are being added to this firm's inventory; all are priced lower than comparable goods marketed by other companies.

Sample Goods: Heavy-duty, air-filled seats for bicycles ($12), motorcycles ($30), and standard and bucket auto seats, aircraft seats, wheelchairs, and trucks ($30 each); also available are an adjustable rearview mirror that fits into the end of most handlebars ($8), a nylon gear bag that fits within the triangular space of a closed-frame bicycle ($15), and nylon panniers and Lexan leg fairings for motorcycles.

Special Factors: PQ by phone or letter with SASE.

ATHLETE'S CORNER; P.O. Box 16993; Plantation, FL 33318 (800) 327-0346/ PL: free/ Save: 10–30%/ Save: C, MO, MC, V **Sells:** tennis racquets, shoes/ Mail order only

$$/ ✉/ ☎

Comment: This firm offers winning savings on name-brand tennis racquets, as well as court and running shoes. Stringing services available.

Sample Goods: Racquets by Prince, Head, Dunlop, Kennex, Donnay, Wilson, Yamaha, etc.; shoes by Asahi, K-Swiss, Nike, Adidas, New Balance, and Ektelon.

Special Factors: PQ by phone or letter with SASE; returns accepted for exchange on unused goods.

THE AUSTAD COMPANY; Dept. WBM-U; P.O. Box 1428; Sioux Falls, SD 57101-1428 (800) 843-6828/ Cat.: free (1, 3, 4, 6, 7, 8, 9, 10, 12)/ Save: to 40%/ Pay: C, MO, AE, CB, DC, MC, V Sells: golf and other sporting equipment, apparel/ Shop: same address; summer hours: M–F 8–8, Sa 8–6, Su 12–5 (Mar. 1–Aug. 30); winter hours: M–Sa 8–6

$$$/ / ☎

Comment: Austad discounts a variety of sports and leisure equipment, but the 62-page color catalog devotes most of its space to golf. Prices are discounted 15% to 40%, and greater savings are offered on overstock and closeout items.

Sample Goods: Golf clubs (sets and singles) for male, female, and junior players by Wilson, Hogan, Pinnacle, etc.; golf balls by Titleist, Hogan, Top Flite, Pinnacle, and Senator; tees, gloves, grips, club-head covers, bags, carts, umbrellas, footwear, apparel, etc. Other sports represented by basketball (Converse shoes), aerobics, and workout equipment for the home.

Special Factors: All goods unconditionally guaranteed against defects for 1 year; returns accepted within 30 days.

BERRY SCUBA CO.; 6674 N. Northwest Hwy.; Chicago, IL 60631 (800) 621-6019/ Cat.: free/ Save: to 30%/ Pay: C,

MO, cert. check, AE, MC, V, **Sells:** scuba-diving gear/ **Shop:** same address; also Palatine and Lombard, IL; Hapeville, GA

$/

Comment: Berry, "the oldest, largest, and best-known direct-mail scuba firm in the country," carries a wide range of equipment and accessories for diving and related activities. Huge brands list. Specials offered regularly.

Sample Goods: Regulators, masks, wet suits, fins, tanks, diving lights, strobes, underwater cameras and housing, Seiko diving watches, pole spears, and much more. Brands include Aquaseal, Arena, Chronosport, Cyalume, Dacor, Desco, Deep Sea, D.B.S., Eska, Fuji, Global, Henderson, Heuer, I.D.I., Ikelite, Mako, Metzeler, Ocean Apparel, Pennform, Scuba Sextant, Scuba Systems, Sea Suits, Seatec, Sherwood, Tabata, Undersea Guns, Underwater Kinetics, U.S. Divers, Voit, Waterlung, Wenoka, etc.

Special Factors: PQ by phone or letter with SASE; complete 244-page catalog, $2; min. order $25 on credit cards.

THE BEST CHOICE; P.O. Box 13-X; Hershey, PA 17033
(800) 233-2175/ **Cat.:** free (2 & 9)/ **Save:** to 35%/ **Pay:** C, MO, AE, CB, CHOICE, DC, MC, V **Sells:** sports gear, apparel/ **Shop:** same address; M, W, F, Sa 9–5, Tu & Th 9–8

$$/

Comment: A great source for running, tennis, aerobics, biking, racquetball, and basketball gear, shown in a color catalog.

Sample Goods: Running shoes by Adidas, Brooks, Etonic, Nike, New Balance, and Reebok; running apparel by Adidas,

Sub 4, Nike, New Balance, Frank Shorter, Bill Rodgers, and Head; TracPac stash pockets, athletic underwear, and shoe products by Spenco, Sorbothane, Eternal Sole, and Shoe Goo. Tennis shoes by Adidas, Bata, Brooks Puma, Fred Perry, K-Swiss, Le Coq Sportif, Nike, Reebok, Asahi, Tretorn, New Balance, and Diadora; racquets by Head, Prince, Wilson, Dunlop, Kennex, and Yonex; name-brand equipment and racquet supplies. Apparel for hiking, biking, aerobics, swimming, and triathaloning also offered.

Special Factors: Many items sold at full retail; shoes resoled; racquets strung; unworn apparel accepted for exchange within 10 days; defective goods replaced.

BIKE NASHBAR; 215 Main St.; New Middletown, OH 44442 (800) 345-2453/ **Cat.:** 50¢ single issue, $2 year's subsc. (2, 5, 8, 10, 12)/ **Save:** 20–50%/ **Pay:** C, MO, CB, DC, MC, V **Sells:** cycling gear, equipment/ Mail order only $$$/ ✉ / ☎

Comment: Bike Nashbar, one of the country's top sources for the serious cyclist, publishes a 64-page catalog of everything from water bottles to top-of-the-line frames. Lowest prices guaranteed.

Sample Goods: Road, touring, dirt, and racing bikes; parts and accessories; frames, clothing, books, etc. Colnago and Guerciotti frames, Campagnolo parts, several lines of tires, saddles by Brooks and Vetta, toe clips and straps, brakes, Bike Porter car racks, helmets, skin shorts, jerseys, cycling gloves and shoes by Detto Pietro and Bata, air pumps, Kryptonite and other locks, and much more.

Special Factors: Satisfaction guaranteed; returns accepted (except used items, specials, and closeouts) within 10 days for refund or credit.

BOWHUNTERS DISCOUNT WAREHOUSE, INC.; P.O. Box 158; Ziegler Rd.; Wellsville, PA 17365 (717) 432-8651/ Cat.: free (quarterly); Save: 30–40%/ Pay: C, MO, cert. check Sells: bow-hunting, hunting, archery equipment/ Mail order only

$$$/ / ☎

Comment: Save up to 40% on a complete range of supplies and equipment for bow hunting, bow fishing, archery, and hunting through the 78-page Warehouse catalog. Specs listed on many items. Est. in 1974.

Sample Goods: Bows, arrows, points, feathers, bow sights, rests, quivers, targets, optics, game calls, camping equipment, camouflage clothing and supplies, rifles and shooting equipment, etc.; brands include Connecticut Valley Arms, Browning, Martin, Jennings, Bear, Darton, Euston, Anderson, PSE, CVA, Bushnell, Simmons, Tasco, Hawken, etc.

Special Factors: Authorized returns accepted; restocking fee may be charged; min. order $10.

CAMPMOR; P.O. Box 999; Paramus, NJ 07652 (800) 526-4784/ Cat.: free/ Save: 20–50%/ Pay: C, MO, MC, V Sells: camping gear, supplies/ Shop: Paramus, NJ

$$$/ ☒ / ☎

Comment: Campmor's 112-page catalog is full of great buys on all sorts of name-brand camping goods, bike touring accessories, and clothing. Huge inventory; savings to 50%. Est. in 1946.

Sample Goods: Swiss Victorinox knives (30% off list); Woolrich, Thinsulate, and Borglite Pile clothing; duofold and Polypro underwear; Timberland boots; Eureka tents; Wenzel, Coleman, and Bristlecone Mountaineering sleeping bags; backpacks by Wilderness Experience, Kelly Camp Trails, and Lowe Alpine Systems; Coleman cooking equipment; Buck knives; Silva compasses; books and manuals, etc.

Special Factors: Returns accepted for exchange, refund, or credit; min. order $20 on phone orders.

CENTRAL SKINDIVERS OF NASSAU, INC.; 2608A Merrick Rd.; Bellmore, NY 11710 (516) 826-8888/ Cat.: free/ Save: to 40%/ Pay: C, MO, cert. check, MC, V **Sells:** scuba-diving gear/ Shop: same address

$$/ ✉ / ☎

Comment: Central has been in business since 1970 and sells name-brand diving gear at savings of up to 40%.

Sample Goods: Tanks from U.S. Divers, Dacor, and Sherwood; jackets from U.S. Divers, Seaquest, Seatec, and Dacor; a full range of regulators; watches and timers from Tekna, Seiko, Chronosport, and Heuer; masks, fins, hunting equipment, and much more available.

Special Factors: PQ by phone or letter with SASE/ shipping included on some items; min. order $50, $75 on credit cards.

CUSTOM GOLF CLUBS, INC.; 10206 N. Interregional Hwy. (I-35); Austin, TX 78753 (800) 531-5025/ Cat.: free (see text)/ Save: 30–50%/ Pay: C, MO, cert. check, MC, V **Sells:** customized golf clubs, accessories/ **Shop:** 3411 N. I-35 and 13048 Research Blvd., Austin

$$$/ ⊠/ ☎

Comment: The "Accessories" catalog from Custom Golf Clubs features its special line of "Golfsmith" clubs, made to order; the "Repairs" catalog shows over 100 pages of replacement parts and repair supplies. Save to 50% on cost of comparable name-brand products.

Sample Goods: Golfing woods, irons, wedges, and drivers offered in a choice of left- or right-handed models, men's and women's styles, 5 degrees of flexibility, any length, weight, color, grip size, etc. House-brand clothing, footwear, bags, carts, gloves, manuals, balls, club covers, and other goods also offered. Pro-shop line includes replacement club heads, grips, refinishing supplies, tools, manuals, etc. Mail-order repairs and services.

Special Factors: Request specific catalog; min. order $10.

CYCLE GOODS CORP.; 2735 Hennepin Ave. So.; Minneapolis, MN 55408 (800) 328-5213/ Cat.: $1, ref./ Save: to 40%/ Pay: C, MO, AE, CB, DC, MC, V **Sells:** cycling gear, equipment/ **Shop:** same address

$$$/ ⊠/ ☎

Comment: Cycle Goods Corp (formerly Cycl-Ology) publishes a 130-page catalog of cycling gear and supplies; valuable tips for improved performance, maintenance, etc. given with product information. Savings to 40%.

Sample Goods: Parts, tools, clothing, supplies, etc. by TTT, Peugeot, Ciocc, Suntour, Campagnolo, Sergal, Cycle Pro, Bata, Protogs, Avocet, Detto Pietro, Sugino, Cinelli, Nadax, Vetta, Omas, Atom, Maillard, Columbus, Reynolds, Kryptonite, Bendix, Gitane, Berec, Citadel, Araya, Fiamme, Mavic, Weinmann, Rigida, Michelin, Brooks, Messinger, Stewart Warner, Tailwind, Carlisle, Kingsbridge, etc.

Special Factors: PQ by phone or letter with SASE.

DYKER HEIGHTS SPORTS SHOP, INC.; 8304 13th Ave.; Brooklyn, NY 11228 (718) 833-8877/ Broch.: free (quarterly)/ Save: to 30%/ Pay: C, MO, MC, V Sells: sports apparel, gear/ Shop: same address
$/

Comment: This is "Joe Torre's" Brooklyn shop, where you can buy all sorts of sports clothing bearing the logos of national teams. Savings to 30% on name-brand sports equipment.

Sample Goods: Jerseys, caps, and duffles with logos of NFL and other teams; pennants, league-endorsed equipment, and football, baseball, softball, basketball, and other sports gear by Rawlings, Wilson, Majestic, Jesco, Empire, Felco, Koho, etc.

Special Factors: PQ by phone or letter with SASE.

GOLF HAUS; 700 N. Pennsylvania; Lansing, MI 48906
(517) 489-8842/ Broch.: free/ Save: 20–60%/ Pay: C, MO,
MC, V Sells: golf clubs, apparel, accessories/ Shop: same
address

$$$/ ✉ / ☎

Comment: Golf Haus has the "absolute lowest prices on pro
golf clubs" anywhere—to 60% below list—on goods by every
possible manufacturer.

Sample Goods: Ping, Titleist, Wilson, Ram, Lynx, Spalding,
MacGregor, Hagen, Powerbilt, Dunlop, and Proline clubs, bags,
balls, putters, etc.; Bag Boy carts; Etonic and Foot Joy shoes;
gloves, umbrellas, spikes, scorekeepers, visors, rainsuits, tote
bags, socks, and much more.

Special Factors: PQ by phone or letter with SASE; shipping,
insurance included; min. order $30.

**HOLABIRD SPORTS DISCOUNTERS; Holabird Industrial
Park; 6405 Beckley St.; Baltimore, MD 21224** (301) 633-
3333/ PL: free (monthly)/ Save: 30–35%/ Pay: C, MO,
CHOICE, MC, V Sells: tennis, racquetball, squash equipment/
Mail order only

$$$/ ✉ / ☎

Comment: Buy here and get the "Holabird Advantage":
prices to 35% below list on equipment for several racquet sports,
service on manufacturers' warranties, and free stringing (tourna-
ment nylon) on all racquets.

Sample Goods: Tennis racquets by AMF Head, Adidas, Davis, Donnay, Dunlop, Durbin, Fila, Kennex, Kneissl, Le Coq Sportif, Match Mate, Prince, Rossignol, Slazenger, Snauwaert, Spalding, Wilson, Yamaha, Bard, Yonex, and Fox; balls by Wilson, Penn, Slazenger, Tretorn, and Dunlop; Prince ball machines; shoes by Adidas, Converse, New Balance, Nike, Foot Joy, AMF Head, K-Swiss, Saucony, Le Coq Sportif, Etonic/Fred Perry, Puma, TBS, Tretorn, Asahi, Reebok, and Diadora. Racquetball racquets by AMF Head, Wilson, Ektelon, AMF Voit, Leach, and Kennex; shoes by Foot Joy, Bata, Adidas, Patrick, AMF Head, and Nike. Squash racquets by AMF Head, AMF Voit, Bancroft, Donnay, Dunlop, Kennex, Slazenger, Manta, and Wilson; eye guards by Voit, Ektelon, and Leader Hogan.

Special Factors: PQ by phone or letter with SASE; authorized returns accepted (except used items) within 5 days.

LAS VEGAS DISCOUNT GOLF & TENNIS; 4813 Paradise Rd.; Las Vegas, NV 89109 (800) 634-6743/ Cat.: free/ Save: 25-40%/ Pay: C, MO, AE, CB, DC, MC, V Sells: tennis, golf, racquetball gear/ Shop: same address

$$$/ /

Comment: Las Vegas sells name-brand gear and equipment for tennis, golf, racquetball, and jogging at savings to 40%. Latest models and styles featured.

Sample Goods: Golf clubs, drivers, putters, wedges, chippers, bags, and balls by Wilson, DDH, Stan Thompson, Spalding, Ram, Lynx, Ben Hogan, Powerbilt, Ping, Tiger Shark, Browning, Dunlop, MacGregor, Toney, Titleist, and PGA; clothing by Izod, Turfer, Lamode, and Foot Joy. Tennis racquets by Head,

Wilson, Donnay, Prince, Dunlop, Kennex, Bancroft, Yamaha, Davis, and Spalding; racquet strings; balls by Penn, Wilson, Dunlop, and Tretorn; name-brand shoes and clothing. Racquetball racquets by Head, Ektelon, and Wilson; eye guards, footwear, Voit jump ropes, and much more.

Special Factors: PQ by phone or letter with SASE.

PEDAL PUSHERS, INC.; 1130 Rogero Rd.; Hacksonville, FL 32211 (800) 874-2453/ Cat.: free/ Save: 10–40%/ Pay: C, MO, AE, CB, DC, MC, V Sells: cycling gear, apparel/ Shop: same address

$$$/ ✉ / ☎

Comment: Pedal Pushers offers 40 pages of frames, parts, accessories, maintenance supplies and tools, and clothing for the cyclist at savings to 40%. Specials offered regularly.

Sample Goods: Lines by Cinelli, Phil Wood, Avocet, Sun Tour, Campagnolo, Zefal, Rigida, Mavic, Weinmann, Ambrosio, Shimano, Brooks, and Dura-Ace; tires by Wolber, Michelin, Clement, and Cycle Pro; frames and parts by Masi, Woodrup, Holsworth, Ciocc, Gios Torini, Guerciotti, and Rossini; Jim Blackburn racks; Cannondale bags and panniers; other equipment and accessories.

Special Factors: PQ by phone or letter with SASE; min. order $15.

PROFESSIONAL GOLF & TENNIS SUPPLIERS, INC.; 7825 Hollywood Blvd.; Pembroke Pines, FL 33024

(800) 327-9243/ Broch.: free with SASE (quarterly)/ **Save:** 30–50%/ **Pay:** C, MO, AE, CB, DC, EC, MC, V **Sells:** golf and racquet-sports gear, apparel/ **Shop:** same address; 5 other locations in FL and AL

$$$/ / ☎

Comment: This firm represents several divisions, which together offer an impressive array of equipment for golf, tennis, racquetball, and squash. Savings to 40%.

Sample Goods: Pro-golf clubs by Acushnet, Titleist, Ben Hogan, Browning, Dunlop, First Flight, Hagen, Jerry Barber, Lynx, MacGregor, PGA, Pink, Pinseeker, Powerbilt, Ram, Rawlings, Sounder, Spalding, Stan Thompson, Taylor Made, Tiger Shark, Tony Penna, and Wilson; gloves, bags, shoes, balls, carts, etc. Tennis racquets by Bancroft, Davis, Donnay, Dunlop, Durbin, Fila, Fischer, Head, Kennex, Kneissl, Le Coq Sportif, Match Mate, P.D.P., Pro Group, Prince, Rossignol, Slazenger, Spalding, Scepter, Snauwaert, Volkl, Wilson, Yamaha, and Yonex; running and tennis shoes, balls, nets, ball machines, hopper, stringing machines, bags, etc. Squash racquets by Donnay, Dunlop, and Head; racquetball racquets by Ektelon, Leach, Head, AMF, Voit, and Wilson; name-brand shoes, bags, balls, gloves, etc. Fashion sportswear.

Special Factors: PQ by phone or letter with SASE; 3% surcharge on MC and V orders; shipping, insurance included on most items.

ROAD RUNNER SPORTS; 1431 Stratford Ct.; Del Mar, CA 92014 (800) 841-0697/**PL:** free (5 & 9)/ **Save:** to 35%/ **Pay:** C, MO, AE, MC, V **Sells:** running shoes, apparel/ **Shop:** 11211

Sorrento Valley Rd., Suite K, San Diego; M–F 10:30–6, Sa 8–3

$$$/ ✉ / ☎

Comment: Road Runner Sports boasts "the absolute lowest running shoe prices," and sells at a 10% markup on the wholesale cost, or to 35% below list prices. Top lines, exhaustive selection.

Sample Goods: Running shoes by Nike, New Balance, Saucony, Brooks, Tiger, Adidas, Etonic, Mizuno, Converse, and Turntec; running shorts, socks, and T-shirts also available.

Special Factors: PQ by phone or letter with SASE.

SOCCER INTERNATIONAL, INC.; P.O. Box 7222; Arlington, VA 22207-0222 (703) 524-4333/ Cat.: $1/ Save: 20–33%/ Pay: C, MO, cert. check Sells: soccer gear, accessories, gifts/ Mail order only

$$$/ ✉

Comment: Soccer International was founded in 1976 by a soccer enthusiast, and offers a 12-page color catalog of items running from novelties to professional equipment. Savings to 33%.

Sample Goods: Soccer-design pillows, soccer "croquet," soccer night lights, clocks, and radios; English and Umbro jerseys, shorts, and hosiery; balls by Brine, Mikasa, and Mitre; PVC leg shields and ankle guards, duffle bags, ball inflators, nets, and practice aids; a range of books and manuals.

Special Factors: Quantity discounts available; min. order $10.

SPORTS AMERICA, INC.; P.O. Box 26148; Tamarac, FL 33320 (800) 327-6460/ PL: free/ Save: 30–40%/ Pay: C, MO, AE, CB, DC, MC, V **Sells:** racquet-sports gear/ Mail order only

$$$/ ✉ / ☎

Comment: Sports America publishes a red, white, and blue "hot list" of tennis and racquetball gear, at prices as much as 40% below list or retail. Excellent selection.

Sample Goods: Tennis equipment by Head, Snauwaert, Yonex, Dunlop, Durbin, Slazenger, Avante Garde, Prince, Rossignol, Wilson, Match Mate, and Kennex; racquetball racquets by Head, AMF Voit, Ektelon, Leach-DP, Kennex, and Wilson; squash racquets by Head, Dunlop, and Ektelon. Shoes by Nike, Adidas, Reebok, Head, Asahi, New Balance, and K-Swiss; bags by Prince, Ektelon, Kennex, Head, Yonex, Snauwaert, and Match Mate; Prince ball machines; strings, eyeguards, socks, Tourna Grip, Shoe Goo, Babolat racquet-head tape, tennis nets, etc.

Special Factors: PQ by phone or letter with SASE; authorized returns accepted (except used, custom-made, or personalized items) within 30 days.

SQUASH SERVICES, INC.; P.O. Box 491; Richboro, PA 18954 (800) 356-9900/ Info: PQ by phone or letter with

SASE/ **Save:** to 35%/ **Pay:** C, MO, cert. check, MC, V **Sells:** tennis and squash racquets, equipment/ Mail order only

$$$/ ✉ / ☎

Comment: Squash Services ranks among the best discounters of squash racquets and equipment. Save to 35%; good service.

Sample Goods: Squash racquets and equipment by Pro Kennex, Goudie, Gray's, Manta, Slazenger, Dunlop, AMF Head, Spalding, Century Sports, and Donnay; court shoes by Nike, Pro Kennex, Foot Joy, Tretorn, and Adidas; Tourna Grip, eyeguards, gloves, bags, and other accessories. Tennis racquets by Wilson, Pro Kennex, Head, Slazenger, Prince, and Dunlop; shoes by Adidas, Nike, Foot Joy, Kennex, and Converse.

Special Factors: PQ by phone or letter with SASE.

STUYVESANT BICYCLE & TOY INC.; 349 W. 14th St.; New York, NY 10014 (212) 254-5200/ **Cat.:** $2.50/ **Save:** 10–30%/ **Pay:** C, MO, cert. check **Sells:** bicycles, equipment/ **Shop:** same address; M–Su 9:30–6:30

$$$/ ✉

Comment: Stuyvesant has been selling bicycles, cycling equipment, and supplies since 1939, and mailing them since 1946. Helpful, experienced staff.

Sample Goods: Cycles ranging from children's bicycles to top-notch track and racing bikes (a specialty), including tandems, city bikes, used bikes, touring bikes, specials, and closeouts. Parts, helmets, jerseys, shoes, toe clips, pumps, locks, water bottles, etc. also available. Brands include Cinelli, Atala, BMX,

Raleigh, Huffy, Bianchi, Ross, Corso, Puch, Bottechia, Campagnolo, Suntour, Regina, and Tipiemme; top-of-the-line Simoncini
frame sets and Sergal clothing featured.

Special Factors: PQ by phone or letter with SASE.

**THE TENNIS CO.; 26441 Southfield Rd.; Lathrup Village,
MI 48076** (800) 521-5707/ Info: PQ/ Save: to 35%/ Pay: C,
MO, cert. check, MC, V **Sells:** squash, tennis equipment/ Mail
order only

$$$/ ✉ / ☎

Comment: The Tennis Co. sells tennis and squash equipment
at savings to 35% on list prices. Custom stringing services also
available.

Sample Goods: Tennis racquets by Head, Wilson, Prince, and
Kennex; squash racquets by Spalding, AMF Head, Dunlop,
Kennex, Donnay, Manta, and Slazenger; Merco squash balls and
other supplies also available.

Special Factors: PQ by phone or letter with SASE.

SEE ALSO:

Bruce Medical Supply . . . small selection fitness equipment
. . . MEDICAL
I. Buss & Co. . . . . military surplus sleeping bags . . .
CLOTHING
Chanute Iron & Supply Co., Inc. . . . . swimming pool
chemicals, supplies . . . HOME—Maintenance

Clothcrafters, Inc. . . . flannel gun-cleaning patches, mosquito netting . . . GENERAL

Custom Coat Co. . . . custom tailoring and dyeing of deer, elk, and moose hides . . . CLOTHING

Danley's . . . name-brand rifle scopes . . . CAMERAS

Eisner Bros. . . . athletic apparel . . . CLOTHING

The Finals . . . athletic, swimming apparel; fitness equipment . . . CLOTHING

47st Photo, Inc. . . . name-brand binoculars . . . CAMERAS

Mass Army & Navy Store . . . camping supplies, equipment . . . SURPLUS

Pagano Gloves . . . deerskin gloves for hunters and archers . . . CLOTHING

A. Rosenthal, Inc. . . . running bras, dance leotards, swimsuits . . . CLOTHING

Ruvel and Company, Inc. . . . camping supplies, equipment . . . SURPLUS

16 Plus Mail Order . . . women's larger size swimwear, running apparel . . . CLOTHING

Weiss & Mahoney . . . camping supplies, equipment . . . SURPLUS

SURPLUS

Surplus and used goods of every sort.

Surplus was probably the original genetic type of "bargain" merchandise, and as you can see from our listings there are still plenty of surplus goods around to make bargain hunters happy. This is the world of military overstock, obsolete electronics, and the 90% discount. It hasn't happened, but we know that one day we're going to graduate from mess kits and heavy-duty flashlights and buy one of those legendary "under $100" G.I. jeeps!

**THE AIRBORNE SALES CO.; P.O. Box 2727; Culver City,
CA 90230** (213) 870-4687/ Cat.: free/ Save: to 90%/ Pay: C,
MO, AE, MC, V Sells: government surplus/ Shop: same ad-
dress

$$$$/ ✉ / ☎

Comment: The Airborne Sales Company has been in business
since 1946, selling all kinds of government surplus. Savings on
comparable retail run up to 90%; anything can turn up here.

Sample Goods: Hobbyist and do-it-yourself materials and
equipment, plus para-military, survival, and outdoor goods; GI
clothing, camping equipment, knives, etc. Extensive selection of
hydraulics, hardware, tools, and unique surplus items.

Special Factors: Authorized returns accepted; restocking fee;
min. order $15.

**BURDEN'S SURPLUS CENTER; 1000-15 W. O St.; P.O.
Box 82209; Lincoln, NE 68501-2209** (402) 474-4366/ Cat.:
free/ Save: to 50%/ Pay: C, MO, cert. check, MC, V Sells:
surplus tools, hardware/ Shop: same address; M–Sa 9–6, Su
12–5

$$$/ ✉ / ☎

Comment: The Surplus Center, established in 1940, offers
great buys on tools and hardware of all sorts.

Sample Goods: Blowers, compressors, hand tools, electrical
equipment, supplies, plumbing equipment and tools, grinders,

and other goods for commercial and industrial use; the Burdex
line of security and surveillance equipment also carried, as well
as other brands.

Special Factors: Order promptly, since stock moves quickly.

**HARBOR FREIGHT SALVAGE CO.; 3491 Mission Oaks
Blvd.; P.O. Box 6010; Camarillo, CA 93011-6010** (800) 222-
6138/ Cat.: free/ Save: to 50%/ Pay: C, MO, cert. check, MC,
V Sells: tools, hardware, surplus/ Shop: same address; also
1387 New Circle Rd. N.E., Lexington, KY

$$$/ / ☎

Comment: Great prices can be found in this firm's "riot-of-
hardware" mailings, which offer toolbox necessities at savings of
up to 50% on list and comparable retail. Specials run frequently;
a valuable source for the hobbyist and do-it-yourselfer.

Sample Goods: Drill and auger bits, Stanley measuring tapes,
Pittsburgh Forge socket wrenches, mildew-proof tarps, Black &
Decker power tools, pipe-sealing tape, camp knives, work ben-
ches, saw blades, wood lathes, heavy-duty bench grinders, disc
sanders, drill presses, and similar goods offered in past bro-
chures.

Special Factors: Min. order $50.

**MASS ARMY & NAVY STORE; 895 Boylston St.; Boston,
MA 02115** (800) 343-7749/ Cat.: free (3 & 9)/ Save: to 40%/
Pay: C, MO, AE, MC, V Sells: government surplus apparel,

accessories/ **Shop:** same address; M, W, F 9–8, Tu, Th, Sa 9–6; also Cambridge, MA

Comment: Mass Army & Navy is among the new breed of surplus centers; its 40-page color catalog offers both reproduction and genuine government surplus, presented as a fashion statement.

Sample Goods: Camouflage clothing, French Foreign Legion caps, pith helmets, leather pilots' caps, U.S. Air Force sunglasses, Canadian battle pants, Vietnam jungle boots, casual and heavy-duty footwear, knapsacks, bandannas, etc.; sleeping bags, air mattresses, backpacks, camping gear, gloves, mess kits, night sticks, handcuffs, duffle bags, insignia and patches, Lee and Levi's jeans, emergency candles, bomber jackets, pea coats, and much more.

Special Factors: "Will not be undersold"; returns accepted for exchange, refund, or credit.

RUVEL AND COMPANY, INC.; 3037 N. Clark St.; Chicago, IL 60657 (312) 248-1922/ **Cat.:** $2/ **Save:** to 70%/ **Pay:** MO, cert. check, MC, V **Sells:** government surplus/ **Shop:** same address; M–Sa 10–4:30

$$$/

Comment: Ruvel is the source to check for good buys on government-surplus camping and field goods—it has a large stock and some of the best prices around on top-quality gear.

Sample Goods: U.S. Army and Navy surplus goods, including G.I. duffle bags, high-powered binoculars, leather flying jackets, mosquito netting, etc.; Justrite carbide and electric lamps, strobe lights, mess kits, dinghies, night sticks, snowshoes, Primus camp stoves, and toxicological aprons have appeared in past catalogs.

Special Factors: List second choices, if acceptable; stock moves quickly.

WEISS & MAHONEY; 142 Fifth Ave.; New York, NY 10011 (212) 675-1915/ Cat.: $1/ Save: to 75%/ Pay: C, MO, AE, MC, V Sells: government surplus, new apparel/ **Shop:** same address

$$/ ✉ / ☎

Comment: Although this firm's discounts on new stock are modest, Weiss & Mahoney is worth noting for its large stock of genuine military surplus at good prices. Everything turns up in the catalog eventually, and inquiries about surplus goods not shown are welcomed.

Sample Goods: New and recycled uniforms, insignia, accessories, parade and camping equipment, trophies, flags, Brasso and Snow-Proof, Eureka and Kirkham tents, Coleman stoves, medals, emblems, enforcement paraphernalia, camping gear, etc.; the clothing featured in past catalogs has included athletic socks and shorts, swim trunks, denim jeans, overalls, watch caps, balaclavas, sneakers, tuxedo jackets, overcoats, and camouflage clothing.

Special Factors: Min. order $10 on credit cards.

TOOLS, HARDWARE, ELECTRONICS, ENERGY, SAFETY, SECURITY, AND INDUSTRIAL

Materials, supplies,
equipment, and services.

This section offers the do-it-yourselfer, hobbyist, logger, and small-time mechanic a wealth of tools and hardware, some of it at rock-bottom prices. Repair and replacement parts for lawn mowers, trimmers, garden tractors, snowmobiles, snow throwers, blowers, go-carts, mini-bikes, and even plumbing and electrical systems are available from these companies. The tools run from pocket screwdrivers and fine wood chisels to complete workbenches and professional machinery, and the hardware includes hard-to-find specialty items as well as stock nuts, bolts, nails, etc.

When you're working, do observe safety precautions and use goggles, dust masks, respirators, earplugs, gloves, and other protective gear as indicated. Make sure blades are sharp and electrical cords are in good repair. Keep tools, hardware, and chemicals out of the reach of children. If you're using a chain saw, make sure it's fitted with an approved anti-kickback device. Most of the firms selling chain-saw supplies should be able to provide one to fit your model.

For more tools and related products, see "Crafts and Hobbies," "General," "Home—Maintenance," and "Surplus."

A.E.S.; P.O. Box 1790-WC; Ft. Bragg, CA 95437 (800) 331-8665/ Cat. & PL: $1/ Save: 20–40%/ Pay: C, MO, MC, V Sells: Makita and Jet power tools/ Mail order only

$$/

Comment: A.E.S., or Appropriate Energy Solutions, is currently marketing the complete lines of Makita and Jet power tools. More manufacturers may be added in the future; savings on these brands run up to 40%.

Sample Goods: Saws (jig, circular, miter, PVC, and chain); drills, routers, trimmers, planers, jointers, sanders, nibblers and shears, polishers, grinders, concrete planers, drywall screwdrivers, cordless tools, and accessories by Makita and Jet; the PL includes both the suggested list and discounted prices.

Special Factors: PQ by phone or letter with SASE; min. order $10.

ALL ELECTRONICS CORP.; 905 S. Vermont Ave.; Los Angeles, CA 90006 (800) 826-5432/ Cat.: free/ Save: to 70%/ Pay: C, MO, MC, V Sells: surplus electronics, tools/ Shop: same address; also 6228 Sepulveda Blvd., Van Nuys, CA

$$$$/

Comment: Electronics hobbyists should see the All Electronics catalog for its huge number of surplus parts, hardware, and tools. The catalog is published 4 times yearly, and the firm keeps a constant inventory of stock items.

Sample Goods: Semiconductors, lamps, heat sinks, sockets, cables and adaptors, fans, connectors, plugs, switches, solenoids, relays, capacitors, wire, fuses, resistors, transformers, potentiometers, keyboards, computer fans, P.C. boards, joysticks, etc.; items of more general interest include replacement phone cords, screwdrivers, socket wrenches, multiple outlet strips, surge suppressors, battery chargers, and replacement knobs for appliances.

Special Factors: PQ by phone or letter with SASE; all parts guaranteed to be in working order; authorized returns accepted within 15 days.

SEE ALSO:

The Airborne Sales Co. . . . hydraulics, tools . . . SURPLUS

Arctic Glass Supply, Inc. . . . replacement thermopane patio-door panes, passive solar panels . . . HOME—Maintenance

Business & Institutional Furniture Company . . . handtrucks, carts . . . OFFICE

Chanute Iron & Supply Co., Inc. . . . Kline, Rigid, Black & Decker power tools . . . HOME—Maintenance

Clothcrafters, Inc. . . . shop aprons, wood-pile covers, tools holders . . . GENERAL

Craft Products Company . . . small selection tools, finishes . . . CRAFTS

Craftsman Wood Service Co. . . . wood-working, power tools . . . CRAFTS

Frank Eastern Co. . . . industrial and institutional supplies, furnishings . . . OFFICE

Great Tracers . . . custom-made name stencils . . . CRAFTS

Harbor Freight Salvage Co., Inc. . . . hardware, tools, parts, shop equipment . . . SURPLUS

L & D Press . . . Sentry safes . . . BOOKS

Plastic BagMart . . . plastic trash-can liners . . . HOME—Maintenance

Protecto-Pak . . . zip-top plastic bags . . . HOME—
Maintenance

The Renovator's Supply, Inc. . . . reproduction house
hardware, brasses . . . HOME—Maintenance

S & S Sound City . . . Fanon surveillance, security equipment
. . . APPLIANCES

Sears, Roebuck and Co. . . . Craftsman tools . . . GENERAL

Southeastern Insulated Glass . . . double-insulated skylights,
glass panels . . . HOME—Maintenance

Sunco Products Corp. . . . heavy-duty protective gloves . . .
CLOTHING

The Surplus Center . . . tools, hardware, security equipment
. . . SURPLUS

Tugon Chemical Corp. . . . wood epoxies, resins . . . AUTO

Wear-Guard Work Clothes . . . work clothes, accessories;
tools, security apparel; enforcement equipment . . .
CLOTHING

Whole Earth Access . . . name-brand hand, power tools . . .
GENERAL

Workmen's Garment Co. . . . new and reconditioned work
clothing, gloves . . . CLOTHING

TOYS AND GAMES

Juvenile and
adult diversions.

For every parent who turned eagerly to this section only to find less than a wealth of sources, we offer our sympathies and apologize. After years of research, we've come to the conclusion that the market is not conducive to discounting. Aside from the large discount chains, there are very few firms selling toys at savings of 30% or more. Why?

Because it's a seller's market, and no one is forced to discount to remain competitive. We are continuing our search for discount toy sources, but we urge parents to sit down and talk with their children about what's on the gift lists they've drafted. All too often they seem to be rosters of what's been run on TV commercials aired on weekend mornings. We believe that there are ways of discussing the manipulative effects of advertising without turning your children into cynics, crushing the holiday spirit, or jeopardizing the myth of Santa Claus. You might be aided by *Penny Power*, published by Consumers Union. It's written for those 8 to 13 years old and includes product reports, juvenile money management, entertainment, and tips on wise shopping. A year's subscription (six issues), at $9.95, can be ordered from Penny Power; Subscription Dept.; Box 2859; Boulder, CO 80321. Good luck!

DINOSAUR CATALOG; P.O. Box 546; Tallman, NY 10982
(212) 582-6343/ Cat.: $1/ Save: to 35%/ Pay: C, MO, MC,
V Sells: dinosaur toys, collectibles, books/ Mail order only
$$/ ✉ / ☎

Comment: Assembled by true aficionados, this beautifully
produced catalog showcases a delightful collection of things di-
nosaur. Although many of the prices are at list or comparable
retail, some are up to 35% below those charged by other catalogs
and gift shops.

Sample Goods: Dinosaur models, rubber stamps, posters,
stationery, T-shirts, mobiles, books, etc.; exact-scale replicas
from the British Museum, glow-in-the-dark dinosaurs, wooden
assembly models, German skeleton kits, hand-finished pewter
models, porcelain dinosaur families, etc.; wooden and board
jigsaw puzzles, dinosaur cookie cutters, ties, jewelry, demitasse
spoons, and much more.

Special Factors: Cat. published biannually.

**DOLL HOUSE & TOY FACTORY OUTLET; 325 Division
St.; Boonton, NJ 07005** (201) 335-5501/ Cat.: $2/ Save:
15–75%/ Pay: C, MO, AE, MC, V Sells: dolls, houses and
furnishings, toys/ Shop: same address
$$$$/ ✉ / ☎

Comment: The color catalog from this firm should please
collector and child alike—it has an excellent selection of doll
houses, miniatures, dolls, and toys at reasonable prices. Est. in
1969.

Sample Goods: Dollhouses in 1″-1′ scale, including Tudor, Southern plantation/estate house, Victorian mansion, American Colonial, and other traditionally favored styles; assembly tools, hardware, and materials also available. Dollhouse "families," miniature towns, and full sets of furnishings and accessories are shown. European wooden toys, Steiff stuffed toys, Effanbee dolls, and other collectible playthings featured as well.

Special Factors: Satisfaction guaranteed; returns accepted within 10 days for exchange, refund, or credit; min. order $25 on credit cards.

DOLLSVILLE DOLLS AND BEARSVILLE BEARS; 373 S. Palm Canyon Dr., Palm Springs, CA 92262 (619) 325-2241/ Cat.: $2, ref./ Save: to 30%/ Pay: C, MO, AE, MC, V
Sells: dolls and bears/ Shop: same address
$$$/ / ☎

Comment: Bears are better by the dozen—30% less expensive from this firm, if you order 12 or more (and 20% less for 6–11). Delightful 20-page catalog of bears of every sort, as well as dolls.

Sample Goods: About 200 different kinds of toy bears, including everything from classic brown Teddy bears to character models ("Humphrey Beargart"). Collectors' dolls are also featured.

Special Factors: Note min. order for discount.

KOUNTRY BEAR COMPANY; P.O. Box 6214; Spartan-burg, SC 29304 Cat.: free/ Save: 50%/ Pay: C or MO Sells: Kountry Bear patterns, kits/ Mail order only

$$/

Comment: This firm features a native South Carolinian "Kountry Bear," distinguished from other varieties by his big black button eyes and jointed limbs. Savings available on orders of 5 or more of the same item.

Sample Goods: "Kountry Bear," stuffed bear with black button eyes, plaid wool body, jointed limbs; available in finished form with registered name tag, kit form, and pattern; "Kuddle Bear," a furry version of his cousin, offered in a limited edition. Three sizes available (9"–19"); bears may be custom-made from your own fabric.

Special Factors: Note min. order of 5 or more items for 50% discount.

PARADISE PRODUCTS, INC.; P.O. Box 568; El Cerrito, CA 94530 (415) 524-8300/ Cat.: $2/ Save: 25%/ Pay: C, MO, MC, V Sells: party paraphernalia/ Mail order only

$$$$/ / ☎

Comment: Paradise Products has been sponsoring bashes, wingdings, and fiestas since 1952, when it began selling party products by mail. The 72-page catalog is a must-see for anyone throwing a theme event.

Sample Goods: Materials and supplies for over 120 different types of events, including Oktoberfest, the 50s, Roaring 20s, St. Patrick's Day, fiesta, "Las Vegas Night," Hawaiian luau, pirate, birthday, football, circus, and July Fourth parties. Balloons, streamers, tissue balls and bells, glassware, party hats, banquet table coverings, crepe paper by the roll, pennants, garlands, and novelties among the items available. A 25% discount is given on *all* purchases.

Special Factors: Goods guaranteed to be as represented in the catalog; shipments guaranteed to arrive in time for the party date specified (terms in catalog); min. order $30 *net*.

LA PIÑATA; No. 2 Patio Market, Old Town; Albuquerque, NM 87104 (505) 242-2400/ PL: free with SASE/ **Save:** to 50%/ Pay: C, MO, cert. check, MC, V **Sells:** piñatas/ **Shop:** same address

$$$/ /

Comment: La Piñata is a marvelous source for piñatas, the hollow papier-mâché animals and characters that are traditionally filled with candy and broken by a blindfolded party guest. Prices here are low; many items under $5.

Sample Goods: Piñatas in the shapes of Sesame Street characters (Big Bird, Cookie Monster, and Oscar); superheroes like Batman and Superman; springing cats, pumpkins, Santa, snowmen, witches, stars, reindeer, and other seasonal characters; all sorts of animals, including bears, burros, cats, elephants, frogs, pigs, kangaroos, penguins, etc. Most offered in 3 sizes.

Special Factors: Gift orders filled; min. order $10.

TOY BALLOON CORP.; 204 E. 38th St.; New York, NY 10016 (212) 682-3803/ PL: free with SASE/ Save: 30–70%/ Pay: C or MO Sells: balloons, inflation equipment/ Shop: same address; M–F 9–5

$$$/ ✉

Comment: Here's a great way to save on a party essential: balloons. The best prices are on gross lots, but many of the models are available in smaller quantities. Great selection; custom printing services available.

Sample Goods: Round balloons, 6″–18″ in diameter; long balloons, round balloons in silver, gold, clear, black, purple, brown, and other hard-to-find colors; marbleized and polka-dotted balloons; novelty shapes; many other sizes, shapes, colors, and designs. Blo-pumps, shower nets, string, vacuum-cleaner inflation devices, metal hand pumps, ribbon, and clips for sealing the balloons also stocked. Imprinting available at a nominal surcharge.

Special Factors: Delivery of helium tanks in the New York City area; specify color, size, shape, and other particulars when ordering.

SEE ALSO:

America's Hobby Center, Inc. . . . model planes, boats, trains, cars, etc. . . . CRAFTS

Bernie's Discount Center, Inc. . . . name-brand video games . . . APPLIANCES

Best Products Co., Inc. . . . name-brand toys . . . GENERAL

Focus Electronics, Inc. . . . name-brand video games, computer games . . . APPLIANCES

Good 'N' Lucky Promotions . . . toys, novelties for adults and children . . . JEWELRY

House of Onyx . . . onyx chess sets . . . JEWELRY

Jems Sounds, Ltd. . . . Atari video games . . . APPLIANCES

Quilts Unlimited . . . patchwork bears . . . ART, ANTIQUES

Regal Greetings & Gifts, Inc. . . . toys, games, novelties . . . GENERAL

RSP Distributing Co. . . . closeout toys, novelties . . . GENERAL

S & S Sound City . . . name-brand video games . . . APPLIANCES

Sales Citi, Inc. . . . Atari video games . . . APPLIANCES

FEEDBACK

Consumers and business, *we want to hear from you!* Your suggestions, complaints, and comments have helped shape this edition of *The Wholesale-by-Mail Catalog,* and are highly valued. We thank every reader who's written in the past and urge you to keep those cards and letters coming in. You can help us by using the guidelines that follow.

Firms: If you'd like to have your company included in the next edition of *WBMC,* send us a copy of your current literature, with prices, and the name of your publicity or marketing director. Firms are listed at the sole discretion of the editors and must meet our basic criteria to qualify for inclusion.

Consumers: If you're writing a letter of complaint, please attempt to work it out yourself first. If you can't remedy the situation on your own, write to us. We'll do our best to help.

If you just want to sound off, we'd like to hear from you too. If you're moved to sing the praises of any mail-order company, please do so—and tell us what's impressed you. If you have suggestions for the next edition of *WBMC,* we're all ears. Remember to include your name and address in all correspondence, and send to:

THE WHOLESALE-BY-MAIL CATALOG ™
P.O. Box 505, Varick St. Sta.
New York, NY 10014

INDEX